SHAKESPEARE'S HISTORIES

COLLEGE OUTLINE SERIES

PLOT OUTLINES OF Shakespeare's Histories SCENE BY SCENE

J. WILSON McCUTCHAN, PH.D.

Late Professor of English
University of Waterloo

BARNES & NOBLE, INC.

PUBLISHERS · BOOKSELLERS · SINCE 1873

Third Printing, 1968

L. C. Catalogue Card No.: 65-26553

Manufactured in the United States of America

ACKNOWLEDGMENTS

First, I express my indebtedness to Mr. Harry Shaw, former Consulting Editor and Director of Publications at Barnes & Noble, Inc., whose vision and foresight were preeminent in launching the Barnes & Noble Focus Books on Shakespeare's plays, whose experience and acumen proved invaluable throughout the preparation of this volume, and whose confidence and reassurance sustained and encouraged me at all times.

I am likewise grateful to Miss Nancy Cone, Assistant to the Editor-in-Chief of Barnes & Noble, and to her colleagues for their patient reviewing of manuscripts, for their keen and perceptive proofreading, and for many helpful emendations.

To Miss Maxine Bechtel and to Mrs. Ina Cahill, I owe appreciation for expert assistance in typing copy and for attending to voluminous correspondence and mailing proofs.

Finally, I record my gratitude to my wife, Betty Combs McCutchan, for absorbing many annoyances and interruptions that would otherwise have hindered or interfered with my work on these books. Her constant attention to my needs and comfort has aided me immeasurably throughout this enterprise.

J. W. McC.

TABLE OF CONTENTS

SYNOPSES OF SHAKESPEARE'S HISTORY PLAYS

When studying or reviewing any play, a reader often wishes to recall the main events and sequence of the action or to locate characters quickly. As a person increases his knowledge of Shakespeare's works, he frequently needs to refresh his memory on the plots, incidents, and characters of plays. This volume provides a ready and convenient reference for this purpose to the ten plays that most editors classify as history (or chronicle) plays.

Users of this book should remember, however, that Shakespeare was a playwright rather than a historian. He based these plays on the historical sources available to him, but he did not concern himself with the accuracy or consistency of this material. Shakespeare compressed events, violated chronology, and altered characters whenever such changes suited his dramatic purpose. In spite of such departures from fact, he usually remained faithful to the broad stream of history, to the atmosphere of the periods he was dramatizing, and to the spirit of the major characters he introduced.

Readers should also keep in mind that a synopsis is the barest outline of the basic elements of any drama and that it can never take the place of a thorough and conscientious reading and examination of the complete text. Helpful as a summary may be, it cannot convey the power, the subtlety, the magic of Shakespeare's genius as a master playwright and poet.

KING JOHN [1596–1597][1]

CHARACTERS

KING JOHN.

PRINCE HENRY, his son.

ARTHUR, Duke of Britain,[2] son of *King John's* elder brother Geoffrey.

EARL OF PEMBROKE.

EARL OF ESSEX.

EARL OF SALISBURY.

LORD BIGOT.

HUBERT DE BURGH.

ROBERT FAULCONBRIDGE, son to Sir Robert Faulconbridge.

PHILIP THE BASTARD [*Sir Richard Plantagenet*], his half brother.

JAMES GURNEY, servant to *Lady Faulconbridge.*

PETER OF POMFRET, a prophet.

PHILIP, King of France.

LEWIS, the Dauphin.

LYMOGES, Duke of Austria.

CARDINAL PANDULPH, the Pope's legate.

MELUN, a French lord.

CHATILLON, ambassador from France to *King John.*

QUEEN ELINOR, widow of King Henry II and mother to *King John.*

CONSTANCE, mother to *Arthur.*

BLANCH OF SPAIN, daughter to the King of Castile and niece to *King John.*

LADY FAULCONBRIDGE, widow of Sir Robert Faulconbridge.

Lords, Citizens of Angiers, Sheriff, Heralds, Officers, Soldiers, Executioners, Messengers, Attendants.

Scene: *England and France*

I,i. England. King John's Palace

In the name of the King of France, Chatillon charges King John with having usurped the title of his nephew, Arthur of Brittany, to

[1] Some editors argue for an earlier date of composition.
[2] "Britain" in Arthur's title stands for Brittany (i.e., Bretagne).

England, Ireland, and various French provinces. Furthermore, the King of France demands, on threat of war, that John yield these to Arthur at once. King John rejects the demand, orders Chatillon to return to France with a declaration of war, and instructs the Earl of Pembroke to provide safe escort for the Ambassador.

Queen Elinor reminds John of her prediction that Constance, widow of Geoffrey, would enlist King Philip's support for Arthur's claims. Elinor also suggests that John's own claim to the throne rests on possession more than on right and that tactful negotiation on his part might have avoided war between the two kingdoms.

A sheriff enters and, through the Earl of Essex, secures John's permission to admit two men who wish to submit a controversy for the King's judgment. While he waits, King John remarks that the abbeys and priories will finance the cost of the expedition against France. The two men approach and identify themselves as Philip and Robert Faulconbridge.

In blunt, forthright fashion Philip explains that Robert, alleging Philip's illegitimacy, would deprive him of an annual income of at least five hundred pounds a year from their father's estate. Philip asks King John to compare him with Robert and says that if Robert resembles their father he is thankful that he does not. At this point Queen Elinor interrupts to point out resemblances in speech and physical appearance between Philip and the late Richard Coeur-de-Lion. John observes that he too has detected the striking similarity between the two men.

To support his charge of Philip's bastardy, Robert relates how Richard Coeur-de-Lion sent the elder Faulconbridge on a diplomatic mission to Germany, during which time the former King sired Philip. King John cynically rejects Robert's argument with the comment that all husbands must risk such infidelity; he decrees that Robert has no legal basis for his suit and that Philip may inherit both title and property despite Sir Robert Faulconbridge's will.

Queen Elinor asks Philip if he would prefer to be a Faulconbridge and enjoy his estate or be the bastard and landless son of Richard Coeur-de-Lion. Conceding his half brother's resemblance in profile to their father in name, Philip replies that he gladly yields the land to Robert in order to accompany Elinor on the French expedition. King John legitimizes Philip by dubbing him Sir Richard Plantagenet. The Bastard shakes hands with his half brother and says that he prefers the honor of his illegitimate ancestry to the property and income he has heretofore wished. All leave except the Bastard, who soliloquizes on his loss of land and acquisition of a legitimate knighthood. While he speculates aloud on how he will adapt himself to his new way of life, he sees his mother and James Gurney approaching.

Lady Faulconbridge explains that she is seeking Robert, who has been maligning her reputation with his claims of Philip's illegitimacy. Referring to his half brother in contemptuous and scornful terms, the Bastard asks Gurney to leave him alone with his mother. Denying that Sir Robert could have been his father, the Bastard asks his mother who his sire really was. After he assures her that he has renounced "land;/Legitimation, name, and all," Lady Faulconbridge confesses that Richard Coeur-de-Lion seduced her and begat him. Exuberantly, the Bastard thanks his mother for giving him such a father and tells her that she was guilty of no sin in thus conceiving him.

II,i. France. In Front of Angiers

Philip, King of France, and the Duke of Austria meet with their respective forces before Angiers. King Philip explains to Arthur of Brittany that the Duke of Austria, responsible for the death of Richard Coeur-de-Lion [1] and wishing to make amends to his heirs, has brought his army to support Arthur's claim and "to rebuke the usurpation" of his uncle, "English John." After Arthur's welcome, the Duke of Austria vows to remain in France until the youth recovers his rightful possessions. Constance adds her thanks to her son's, and King Philip declares that they will launch an attack on Angiers to force the city's recognition of Arthur. Constance advises delaying until Chatillon returns from England, but the Ambassador arrives with word of the imminent invasion by King John in the company of Queen Elinor, Blanch of Spain, the Bastard Faulconbridge, and an army "of dauntless spirits." Having been delayed by contrary winds, Chatillon barely delivers his message before King John and his followers appear.

After an exchange of formal greetings, Philip of France challenges John to yield his throne and territories to Arthur, the rightful heir. John asks by what authority the King of France issues such a demand, and Philip replies that the Almighty has made him guardian of Arthur and responsible for his cause. While the two

[1] One of Shakespeare's sources for *King John* confused Leopold, Duke of Austria, who captured Richard I in 1192, with Widomar, Viscount of Limoges, who opposed Richard at the time of his death in 1199.

monarchs defy each other, Queen Elinor and Constance trade insults until the Duke of Austria shouts "Peace!" Irritated by the Austrian's intervention, the Bastard threatens to smoke the Duke's lion-skin or, better still, pluck it off. Silencing the "Women and fools," King Philip asks John if he will surrender England and Ireland, Anjou, Touraine, and Maine. King John boldly defies his rival monarch and promises Arthur to deal more generously with him than King Philip will.

Queen Elinor calls Arthur to come to his grandmother while Constance mocks her mother-in-law with baby-talk. Arthur protests that he is not worth the strife that his title is causing, and his mother and grandmother start quarreling again. King Philip orders Constance to be quiet or to control her emotions and suggests that they summon the citizens of Angiers in order to learn where the city's loyalty lies. In response to the trumpet call, a citizen appears on the walls of the town.

Declaring that Philip of France has intended to besiege and raze the city, King John pleads with the people to acknowledge him as their rightful ruler and give him harborage within their walls. In rebuttal, the King of France maintains that he has come merely to support the just claims of Arthur and promises that if the citizens recognize him as their prince the French army and its allies will withdraw peaceably.

To these arguments the citizen answers that Angiers belongs to the King of England and will be loyal to whoever establishes a claim to that title. Until then the city has fortified itself against the world. With taunts and boasts the French and English forces prepare for battle. After a series of marches and engagements the Herald of France declares that the French have been victorious and demands that the city admit Arthur as King of England. Immediately the English Herald appears and similarly claims victory for King John. The citizen states, however, that he and his fellow townsmen have watched the battle from the walls, that they judge the outcome to be inconclusive, and that one force or the other must prove superior before the city owns allegiance to either.

At this point, both Kings return with their retinues and continue to defy each other. Impatient with the parley, the Bastard praises the glory of war and urges that they settle the issue on the field. Once more the Kings demand that the citizens indicate their allegiance, but the town's spokesman obstinately insists that someone must prove himself King of England beyond doubt. Impetuously, the Bastard advises King John and King Philip to lay aside their controversy temporarily, join forces, conquer the impertinent people of Angiers, and then resolve their dispute in battle. King John approves the suggestion, and the Bastard persuades King Philip to support the plan. John says that he will attack from the west; the Duke of Austria chooses the south, and King Philip the north. The Bastard, in an aside, notes that the Austrian and French armies will be shooting into each other and he determines to encourage this rash strategy.

Diplomatically, the citizen delays the monarchs by proposing a scheme that will save the city. He advises that the Kings arrange a marriage between Lewis, Dauphin of France, and Blanch, niece of King John. He promises that if the rulers compromise their dispute in this way the city will open its gates to both. Despite the Bastard's scathing distrust of the compromise, Queen Elinor urges John to contract the marriage as a means of effecting an alliance with France and blocking Arthur's claim to the English throne. King Philip hesitatingly asks John his opinion. Immediately John answers that if Lewis the Dauphin finds Blanch appealing as a bride, he will endow her with all his French possessions except the city of Angiers. Lewis professes himself dazzled by Blanch's beauty and perfection, and Blanch agrees to obey her uncle's wish. Speedily, the Kings complete their arrangements, King John adding thirty thousand marks to the five provinces he has already promised as dowry. King Philip requests the citizens to open the gates so that the marriage may be celebrated at once in Saint Mary's Chapel.

Noting the absence of Constance, King Philip inquires where she and her son may be. The Dauphin says that she is in Philip's tent, and the King comments that she will find little comfort in the new alliance, which he has accepted for his own advantage rather than Arthur's, for which cause he took the field. King John observes that he will create Arthur Duke of Brittany, Earl of Richmond, and Lord of Angiers—rewards that he trusts will satisfy Constance. All leave for the wedding except the Bastard Faulconbridge, who delivers a cynical soliloquy on "commodity," the self-gain and expediency that have prompted King Philip to abandon an honorable cause and King John to cede his claim to five provinces "to stop Arthur's title in the whole." Comparing "this commodity" to the weight on a bowling ball that causes it to veer from a true course, the Bastard vows that he will henceforth pursue gain instead of honor.

III,i. France. The French King's Tent [1]

Dismayed, Constance argues with the Earl of Salisbury that he has erred in reporting the recent compromise between King John and King Philip. When Salisbury reaffirms the fact, Constance finds him "a most ugly man" and commands him to leave. Arthur tries to calm his mother, but she decries "That strumpet Fortune" for having corrupted King Philip and favored John. She orders Salisbury to depart, but he says that he must escort her to the monarchs. Constance obstinately seats herself on the ground and refuses to move as the two Kings and their followers appear.[2]

While King Philip is telling his new daughter-in-law (Blanch) that the date of her wedding will forever be a holiday, Constance rises and declares that it will be "A wicked day" on which "all things begun, come to ill end." The French King advises Constance that she will have no cause to curse the day's events, but she charges him with breaking his oath and prays that "ere sunset" the heavens will "Set armed discord 'twixt these perjur'd kings!" When Lymoges tries to quiet her, she turns her fury on him, calling him an opportunist, a cold-blooded slave, and a cowardly fool. The Bastard joins Constance in taunting Lymoges until King John silences him.

At this point Pandulph, "the holy legate of the Pope," arrives to demand why King John has refused to approve Stephen Langton's appointment as Archbishop of Canterbury. Bristling, John replies that as an anointed king he does not recognize the Pope's jurisdiction or authority. He further decrees that no Italian priest "Shall tithe or toll" in his dominions. King Philip remonstrates, but John defies excommunication, condemns purchased pardons, and says that he alone will oppose the Pope. Pandulph speedily excommunicates John, pronounces a blessing on all who rebel against him, and promises canonization on whoever "takes away by any secret course" his hateful life. Constance adds her curses to the legate's, and Pandulph orders the King of France to break his alliance with John and to "raise the power of France upon his head/Unless he do submit himself to Rome." Queen Elinor urges King Philip to keep the treaty; Lymoges advises him to heed Pandulph; and the Bastard resumes

[1] Although a few editors designate this division of the play as scene ii of Act II, the majority begin Act III at this point.

[2] Some editors terminate Act II here and begin Act III with the ensuing episode.

his needling of the Duke of Austria. Lewis, the Dauphin, advises his father to forfeit England's friendship rather than incur the curse of Rome, but Blanch interposes on the side of King John. When King Philip demurs and admits that he does not know what to say, Pandulph threatens to excommunicate him also.

Troubled by the thought of violating his recently sworn amity to England and of precipitating more bloodshed, King Philip pleads with Pandulph to devise and impose some "gentle order." The papal legate, however, demands immediate war against England. As King Philip ponders his dilemma, Blanch appeals for peace; Constance and the Dauphin counsel war; and Pandulph repeats his threat to excommunicate the French monarch.

Finally King Philip declares that he will break the treaty. Constance commends him; Queen Elinor reviles him; King John and the Bastard predict that he will rue his decision. Blanch, her loyalties divided, cannot wish success to either side and concludes, "Whoever wins, on that side shall I lose:/Assured loss before the match be play'd." Trading defiant boasts, the two Kings separate to prepare for battle.

III,ii. France. Plains near Angiers

Philip the Bastard appears with the severed head of Lymoges, Duke of Austria. King John places Arthur of Brittany in Hubert's custody and expresses fear that the enemy has captured Queen Elinor. The Bastard reports that he rescued her and that she is safe.

III,iii. France. Plains near Angiers [1]

King John and his followers are marching across the field. The King leaves Queen Elinor under the protection of a strong guard; he assures Arthur that he will receive as much love from his grandmother and captor uncle as he did from his own father; then he directs the Bastard to return to England and ransack the abbeys to subsidize the campaign in France. The Bastard departs, and Queen Elinor draws Arthur aside.

In cautious and roundabout phrases, King John flatters Hubert, reminds him of the royal favors he has received, and indicates that he would serve his master well by killing Arthur. Hubert says, "He shall not live," and the King directs Arthur to set out for England under Hubert's care.

[1] Some editors continue scene ii here instead of introducing scene iii.

III,iv. France. The French King's Tent

King Philip objects to Pandulph's optimism with the observation that the French army has suffered defeat, the English have captured Angiers and Arthur, many dear friends have died, and John has left for England. While the two men and the Dauphin converse about their situation, Constance joins them. In reply to King Philip's courteous greeting, Constance invokes death and hopes that it will seize her. Pandulph tells her that she utters madness, but she tears her hair and laments more loudly than before. The King urges her to bind up her hair. Constance continues to bewail Arthur's capture. Pandulph remonstrates with her, but she reminds him that he never had a son and can easily give such advice. Still voicing her grief, she leaves. The King, fearing that she may do herself injury, follows her.

To Pandulph, the Dauphin deplores the weariness of life. The Cardinal predicts that events will lead the Dauphin to the throne of England and that King John will not enjoy one quiet hour's rest so long as Arthur lives. Pandulph is certain that John will effect Arthur's death, after which event Lewis can claim the throne of England through his wife, Blanch. Lewis is doubtful that he can prove more successful in opposing John than Arthur has been, but Pandulph prophesies that John's violence to Arthur will cost him much popularity and turn his people against him. The wily legate also convinces Lewis that the Bastard's confiscation of church establishments in England will cause many to desert John, and the Dauphin invites Pandulph to accompany him in securing King Philip's support for an attack on England.

IV,i. England. A Room in a Castle

Hubert instructs the executioners to heat their irons and on signal to rush forth and bind Arthur to his chair. One executioner hopes that Hubert's commission for the act is in order. Hubert reassures his helpers, who withdraw as he summons Arthur to him.

Observing Hubert's sadness, Arthur chats innocently about his former life in France and wisely comments that King John is as much afraid of him as he is of his uncle. His compassion awakened by the friendliness of the "little Prince," Hubert says to himself that he must kill Arthur quickly before his resolution vanishes. He shows Arthur the order to burn out the Prince's eyes with hot irons. Arthur, mentioning his many attentive services for Hubert's comfort, appeals for mercy and says that he cannot believe that Hubert would commit such an act of violence. Impatiently, Hubert calls forth the executioners with their searing irons. He commands the men to hand him an iron and to tie Arthur. Frightened by the roughness of the executioners, Arthur promises that if Hubert dismisses the henchmen and leaves him unbound, he will "sit as quiet as a lamb" and "will not stir nor winch nor speak a word." Hubert orders the executioners to leave him alone with the boy, and one of the men expresses relief to be excused from committing such a deed. Again Hubert prepares to blind the lad and, when he continues to plead for mercy, chides him for breaking his promise. Arthur says that he would rather lose his tongue than his eyes. Then he argues eloquently that the instruments and fire are not hot enough to perform the task. At long last Hubert yields to the boy's petitions and declares that, although he risks much danger in crossing the King, he will not touch the Prince's eyes for any reward. Hubert comforts Arthur, vows never to harm him, and goes to circulate false reports of Arthur's death.

IV,ii. England. King John's Palace

King John, stating that he is "once again crown'd," seeks his court's approval. The Earl of Pembroke regards the second coronation as a mistake, and the Earl of Salisbury characterizes the ceremony as "wasteful and ridiculous excess," as practical as "To gild refined gold, to paint the lily, . . . or add another hue/Unto the rainbow." Defending his action against this criticism, King John inquires what he has done that the lords would change. Speaking for the others as well as for himself, Pembroke vigorously argues for the liberation of Arthur on the grounds that the Prince's continued imprisonment is both unnecessary and injurious to the King's reputation and popularity.

At this moment, Hubert enters, and the King takes him apart to confer. Pembroke has heard of the order for Arthur's execution and identifies Hubert as the agent delegated to carry it out. Salisbury remarks that John is changeable, but Pembroke fears that Arthur will perish. King John then announces that Arthur is already dead. Ironically, Salisbury and Pembroke say that they suspected his disease "was past cure" and that he was near death. King John asks why his lords "bend such solemn brows" on him and protests that he cannot control "the shears of destiny" or "the pulse of life." In disgust the lords denounce the King's foul play and stalk out, as a messenger enters with news of the immense force the Dauphin is assembling in France for the invasion of England. King John cannot understand why Queen Elinor has failed to alert him to these preparations, and the messenger reports the death of the Queen Mother and the rumor of Lady Constance's death "in a frenzy." Disheartened by the defection of his peers, the loss of his mother, and the menace of war, King John turns to receive the Bastard, who approaches with Peter of Pomfret.

With direct bluntness, the Bastard says that he has collected the sums of money required but that he has found the people "strangely fantasied" and "full of fear." He then declares that Peter of Pomfret has been publicly prophesying that King John would lose his crown before the next Ascension Day at noon. Summarily, the King commits Peter to Hubert with orders to hang the prophet on the fateful day he has designated. Turning to the Bastard, John directs him to fetch Salisbury, Lord Bigot, and their fellows.

While John is reflecting briefly on his mother's death, Hubert returns with an account of omens, prodigies, and rumors associated with Arthur's supposed death. Petulantly, King John accuses Hubert of instigating the murder of the young Prince and says that it is the curse of rulers "to be attended/By slaves that take their humours for a warrant" to commit deeds of violence. In self-justification Hubert shows John the decree for Arthur's assassination. Although the document is written in the King's hand and bears the royal seal, John insists that Hubert's presence, villainous appearance, and malevolent attitude prompted him to issue the order. Convinced that the King sincerely wishes Arthur alive, Hubert confesses that he did not carry out his orders and tells John that the Prince lives. Relieved, King John apologizes for his unflattering comments about Hubert's fierce appearance and orders him to appease the rebellious peers and bring "The angry lords with all expedient haste."

IV,iii. In Front of the Castle

Resolved to escape his confinement, Arthur leaps from the castle walls, falls on the stones below, and dies. At this instant Pembroke, Salisbury, and Bigot appear. They are discussing a letter from the French that Count Melun has brought to Salisbury and decide to confer with the invaders at St. Edmundsbury. The Bastard approaches and summons the "distemper'd lords" to the King, but they have forsworn allegiance to their ruler and refuse to accompany him. While the Bastard and Salisbury are arguing, Salisbury sees the corpse of Arthur. Horrified by this discovery, the lords conclude that Hubert has carried out the King's instructions and murdered the boy. Salisbury, Pembroke, and Bigot vow to avenge Arthur's death.

Hubert, arriving to fetch the peers to the King, announces that Arthur lives. Salisbury and Bigot denounce him as an archvillain and assassin, and the rival lords draw their weapons while the Bastard commands them to keep the peace. Refusing to believe Hubert's protestations of innocence, the outraged peers depart to ally themselves with the Dauphin. The Bastard, likewise discrediting Hubert's avowal of guiltlessness, berates him and orders him to remove Arthur's body. Bewildered by all that has happened, the Bastard foresees confusion to England because of the impending war with France and "discontents at home."

V,i. England. King John's Palace

King John, in a symbolic gesture of submitting to papal authority, yields his crown to Pandulph, who immediately returns it. John then requests Pandulph to keep his "holy word" and use his ecclesiastical authority to halt the French invasion. Pandulph promises "on this Ascension Day" "to make the French lay down their arms." His mention of the date reminds King John of Peter's prophecy that he would lose his crown on this date, and he finds comfort in the thought that his voluntary submission to the Pope has fulfilled the prediction.

Philip the Bastard enters with news that all Kent (except for Dover Castle) has surrendered to the French and that London has opened its gates to the Dauphin's forces. When John asks why his lords would not return "After they heard young Arthur was alive," the Bastard informs him of Arthur's death, and John thinks that Hubert has played him false. Admitting the possibility of Hubert's innocence, the Bastard implores King John to seize the initiative and meet the French armies with boldness and confidence. John then tells the Bastard of his recent submission to papal authority and of his hope that Pandulph will negotiate a peace. Deeming the King's action base and inglorious, the Bastard exhorts John to take the field, whereupon the King delegates him commander in chief.

V,ii. England. The Dauphin's Camp near St. Edmundsbury

Lewis, the Dauphin, orders Count Melun to make copies of the alliance to which he and Salisbury, Pembroke, and Bigot have sworn.

Salisbury deplores the injustice and grievances that have led him and his fellow peers to desert England and join the Dauphin. The French Prince commends Salisbury's patriotic emotions and promises suitable rewards to the English lords for their service. Lewis assumes that Pandulph is approaching to pronounce a blessing on his cause. Instead, Pandulph discloses John's reconciliation with Rome and orders Lewis to abandon the war and make peace. Disgusted, Lewis reminds Pandulph that he launched the invasion on the Cardinal's instigation, that Rome has provided neither manpower nor financial support, and that the time is ripe for him to establish his rightful claim to the English throne. Defiantly Lewis refuses to withdraw and declares that he will not return to France.

A trumpet announces the arrival of the Bastard, who inquires about the success of Pandulph's negotiations for peace. The Cardinal tells him of Lewis's rejection of compromise and his determination to settle the issue on the battlefield, and the Bastard warmly applauds the nobility of the Dauphin's decision. The Bastard boldly challenges the French and scornfully censures the English peers who have deserted. Refusing to listen longer to the Bastard or to Pandulph, Lewis orders immediate preparations for battle, and the Bastard boasts of the coming English victory.

V,iii. England. The Battlefield

Hubert gives a pessimistic report on the course of the battle, and King John complains of a fever. A messenger appears with the Bastard's request that the King leave the field. John says that he will go to Swinstead Abbey, and the messenger tells of the loss of a large French convoy on the Goodwin Sands. The French are beginning to weaken, but King John is too sick to "welcome this good news."

V,iv. England. Another Part of the Battlefield

Salisbury, Pembroke, and Bigot express amazement at the resistance the English army has offered, attribute this success to the Bastard's leadership, and fear the fate they themselves are facing. Count Melun, mortally wounded, joins them and urges them to return to King John and seek his pardon. The Count warns that Lewis and his staff have sworn to behead the English traitors if the French emerge victorious. Salisbury questions Melun's veracity, but the Frenchman insists that he would not lie when at the point of death. He further explains that his grandfather was an Englishman. Heeding Melun's advice, Salisbury and his companions decide to abandon their rebellion and return to King John. They assist the dying Melun off the field.

V,v. England. The French Camp

As the Dauphin reviews the day's action, a messenger reports Melun's death, the return of the English peers, and the loss of French supplies in the Channel. Wearily, Lewis resolves to "try the fair adventure of to-morrow."

V,vi. England. An Open Place near Swinstead Abbey

Challenging and recognizing each other in the dark, Hubert and the Bastard discuss the poisoning of King John by a monk who posed as food-taster to the monarch. Still alive, John has, at Prince Henry's request, pardoned the English deserters. The Bastard, who has lost half his army in the "Lincoln Washes [estuary]," hastens to join the dying King.

V,vii. The Orchard at Swinstead Abbey

Prince Henry, despairing of his father's recovery, orders Bigot to bring the King into the orchard. Pembroke says that King John is calmer and has been singing. Prince Henry reflects on the strangeness of death and on his imminent succession to the throne. Bigot and attendants carry in the King, who is suffering severe pain and complaining of the heat. As the King dies, the Bastard appears and starts to describe the loss of his troops. Vowing to avenge John's death, the Bastard exhorts the peers to accompany him into battle, but Salisbury tells him that Pandulph has come "half an hour since" with an offer of peace from the Dauphin. The Bastard suspects a trap, but Salisbury assures him that the French are already withdrawing from the field and that Pandulph is fully commissioned to arrange a treaty. Accepting this conclusion to the war, the Bastard advises Prince Henry to make preparations for King John's funeral. Henry orders that the burial take place at Worcester. The Bastard and Salisbury pledge their allegiance to Henry III, their new king. In a concluding speech the Bastard prophesies the independence of England so long as the nation avoids civil war.

> . . . Naught shall make us rue
> If England to itself do rest but true.

RICHARD II [1595–1596]

CHARACTERS

KING RICHARD THE SECOND.

JOHN OF GAUNT, Duke of Lancaster, } uncles to the King.
EDMUND OF LANGLEY, Duke of York, } uncles to the King.

HENRY, surnamed BOLINGBROKE, Duke of Hereford, son to *John of Gaunt;* afterwards *King Henry IV.*

DUKE OF AUMERLE, son to the *Duke of York.*

THOMAS MOWBRAY, Duke of Norfolk.

DUKE OF SURREY.

EARL OF SALISBURY.

LORD BERKELEY.

BUSHY, } servants to *King Richard.*
BAGOT, } servants to *King Richard.*
GREEN, } servants to *King Richard.*

EARL OF NORTHUMBERLAND.

HENRY PERCY, surnamed HOTSPUR, his son.

LORD ROSS.

LORD WILLOUGHBY.

LORD FITZWATER.

BISHOP OF CARLISLE.

ABBOT OF WESTMINSTER.

LORD MARSHAL.

SIR STEPHEN SCROOP.

SIR PIERCE OF EXTON.

Captain of a band of Welshmen.

Two Gardeners.

QUEEN [ISABELLA] to *King Richard.*

DUCHESS OF YORK.

DUCHESS OF GLOUCESTER [widow of Thomas of Woodstock].

Lady attending on the *Queen.*

Lords, Heralds, Officers, Soldiers, Keeper, Messenger, Groom, and other Attendants.

Scene: *England and Wales*

I,i. London. The Palace

Henry Bolingbroke, Duke of Hereford, has previously impugned the honor and reputation of Thomas Mowbray, Duke of Norfolk. King Richard asks John of Gaunt if he has brought Henry to court in order that he may state his accusations and support them publicly. In reply John of Gaunt says that the charge relates to Richard's security and that Henry is ready. After an attendant has ushered in Bolingbroke and Mowbray, the King orders Henry to speak first. Wishing his sovereign well, Henry directly accuses Mowbray of being "a traitor and a miscreant." Scornfully the Duke of Norfolk denies the allegation and calls Bolingbroke "a slanderous coward and a villain." Haughtily Henry throws his gage [1] at Mowbray's feet and dares him to pick it up. Mowbray seizes it and vows to answer Bolingbroke "in any fair degree/Or chivalrous design of knightly trial." Specifically Bolingbroke then accuses Mowbray of: (1) misappropriating eight thousand nobles allocated for his soldiers' pay; (2) inspiring treasons for the past eighteen years; and (3) plotting the recent murder of Thomas of Woodstock, Duke of Gloucester, at Calais.

Richard invites Mowbray to answer the charges, guaranteeing him the right of free and fearless speech. Mowbray claims that he properly compensated his troops and held back the remainder in payment of a debt the King owed him; he further argues that he did not slay the Duke of Gloucester although he neglected his sworn duty to do so.[2] In final defiance Mowbray throws his gage in front of Henry.

Having heard the charges and countercharges, Richard appeals for peace between the two peers. Saying that he will calm Mowbray, Richard orders John of Gaunt to soothe Bolingbroke. Both dukes obstinately defy royal command, neither being willing to incur dishonor by conceding to the other first. Frustrated in his efforts to reconcile the two men, Richard orders them to settle the issue with their swords and lances "At Coventry upon Saint Lambert's day [September 17]."

[1] A token of defiance and a symbolic challenge to trial by combat. Most editors believe that Shakespeare had a glove or gauntlet in mind, although the gage could have been a hood.

[2] Shakespeare apparently wanted his audience to understand that Mowbray identified Aumerle as the actual agent of Gloucester's death. See IV,i, 1–12, and 80–83.

I,ii. London. The Duke of Lancaster's (John of Gaunt's) Palace

John of Gaunt tells the Duchess of Gloucester that they can do nothing to avenge the death of Thomas of Woodstock, Duke of Gloucester, who was her husband and his brother. Only King Richard, who arranged the murder, can punish the offenders. In a highly emotional outburst, the Duchess chides John of Gaunt for exhibiting despair rather than patience and suggests that the best way for him to safeguard his own life is to avenge Gloucester's death. To this, Gaunt replies that he can never lift "An angry arm" against Richard, God's anointed deputy. The Duchess asks to whom she can complain, and Gaunt says, "To God, the widow's champion and defence." Thereupon the Duchess prays for Bolingbroke's triumph and Mowbray's defeat. Gaunt prepares to go to Coventry. The Duchess sends greetings to the Duke of York and departs for Plashy, where she will die in grief.

I,iii. The Lists at Coventry

Aumerle, High Constable of England, informs the Lord Marshal [1] that the two contestants are ready for combat. At the sound of trumpets, King Richard and his retinue appear, followed by Mowbray and the herald. On the King's command, the Lord Marshal demands Mowbray's identification and purpose. Immediately Bolingbroke appears and in like manner proclaims his identity and his aim of proving the Duke of Norfolk "a traitor, foul and dangerous." Both knights take formal leave of their sovereign and friends. With a suggestion of hypocrisy Richard embraces Bolingbroke, who bids farewell to the King and to Aumerle, his "noble cousin." John of Gaunt invokes divine guidance on his son, and Mowbray persists in maintaining himself "A loyal, just, and upright gentleman." On Richard's orders, the Lord Marshal directs the heralds to alert the two opponents. A trumpet signals the start of the combat, but King Richard throws down his warder (staff) to stop the fight and commands Bolingbroke and Mowbray to lay aside their arms and return to their chairs. Protesting his distaste for bloodshed and civil war, Richard banishes Bolingbroke from England for ten years and Mowbray for life.

[1] Shakespeare appears to have overlooked the fact that the Duke of Surrey was also the Lord Marshal. See I,iii, 251–252.

Bolingbroke accepts his sentence with dignity, but Mowbray, who expected more lenient treatment, laments his fate, especially the fact that he will no longer be able to speak or hear his "native English" language. Bolingbroke and Mowbray prepare to leave, but Richard calls them back and requires them to swear that they will never embrace "each other's love in banishment," communicate with each other, or plot or contrive any ill against "us, our state, our subjects, or our land." Both men swear, and Bolingbroke demands that Mowbray confess his treasons before he goes. Stoutly protesting his innocence, Mowbray departs with a veiled prediction that King Richard will soon rue Henry's character.

Turning to John of Gaunt, Richard says that out of pity for his aged uncle he reduces Bolingbroke's banishment to six years. Gaunt thanks the King but prophesies that he will die before the time runs out. Richard repeats his sentence and leaves with his court. Aumerle says good-by to his cousin, and the Lord Marshal vows to accompany Bolingbroke as far as he can on land. In a philosophical farewell, John of Gaunt tries to encourage his son, and they all walk away.

I,iv. London. The Court

Aumerle reports the manner of Bolingbroke's recent departure to Richard, Bagot, and Green. Aumerle also indicates that he has no fondness for his banished cousin. Richard comments that he and his servants have noted how Bolingbroke ingratiated himself with the common people. Green observes that Henry has gone and that Richard should turn his attention to the Irish rebels. Richard declares that he will assume command of the Irish campaign and empower deputies with "blank charters" to levy large sums on the rich to finance the expedition. Bushy enters with news that John of Gaunt is seriously ill at Ely House and wishes to confer with the King. Sardonically hoping that Gaunt's physician speedily assists the old man to his grave, Richard starts with his companions to see his uncle.

II,i. London. Ely House

Near death, John of Gaunt tells his brother, the Duke of York, that he has advice for Richard and hopes that his last words may impress the young monarch. York says that Richard has opened his ear to flattery and "Lascivious metres" and that Gaunt's counsel will be in vain and his breath lost. In an inspired prophecy Gaunt delivers a tribute to "This blessed plot, this earth, this realm, this England," concluding with the sad observation that this nation "that was wont to conquer others/Hath made a shameful conquest of itself." At this moment the King, Queen, and their attendants enter.

Punning on his title, the Duke declares that he is gaunt from worrying and watching over England. More seriously, he warns Richard that he has surrendered himself to flatterers and is squandering the resources of the crown and realm. Infuriated, the King calls the old duke "A lunatic lean-witted fool" and says that he would forfeit his life if he were not the brother of Edward the Black Prince (Richard's father). Accusing Richard of inspiring the murder of the Duke of Gloucester (Richard's uncle), Gaunt dares the King to execute him and commands his retainers to carry him away. While the Duke of York begs Richard to attribute Gaunt's denunciation to sickness and age, Northumberland announces that John of Gaunt has died.

Shrugging off his uncle's death, Richard declares his determination to set out for Ireland and to confiscate to himself all the property belonging to the Duchy of Lancaster. At once, the Duke of York, as the last surviving son of Edward III, protests and denounces this action as worse than Richard's slaying of Gloucester, banishing of Bolingbroke, or other offenses. Vigorously York beseeches the King not to deprive Henry of his rightful title and inheritance, pointing out that Richard will alienate many people and imperil his own claims to the throne. The King is adamant, and York leaves with the warning that good events can never come of bad means. Richard dispatches Bushy on an errand, reveals his intention to appoint the Duke of York Governor of England, and leaves with the Queen and members of the court.

Northumberland, Willoughby, and Ross discuss the injustice Richard has afflicted on Bolingbroke. Fearful of Richard's susceptibility to flattery, aware that he has earned the animosity of the commons and the nobility, and disgusted with his display of avarice and ignobleness, the three lords set out for Ravenspurgh to meet Bolingbroke and his followers.

II,ii. Windsor Castle

Bushy and Bagot attempt to cheer the Queen in Richard's absence, but the young consort has a presentiment of impending danger and a "nameless woe." Green enters with news of Bolingbroke's landing at Ravenspurgh. He identifies several peers who have allied themselves with Bolingbroke. Among these is the Earl of Worcester, who, upon hearing the noblemen proclaimed traitors, resigned the Lord Stewardship and went to join them. In deep despair the Queen sees the Duke of York approaching and begs him to "speak comfortable words," but York, "weak with age," offers no cheer. A servingman announces Aumerle's departure,[1] and York sends the fellow to the Duchess of Gloucester with a request for a thousand pounds. The servingman then tells York that the Duchess has died. Greatly perplexed and upset, York views Richard as his sovereign, whom he has sworn to defend, and Bolingbroke as his kinsman "whom the King hath wrong'd." Faced with the necessity of doing something, York leads the Queen out and plans to assemble his forces at Berkeley Castle.

Realizing that their intimacy with Richard places them in a perilous position, Bushy, Green, and Bagot separate to find their own safety. Bushy and Green will find refuge in Bristow (Bristol) Castle with the Earl of Wiltshire; Bagot will attempt to join Richard in Ireland.

II,iii. In Gloucestershire

Northumberland and Bolingbroke chat while they await the arrival of Lords Willoughby and Ross. Henry Percy (Hotspur) brings the news that the Earl of Worcester has broken his staff of office and has gone to Ravenspurgh to enlist with Bolingbroke; he also reports that Northumberland has been proclaimed traitor. Northumberland introduces Hotspur to Bolingbroke, and the younger Percy points out Berkeley Castle, which York, Berkeley, and Seymour are occupying with a garrison of three hundred men. Bolingbroke welcomes Willoughby and Ross, who ride up at top speed.

Lord Berkeley approaches with a message to "My Lord of Hereford." Bolingbroke insists that Berkeley address him as "Lancaster" and says that he returns to England only to recover the title that is rightfully his. Berkeley replies that he does not care what title Bolingbroke uses but that the Duke of York, as Regent, demands to know why his nephew takes advantage of Richard's absence from the kingdom to "fright our native peace with self-borne arms."

On York's arrival Bolingbroke kneels, but the old lord adjures his

[1] J. Dover Wilson notes that Aumerle had gone to join Richard in Ireland, a point that Shakespeare does not make clear in the play.

nephew to show a humble heart rather than a bended knee. York condemns Bolingbroke's display of force and says that if he were younger and stronger he would punish Henry for his presumption. Bolingbroke demands to know his "fault." York answers that he has broken the terms of his banishment and stands in "gross rebellion and detested treason." In intimate and emotional language Bolingbroke argues that his claims to the Duchy of Lancaster are similar to Richard's claim to the throne, that York should support him even as John of Gaunt might have aided an orphaned Aumerle, and that since he has no recourse to attorneys he must personally lay claim to his inheritance. Northumberland, Ross, and Willoughby affirm the justice of Bolingbroke's case. York admits that he has sympathized with Bolingbroke's plight, but he insists that Henry has no right to take up arms and that all who assist him are rebels.

Northumberland's answer is that Bolingbroke has sworn that his sole purpose is to regain the title and property of Lancaster and that his fellow peers have vowed to help him. Seeing the futility of opposing a force he cannot quell, York says that he will remain neutral. He invites Bolingbroke to spend the night in Berkeley Castle, but Bolingbroke is determined to hasten to Bristol in order to punish Bushy and his accomplices, "The caterpillars of the commonwealth." York, reluctant to break his country's laws, demurs when Bolingbroke asks him to accompany this expedition.

II,iv. A Camp in Wales

Impatient because Richard has not appeared or sent news, the Welsh Captain tells the Earl of Salisbury that he and his countrymen are dispersing. In addition, divers omens and prodigies in nature have convinced the superstitious Welshmen that Richard is dead. The Captain goes, and Salisbury reflects that Richard's glory, "like a shooting star," is falling.

III,i. Bristol. Bolingbroke's Camp

In the presence of his fellow peers Bolingbroke arraigns Bushy and Green for corrupting Rinchard's character and morals and for squandering and vandalizing Henry's own property and estate. He summarily orders Northumberland to see to their execution. After sending his greetings to the Queen, Bolingbroke departs with his companions to suppress Glendower and his accomplices.

III,ii. The Coast of Wales. A Castle in View

King Richard expresses to Aumerle and the Bishop of Carlisle his joy and satisfaction on returning to English soil, but he voices concern regarding the rebellion. The Bishop exhorts the King to trust in Heaven's power to keep him on the throne; Aumerle suggests that they have been remiss in permitting Bolingbroke to gain strength. Richard rebukes Aumerle with the observation that his return from Ireland will put an end to the uprising, that "Not all the water in the rough rude sea/Can wash the balm off from an anointed king," and that "heaven still guards the right." At this moment, Salisbury brings the news that Richard has arrived one day too late and that the Welsh troops on whom the King depended have dispersed and fled. Richard is depressed, but Aumerle bids him remember who he is; and Richard, recalling his glory as a king, hopes that the Duke of York will lend assistance.

At this instant, Scroop reports that Bolingbroke's power is growing and his popularity increasing more rapidly than anyone could have anticipated. Richard inquires about his favorites and the Earl of Wiltshire and learns that they have been beheaded. The King, now low in spirit, ruminates on death and the sad fate of monarchs until Aumerle and the Bishop stir him to action, and he inquires the whereabouts of the Duke of York. Scroop confesses that York and his troops have also joined the rebellion. Ignoring Aumerle's attempt to speak, Richard decides to take refuge in Flint Castle.

III,iii. Wales. In Front of Flint Castle

Northumberland advises Bolingbroke that "Richard" cannot be far away, and the Duke of York rebukes the old peer for omitting the royal title before the King's name. Bolingbroke enters the argument, but Hotspur interrupts with the news that King Richard and his party are in Flint Castle. Bolingbroke commands his supporters to convey his allegiance and "true faith of heart" to the King. He proposes to lay down his arms if Richard will restore to him the title and estate of Lancaster. Otherwise, he vows to seize by force what is rightfully his. Alerted by a flourish of trumpets, King Richard and his followers emerge upon the castle walls. Bolingbroke and York marvel at the splendor and magnificence of Richard's appearance.

Invoking the aid and protection of the Almighty, Richard chides Northumberland for failing to kneel and then orders him to warn

Bolingbroke of the bloodshed that will result from the war he threatens. Northumberland insists that Bolingbroke approaches only to claim his hereditary title and that upon recovering it, he will disband his forces. Richard instructs Northumberland to convey his acceptance of Bolingbroke's terms. Immediately Richard has misgivings and fears that he has debased himself, but Aumerle advises that they should "fight with gentle words" until they recoup their strength. While they watch Northumberland coming again from Bolingbroke, Richard sadly philosophizes on the burdens of kingship and wishes that he might enjoy the pleasures and comforts of a private and solitary life. Sardonically Richard asks if "King Bolingbroke" will "Give Richard leave to live till Richard die," but Northumberland says that Henry wishes to speak with the King in the lower courtyard.

Again Richard concedes to his rival's demands, and in a moment the two cousins meet. Kneeling, Bolingbroke repeats his statement that he comes but for his own. Ironically suggesting that Henry has seized the kingdom, Richard promises that he will give Bolingbroke what he "will have . . . and willing too," and they set out for London.

III,iv. The Duke of York's Garden

Two ladies in waiting are attempting to amuse the Queen, who is sad and heavyhearted. They step aside as a gardener and two servants appear. While the men work, they contrast their carefully tended garden with the unpruned and disordered condition of England. The gardener mentions the recent executions of the King's favorites and Bolingbroke's usurpation and says that Richard will soon be deposed. Stepping forward, the Queen rebukes the gardener but asks him for confirmation of his report. Respectfully, the gardener repeats his story and suggests that the Queen go to London to learn the truth. Summoning her ladies to accompany her, the Queen places a curse on the gardener's plants as punishment for the news he has brought. Sympathetically the gardener plants "a bank of rue" where the Queen has shed a tear.

IV,i. Westminster Hall

Before a meeting of Parliament, Bolingbroke interrogates Bagot on the death of Thomas, Duke of Gloucester (see I,i and ii; and II,i). Bagot accuses Aumerle to his face of complicity in the death of Gloucester and of plotting the death of Bolingbroke. Aumerle replies by throwing down his gage to support his charge that Bagot is lying. Fitzwater hurls his gage in defiance of Aumerle and implicates him in Gloucester's death. When Aumerle berates Fitzwater, Hotspur (Henry Percy) and another lord cast their gages against Aumerle's honor. Fitzwater appeals to the Duke of Surrey to corroborate his statement, but Surrey denounces Fitzwater as a liar and challenges him with another gage. Defying Surrey, Fitzwater testifies that Mowbray once said that Aumerle sent two men to execute Gloucester at Calais, and Aumerle hurls another gage as a challenge to the absent Mowbray. Bolingbroke promises to recall Mowbray from exile in order that he and Aumerle may settle their quarrel. The Bishop of Carlisle, however, reports that Mowbray, after participating in various campaigns against "black pagans, Turks, and Saracens," has died in Venice. Bolingbroke tells the bickering lords that he will appoint a day for their trials of honor.

At this point the Duke of York enters, addresses Bolingbroke as Henry the Fourth, and says that Richard has abdicated in his cousin's favor. Bolingbroke declares that he will ascend the throne, but the Bishop of Carlisle, endorsing the doctrine of the Divine Right of Kings, praises Richard, brands Bolingbroke a traitor, and prophesies that "The blood of English shall manure the gound,/And future ages groan for this foul act."[1] Immediately Northumberland arrests Carlisle for "capital treason" and commits him to the custody of the Abbot of Westminster. Bolingbroke directs that Richard come to abdicate publicly, and York goes to fetch him.

In a moment Richard and the Duke of York appear, accompanied by officers carrying the crown and other symbols of the royal office. Comparing himself with Christ betrayed by Judas, Richard asks why he has been sent for. York tells him that he is to resign the kingship and crown to Bolingbroke. Taking the crown in his hands, Richard passes it to Bolingbroke and compares their relationship to that of two buckets in a well, one empty and the other full. Bolingbroke remarks that he thought Richard was willing to abdicate. Richard answers that he willingly resigns the crown; but he is still king of his griefs, and the cares that attend the crown will remain with him. Quibbling on words, Richard sadly passes the symbols of rule to Bolingbroke and renounces all pomp and majesty together with his royal estates and revenue. He invokes God's pardon on those who have broken their oaths to him and hopes (perhaps ironically) that

[1] Carlisle is prophesying the Wars of the Roses, which began with the Battle of St. Albans in 1455 and ended at Stoke Field in 1487.

the Almighty will preserve the vows of allegiance sworn to Bolingbroke.

Peremptorily, Northumberland interrupts and insists that Richard read the list of indictments against himself and his followers. Richard protests that Northumberland might also find an article condemning himself and others who violate their loyalty and depose their King, but Northumberland is inexorable. Through tears, Richard says that he can see "a sort of traitors" around him and that he is one of them because he has consented to his own abdication. He calls for a mirror in order that he may gaze on a face bankrupt of majesty. Bolingbroke commands an attendant to fetch a looking glass and tells Northumberland to spare Richard further embarrassment.

Commenting that he will see more sins in his own countenance than in the bill of indictment, Richard seizes the mirror and describes his reflection. In bitterness, he dashes the glass to the floor and shatters it, but spontaneously asks Bolingbroke to repeat a striking phrase he has uttered concerning the shadow of the King's grief. Seeking one last boon, Richard asks permission to depart. Henry sends Richard under guard to the Tower and sets his own coronation for the following Wednesday. After Henry walks away, Carlisle predicts that "children yet unborn" will suffer the consequences of Bolingbroke's usurpation, and Aumerle asks if there is no "plot/ To rid the realm of this pernicious blot." The Abbot of Westminster intimates that he is already devising a scheme against Bolingbroke, but Aumerle must "take the sacrament" to preserve secrecy before the Abbot divulges his plan.

V,i. London. A Street Leading to the Tower

The Queen, with ladies and attendants, is waiting to see Richard pass on his way to the Tower. Richard approaches under guard, greets the Queen, urges her not to grieve and to flee to France where she may enter the sanctuary of "some religious house."[1] The Queen chides Richard for having abandoned his lionlike nature in submitting to Bolingbroke, but he again tells her to return to France and to think of him as dead. Northumberland appears and informs Richard that Bolingbroke is transferring him from the Tower to Pomfret and that the Queen "must away to France." With prophetic insight, Richard predicts that Northumberland, having aided Boling-

[1] In actual history, Henry captured Isabella and did not release her until after Richard's death. She returned to France in 1401 and married Charles, Duke of Orleans and Count of Angoulême, in 1406.

broke, will turn against the new monarch.[1] Northumberland separates Richard and the Queen, and Richard accuses the Earl of divorcing him from his crown and from his wife. The Queen prays Northumberland to banish Richard and her together. Northumberland retorts that such an action would be "some love, but little policy [statecraft or diplomacy]." Sadly Richard and the Queen pledge their love and say their farewells.

V,ii. The Duke of York's Palace

Edmund Langley, Duke of York, is describing to his Duchess the sad circumstances of Henry's and Richard's arrival in London. In sympathy with the public's repudiation of Richard, York comments that heaven has controlled "these events" and that they are now the sworn subjects of Bolingbroke. The Duchess sees Aumerle entering, but York tells her that he has lost his title and she must now address him as Rutland. Having taken an oath guaranteeing Aumerle's loyalty to Henry, York warns his son to conduct himself prudently. Perceiving that Aumerle is carrying a document, York asks what it is. Aumerle turns pale but insists " 'tis nothing." Snatching the parchment from his son's bosom, York discovers a compact to assassinate the new King. Denouncing Aumerle as a traitor and villain, York calls for his boots and horse in order that he may warn Henry of the plot against his life. Resisting the Duchess's frantic cries that he is effecting their son's death, York rushes out. In desperation the Duchess tells Aumerle to seek Henry's pardon before York reaches him; she promises to follow and plead in her son's behalf.

V,iii. Windsor Castle

Bolingbroke, now Henry IV, inquires if anyone can reveal the whereabouts of Prince Hal, who has absented himself from court and is rumored to be reveling with dissolute companions in the taverns of London. Hotspur says that he saw the Prince two days before, told him of the jousting at Oxford, and received an insulting and irresponsible answer. Hopefully, King Henry predicts that the Prince will exhibit nobler qualities as he grows older.

Aumerle, staring wildly, dashes in and seeks a private audience with the King. Alone with Henry, Aumerle kneels and pleads for

[1] Shakespeare here anticipates the Percy rebellion of *1* and *2 Henry IV*. Especially see *2 Henry IV,* III,i, 70–77.

pardon before he confesses his fault. Receiving the King's promise of mercy, Aumerle asks and receives permission to lock the door until he finishes his story. No sooner has he turned the key, however, than the Duke of York knocks and shouts to Henry to beware of the traitor in his presence. The King draws his sword and then admits the clamoring York.

Henry reads the document setting forth the plot against his life while Aumerle reminds him of his promised pardon. Somewhat ruthlessly, York scorns Aumerle's professed repentance and advises Henry to punish him regardless of his oath to spare him. Henry praises York's loyalty and says he will forgive Aumerle because of his father's goodness, but York repeats his counsel to execute the offender, who has shamed and dishonored his father. In the midst of their conversation, the Duchess cries for admittance to the King. Henry knows that she comes to plead for her son and instructs Aumerle to admit her. York once more exhorts the King to kill Aumerle lest his proffered leniency encourage later attempts against him. While the Duchess and Aumerle kneel beseeching Henry's pardon, York kneels to oppose their suit. Charging York with hard-heartedness, unnatural cruelty, and "false hypocrisy," the Duchess refuses to rise until Henry pardons her son. At last he does so and then directs the Duke of York to undertake the apprehension and execution of the other conspirators, including his brother-in-law [1] and the Abbot of Westminster.

V,iv. Windsor Castle

Sir Pierce of Exton, recalling King Henry's question "Have I no friend will rid me of this living fear?" tells his servant that he has resolved to kill Richard at Pomfret.

V,v. Pomfret Castle

Philosophizing on his imprisonment, Richard thinks of himself first as a beggar and then as a king and finally decides that he is nothing. He hears music, but time is heavy and tedious and he thinks that the sound will madden him. A groom enters and recalls how grieved he was when Henry, going to his coronation, rode through the London streets on "roan Barbary," Richard's favorite horse. Sadly Richard observes that even the horse deserted his

[1] John Holland, Duke of Exeter, had married Elizabeth, daughter of John of Gaunt and sister of Henry IV.

former master and proudly bore the usurper. A keeper appears with food; Richard dismisses the groom and commands the keeper to taste the food first as he is accustomed to do. When the keeper says that Sir Pierce of Exton has forbidden him to do so, Richard curses Henry and beats the keeper.

As the keeper shouts for help, Exton and his servants rush in. Richard defends himself vigorously, killing two of his would-be assassins before Sir Pierce strikes him down. Accusing Sir Pierce of regicide, Richard dies. Instantaneously Exton comprehends the enormity of his crime but determines to convey Richard's body to Henry.

V,vi. Windsor Castle

Henry has received news of the rebels' razing of Ciceter. While he awaits additional information, Northumberland arrives and announces the execution of various traitors. Fitzwater enters and lengthens the list. Then Hotspur, with the Bishop of Carlisle as his captive, reports the death of the conscience-stricken Abbot of Westminster. Henry, who has detected sparks of honor in Carlisle despite his enmity, sentences the Bishop to spend the remainder of his life in peaceful religious retirement.

Sir Pierce of Exton brings in the coffin and corpse of Richard of Bordeaux, Henry's mightiest enemy, but the King repudiates the murder, castigates Exton as a murderer,[1] and condemns him to perpetual banishment. Proclaiming a period of mourning for Richard, Henry vows that he will make a pilgrimage to the Holy Land "To wash this blood off from my guilty hand."

[1] Compare this scene with that between King John and Hubert in *King John*, IV,ii.

HENRY IV (PART ONE) [1597–1598]

CHARACTERS

KING HENRY THE FOURTH.

HENRY, PRINCE OF WALES, PRINCE JOHN OF LANCASTER, sons to the *King*.

EARL OF WESTMORELAND.

SIR WALTER BLUNT.

THOMAS PERCY, Earl of Worcester.

HENRY PERCY, Earl of Northumberland.

HENRY PERCY, surnamed HOTSPUR, his son.

EDMUND MORTIMER, Earl of March.

ARCHIBALD, Earl of Douglas.

RICHARD SCROOP, Archbishop of York.

SIR MICHAEL, friend to the *Archbishop*.

OWEN GLENDOWER.

SIR RICHARD VERNON.

SIR JOHN FALSTAFF.

[NED] POINS.

BARDOLPH.

PETO.

GADSHILL.

LADY PERCY, wife to *Hotspur* and sister to *Mortimer*.

LADY MORTIMER, wife to *Mortimer*, and daughter to *Glendower*.

MISTRESS QUICKLY, hostess of the Boar's Head in Eastcheap.

Lords, Officers, Sheriff, Vintner, Chamberlain, Drawers [*Francis, Tom, Dick*], two Carriers [*Mugs*], Travellers, and Attendants.

Scene: *England and Wales*

I,i. London. The Palace

Weary of the bloodshed and civil strife that have accompanied his accession to the throne, King Henry recalls his vow to make a pilgrimage to the Holy Land and asks Westmoreland what preparations the Council has made for the journey. The Earl replies that in the midst of that body's deliberations a messenger brought word from Wales that Glendower had captured Mortimer [1] and slain a thousand of his soldiers, whose corpses the Welsh women mutilated. King Henry observes that this uprising has interfered with his projected pilgrimage, and Westmoreland mentions the uncertain rumor of a sharp battle between Hotspur and Archibald, Earl of Douglas, at Holmedon (or Homildon Hill). Henry has already received Sir Walter Blunt's account of Hotspur's glorious victory, which involved heavy casualties on the enemy and the capture of several noble Scots. The King sadly notes how fortunate the Earl of Northumberland is in having "so blest a son" as Hotspur, "sweet Fortune's minion and her pride," whereas he sees "riot and dishonour stain the brow" of his young Harry (Prince Hal). He wishes that "some night-tripping fairy had exchang'd" the two children in their cradle-clothes. Dismissing Prince Hal from his thoughts, Henry turns to the problem of Hotspur's refusal to surrender any prisoners, except Mordake, to his monarch. Westmoreland believes that the Earl of Worcester (Hotspur's uncle) has prompted this defiance. Having summoned Hotspur for an explanation, Henry must postpone his trip to the Holy Land.

I,ii. London. Prince Henry's House

Falstaff, who has been eating, drinking, and sleeping, asks Prince Hal the time of day. The two men amuse themselves with jesting and wordplay until the Prince inquires where they will steal a purse the following night. At this moment Poins enters and tells them that Gadshill [2] is in Rochester looking for pilgrims and traders whom they may rob the next day on the highway to Canterbury. Poins has procured masks for everybody; they have their own horses; and they can sup in Eastcheap afterward. Poins predicts rich booty, and Falstaff urges Prince Hal to join the venture. At first Hal agrees to "be a madcap" and accompany them, but then he wavers and says he will "tarry at home." Poins asks Falstaff to leave him alone with the Prince, whom he will persuade to go along. Quickly Poins proposes to Prince Hal that, after Falstaff, Bardolph, Peto, and Gadshill have waylaid the travelers, the two of them rob the robbers. Prince Hal raises a few feeble objections, but Poins has

[1] Relying on Holinshed, Shakespeare here confuses Edmund Mortimer, 5th Earl of March, with Sir Edmund Mortimer, the Earl's uncle.

[2] Shakespeare borrowed this nickname from one of his sources.

thought of everything. He assures the Prince that their prospective victims are "true-bred cowards" and adds that the real enjoyment of the jest will derive from the "incomprehensible lies" and boasts Falstaff will utter afterwards. Securing Hal's promise to share in the prank, Poins leaves to complete his preparations. In a soliloquy, Prince Hal explains that he is fully aware of the "unyok'd humour" of his idle companions, that he is temporarily consorting with rogues and roisterers, and that in due season he will throw off "this loose behaviour" and win admiration for having changed his way of life.[1]

I,iii. London. The Palace

Describing himself as excessively patient and tolerant with insubordination and disobedience, King Henry angrily dismisses the Earl of Worcester (Thomas Percy) from court. Northumberland (Henry Percy the elder) interposes with the explanation that someone has distorted the spirit in which Hotspur declined to turn his Scottish prisoners over to the King. In his own defense, Hotspur insists that he did not positively refuse to deliver the captives to the King but says that the foppish manners of an elegantly dressed and perfumed lord enraged him and provoked his curt statement before he had cooled from the heat of battle. Sir Walter Blunt argues that the King would do well to ignore and forget any remarks attributed to Hotspur under such circumstances.

King Henry observes that Hotspur's willingness to yield the prisoners is, however, conditioned on Henry's ransoming Edmund Mortimer (Hotspur's brother-in-law) from Owen Glendower. The King refuses to deplete his treasury to redeem a traitor who betrayed his troops and then married the daughter of his captor. Hotspur vigorously defends Mortimer's reputation and in flowery language describes a hand-to-hand struggle between his brother-in-law and Glendower. The King retorts that Mortimer would rather have faced the devil alone than fight Glendower, that he never met the Welshman in combat, and that Northumberland and Hotspur must deliver their prisoners or suffer the consequences.

After King Henry, Sir Walter Blunt, and their attendants have departed, Hotspur vows that he will not release his Scottish captives to the King. His father urges him to control his rage, but Hotspur

[1] Many editors agree that this soliloquy is a "kind of chorus" in which Shakespeare disregards dramatic propriety in order to safeguard the Prince's reputation in the eyes of the audience.

declares that he will take up arms in Mortimer's behalf. The Earl of Worcester returns, and Northumberland explains the cause of Hotspur's anger. Worcester and Northumberland recall that Richard II proclaimed Mortimer heir to the throne[1] and suggest that this fact explains King Henry's dislike for the man. Immediately Hotspur seizes the opportunity to plead that his family atone for its part in overthrowing Richard II by advancing Mortimer's claim to the throne and thus deposing Henry, "this thorn, this canker, . . . this proud king." Worcester agrees to reveal a "deep and dangerous" scheme to his nephew but has difficulty in restraining the excited Hotspur long enough to explain what he has in mind. Hotspur finally ends his tirade, and Worcester advises him to free his Scottish captives without ransom, thus winning their support. Meanwhile Worcester and Northumberland will enlist the assistance of the Archbishop of York, who has personal reasons for detesting the King.[2] Worcester remarks that Henry, knowing himself indebted to the Percy family, will grow more and more distrustful of its members. Confident of their success in forming a coalition with Scotland, Mortimer, and the Archbishop of York, the three Percies leave, Hotspur eager for the blows and groans of the battlefield.

II,i. Rochester. An Inn Yard

By lantern light in the darkness of early morning, two Carriers are packing their horses for the road. Gadshill appears and attempts to learn details of their journey. The Carriers are suspicious and avoid giving him direct answers, but they innocently reveal that gentlemen with a large amount of money are traveling with them. As soon as they leave, Gadshill calls the employee of the inn (the "Chamberlain"). This man is in league with the highwayman and briefs him on the identity and wealth of the travelers, who are ordering breakfast prior to their departure. The Chamberlain teases Gadshill about his occupation, but the robber boasts that if he hangs, "old Sir John" will hang with him. Promising his confederate a share of the loot, Gadshill calls for his gelding and leaves.

[1] Again Shakespeare, following Holinshed, confuses the members of the Mortimer family. Richard first proclaimed Roger Mortimer his heir; on Roger's death in 1398, Richard similarly designated Edmund Mortimer (son of Roger and 5th Earl of March) as his successor. The Edmund Mortimer who married Glendower's daughter was Roger's brother and the Fifth Earl's uncle.

[2] Shakespeare follows Holinshed in erroneously identifying Richard Scroop, the Archbishop, as a brother of William Scroop, Earl of Wiltshire, whom Henry executed at Bristol in 1399.

II,ii. The Highway near Gadshill

Poins has hidden Falstaff's horse, and he and the Prince step aside as Falstaff appears shouting for Poins. Prince Hal joins Falstaff, rebukes him for making so much commotion, and says that he will look for Poins on top of the hill. Alone, Falstaff bewails his misfortune in having such rogues and tricksters for companions. He shouts for his horse, and the Prince orders him to be quiet and listen for approaching travelers. Gadshill, Bardolph, and Peto come up with news that wayfarers are drawing near. Prince Hal suggests that he and Poins retire and hold themselves in reserve; he tells Falstaff the whereabouts of the missing horse; and Poins assures Prince Hal that their disguises are close at hand.

Without Prince Hal and Poins, Falstaff and his accomplices attack the unsuspecting travelers, rob them, bind them, and depart. Immediately the Prince and Poins return and wait until Falstaff and his partners in crime come back. Falstaff sneers at the cowardice Poins and Prince Hal have exhibited and starts dividing the booty with his accomplices. Emerging from their concealment, the Prince and Poins easily frighten the thieves, who flee, abandoning the spoil. Chuckling over their prank, Poins and Prince Hal leave.

II,iii. Warkworth Castle

Hotspur is reading and commenting contemptuously on a letter from a lukewarm and hesitant adherent to the Percy conspiracy. Lady Percy, whom he addresses as Kate,[1] enters and inquires why he has banished her from his bed and why he has appeared so deeply preoccupied. Ignoring her, Hotspur calls a servant and asks about his horse. When the servant withdraws, Lady Percy renews her questioning. She suspects that her brother has induced him to undertake some perilous enterprise, but Hotspur tells her nothing. Pretending to scorn her love, he warns her of the need for absolute secrecy and says that he must leave at once.

II,iv. Eastcheap. The Boar's Head Tavern

Prince Hal is boasting to Poins how he has won the friendship of the Drawers and learned their slang. They decide to make sport of Francis. Calling for service, the Prince pretends to offer the Drawer

[1] Historically Hotspur's wife was Elizabeth Mortimer, sister of Roger Mortimer, 4th Earl of March. The chroniclers called her Eleanor.

a place in his retinue. Poins, who has gone into another room, constantly interrupts by shouting "Francis!" Trained to answer "Anon," the Drawer keeps breaking into the conversation of the Prince, who finally tells the confused lad to take Poins's order. The Vintner enters, sends Francis to Poins, and asks the Prince if he should admit Falstaff and his fellows. Calling Poins, Prince Hal proposes that they amuse themselves at Falstaff's expense. After a last jibe at Francis, Prince Hal impersonates Hotspur and intimates that he and Falstaff will play the roles of Hotspur and Lady Percy.

Entering with his fellow thieves, Falstaff quenches his thirst with wine and accuses Prince Hal and Poins of cowardice in the recent Gadshill episode. When Falstaff claims that he and his cronies robbed the travelers of a thousand pounds, the Prince demands to see the money. Then Falstaff and Gadshill relate how a large body of men attacked them and hijacked their booty. The Prince goads Falstaff into exaggerating his tale until he has contradicted himself with absurdities and impossibilities. At last Hal tells Falstaff that he and Poins were the hijackers and have the loot to prove it. Instantly Falstaff insists that he recognized Hal in disguise and that his own lionlike instinct kept him from resisting or fighting with a true prince. Seeking other amusement, Falstaff and Prince Hal agree to "have a play extempore," but Mistress Quickly enters to announce that a courtier has come from the King in search of Prince Hal. Falstaff goes to get rid of the messenger. The Prince learns from Bardolph and Peto how Falstaff hacked his own sword and induced his companions to make their noses bleed in order to produce spurious evidence of a ferocious melee. Falstaff comes back with news of the Northumberland uprising and says that Prince Hal must report to court the following morning. Falstaff asks if the King will chide the Prince for his conduct, and Hal proposes that they dramatize the anticipated event. Falstaff assumes the role of King Henry and interrogates the Prince on his disgraceful behavior. Mistress Quickly is convulsed with merriment as Falstaff regally and paternally admonishes Prince Hal and praises himself as a man of "most noble carriage" and much virtue.

Changing roles, Prince Hal speaks in his father's person, and Falstaff impersonates the Prince. Wittily the Prince describes Falstaff as "a tun of man" a "roasted Manningtree ox with the pudding in his belly, that reverend vice, that grey iniquity." Speaking in the person of Prince Hal, Falstaff starts to defend himself and his habits when Bardolph, who has gone with the hostess and Francis to investigate a knocking at the door, brings word that the Sheriff and a large band are outside. The Hostess follows to say that they have come to search the house. Telling Falstaff to hide behind the drapes, the Prince prepares to meet the searchers.

The Sheriff and one of the Carriers from Gadshill have traced a "gross fat man" to the Boar's Head. Assuring them that the man is not "here," the Prince pledges to send Falstaff to the Sheriff the following day to answer any charges that anyone may lay against him. The Sheriff and the Carrier withdraw, and the Prince tells Peto [1] to call Falstaff from behind the tapestry. Sir John is peacefully snoring, however, and the Prince and Peto search him. All they find are tavern bills itemizing an "intolerable deal of sack" and "but one halfpennyworth of bread." The Prince promises Peto a place in the army, indicates that he will give Falstaff a command in the infantry, and says that the loot of the robbery will be paid back "with advantage [addition]."

III,i. Bangor. The Archdeacon's House [2]

Hotspur and Worcester have met with Glendower and Mortimer to plan the rebellion. Glendower vaingloriously boasts of the prodigies and earthquake accompanying his birth. Hotspur, rashly skeptical, denies that nature trembled because of Glendower's nativity. The Welsh chieftain grows increasingly angry at Hotspur's mockery. Mortimer tries to quiet the two men and at Glendower's suggestion analyzes the map on which the Archdeacon has divided Henry's kingdom of England and Wales "Into three limits very equally." Mortimer, Hotspur, and Worcester will meet Northumberland and the Scottish army at Shrewsbury; Glendower, with his forces and Ladies Mortimer and Percy, will join them later. Hotspur, dissatisfied with his share of territory, threatens to dam the Trent River and divert its course so as to gain more land. Tempers mount again until Glendower concedes to Hotspur's demand and leaves to inform the ladies of their husbands' departure.

Mortimer rebukes Hotspur for vexing and contradicting Glendower, but young Percy argues that the old Welshman is tedious, impractical, and exasperating. Mortimer defends his father-in-law and insists that Glendower's admiration for Hotspur is the only factor that has led the chieftain to restrain himself as well as he has done. Worcester also criticizes Hotspur for his tactlessness and lack

[1] Some editors assign Peto's lines to Poins at this point in the scene.
[2] Some editors locate this scene in Glendower's House or Castle.

of self-control. At this moment Glendower returns with the two ladies. Lady Mortimer can speak no English, Mortimer no Welsh. Overcome with emotion at parting, Lady Mortimer speaks through her father as interpreter. While Hotspur and Kate listen, Lady Mortimer sings a Welsh ditty. Hotspur invites his wife to sing, but she refuses. Hotspur leaves, and the others follow him.

III,ii. London. The Palace

Dismissing his attending Lords, King Henry roundly rebukes Prince Hal for his dissoluteness and irresponsibility. Admitting that he has erred at times and asking pardon for past offenses, the Prince pleads that flatterers and "base newsmongers" have exaggerated reports of his wild behavior. King Henry reminds the Prince that he has forfeited his place on the Privy Council to his younger brother, Thomas, Duke of Clarence. Disturbed by Prince Hal's bad reputation and preference for disreputable companions, the King recalls his own assumption of affability and modesty in order to win popular support during his rebellion against Richard II. Henry also took pains to display traits of simplicity and economy in contrast to the haughtiness and frivolity of Richard, in whose model Prince Hal has cast himself.

Prince Hal promises henceforward to "be more" himself, but the King says that the Prince now plays the part Richard played when Henry landed at Ravenspurgh, "And even as I was then is Percy now." Enlarging on this theme, King Henry observes that Hotspur has "more worthy interest to the state" than Hal has as Prince of Wales. After describing the rebellion against him, the King charges Prince Hal with being his "nearest and dearest enemy." Repudiating this picture of himself, the Prince seriously vows to take the field and personally "redeem all this" on Hotspur's head. The King confers "charge [an army command] and sovereign trust" on the Prince as Sir Walter Blunt enters with a report of the assembling of the rebel armies at Shrewsbury. Quickly the King issues campaign orders to the royal forces that are to meet at Bridgenorth in twelve days.

III,iii. Eastcheap. The Boar's Head Tavern

In a characteristic exhibition of wordplay, Falstaff chafes Bardolph on the fiery redness of his nose, a condition produced by many years of heavy drinking. Mistress Quickly appears but maintains that she and her husband have been unable to learn who picked Falstaff's pocket. When Falstaff insists that the Hostess is lying, she turns the tables on him by naming his heavy debts to her. While they are arguing, Prince Hal and Poins [1] march in, and Falstaff plays on his truncheon (short staff) as if it were a fife. Mistress Quickly begs the Prince to settle the quarrel over the pocket-picking and repeats Falstaff's threat to cudgel the Prince for saying that his ring was copper only. Prince Hal sides with the Hostess and exposes Falstaff's grandiose claims of the belongings he says he has lost. Finally the Prince confesses that he picked Sir John's pocket, and Falstaff sends the Hostess to prepare breakfast. Prince Hal informs Falstaff that he has repaid the travelers' stolen money and procured Falstaff a commission in the army. Sir John wishes that he could serve in the cavalry and says that he needs money for equipment. The Prince dispatches Poins on military errands and directs Falstaff to meet him in the Temple Hall the following day.

IV,i. The Rebel Camp near Shrewsbury

Hotspur and Douglas are concluding a conversation as a messenger appears with word that Northumberland is ill and cannot take the field. Worcester and Hotspur deplore the elder Percy's absence at a time when they cannot postpone the battle. Douglas agrees with them that Northumberland's strength will, nevertheless, provide a nucleus around which they may regroup in the event that their efforts do not prosper. Worcester fears that many will interpret Northumberland's failure to join battle as evidence of his dislike for the enterprise, but Hotspur sees an opportunity to gain greater glory with a smaller force. Sir Richard Vernon comes up to describe the approach of the royalist armies, and Hotspur immediately looks forward to personal combat with Prince Hal. Vernon adds the disappointing news that Glendower has been delayed and cannot participate, but Hotspur jauntily ignores the enemy's superiority in numbers and calls his companions to prepare for battle.

IV,ii. A Public Road near Coventry

Falstaff sends Bardolph to bring him a bottle of sack from Coventry. Falstaff then confesses to himself that he has abused his authority as an officer, lined his own pockets, and collected a dis-

[1] Some editors follow the early texts in assigning this role to Peto; most prefer to substitute Poins. See II,iv above, p. 35, note 1.

reputable group of "tattered Prodigals" as soldiers. Prince Hal and the Earl of Westmoreland join him, exhort him to resume his march, and criticize the poverty and bareness of his troops. Falstaff cynically comments that they are "food for powder and will fill a pit as well as better [men]."

IV,iii. The Rebel Camp near Shrewsbury

Worcester and Vernon are attempting to dissuade Hotspur and Douglas from attacking immediately. While the four commanders argue, Blunt approaches with King Henry's invitation to confer and mediate the causes of the rebellion. Hotspur reviews the assistance Northumberland gave Henry in his insurrection against Richard II, after all of which Henry has insulted the Percies and their kinsmen and has broken his promises to them. Willing to play for time, Hotspur proposes a truce until the following morning, when Worcester will carry the rebels' answer to Henry's offer of peace and amnesty.

IV,iv. York. The Archbishop's Palace

Apprehensive about the outcome of the imminent battle at Shrewsbury, the Archbishop gives Sir Michael several messages which are designed to forestall reprisals for the Archbishop's complicity in the rebellion.

V,i. The King's Camp near Shrewsbury

At sunrise King Henry and Prince Hal, with other officers, are forecasting the weather. Worcester and Vernon approach for a parley. The King charges Worcester with disloyalty and asks if he will help restore peace in the realm. Claiming that he has not wanted war, Worcester replies that Henry has violated his promises by usurping the throne and oppressing the kingdom. King Henry retorts that there has never been an insurrection based on such flimsy pretexts or excuses. Prince Hal interrupts with an offer to settle the entire issue in personal combat with Hotspur, whose valor and prowess he greatly admires. Reluctantly, the King agrees to Prince Hal's plan and directs Worcester and Vernon to carry the challenge to Hotspur and return with an answer. Prince Hal and his father agree that Hotspur and Douglas are unlikely to risk their chances in such a trial, and the King departs with most of his staff to prepare for the coming battle. Prince Hal exchanges a couple of jests with Falstaff and leaves. Falstaff somewhat cynically soliloquizes on the emptiness of honor that demands death from him who practices it.[1]

V,ii. The Rebel Camp

As the two men make their way back from the parley, Worcester insists that Hotspur must not learn of "The liberal and kind offer of the King." To Vernon's opinion that they should report the truth, Worcester replies that, although Henry may pardon and forget Hotspur's rashness and previous offenses, he will eventually punish the two elder Percies (Northumberland and Worcester). When Hotspur and Douglas appear, Worcester says that King Henry is resolved to engage in battle, and Hotspur sends his defiance by the Earl of Westmoreland, who has been held as a hostage during the parley. Worcester misrepresents his recent conversation with the King; Douglas returns with news that battle is in the offing; and Worcester tells Hotspur of Prince Hal's chivalric offer "to single fight." Ignoring arriving messengers, Hotspur embraces his comrades as trumpets sound the commencement of the conflict.

V,iii. The Field between the Camps

King Henry and his army march past; Douglas slays Sir Walter Blunt, who has arrayed himself in armor like that of the King. Hotspur arrives, identifies Blunt, and leaves with Douglas in pursuit of other foes. Falstaff, praying that God will keep lead out of him and commenting on the heavy casualties his company has sustained, finds the body of Sir Walter. Prince Hal overtakes Falstaff, chides him for malingering, and asks for his sword. Falstaff refuses, but offers Hal his pistol instead. Opening Falstaff's holster, Prince Hal draws out a bottle of sack and disgustedly throws it at the old soldier.

V,iv. Another Part of the Field

King Henry commands John of Lancaster to escort the wounded Prince Hal from the field, but both Princes implore the King to continue the battle with renewed courage. Prince Hal praises the manly spirit of his young brother and leaves. Douglas discovers the King and is about to vanquish him when Prince Hal returns

[1] Critics differ in their interpretation of Falstaff's "catechism," some arguing that it reflects cowardice in Sir John. Others hold that he is only half-serious and is expressing "the half-cynical mood of a veteran soldier who has outlived the romance of warfare" (Kittredge).

and quickly forces the Scot to flee. Prince Hal vindicates his reputation by telling the King that if he had wanted him dead he could have permitted Douglas to kill him. After Henry leaves, Hotspur finds Prince Hal, and they fight furiously. Falstaff appears and starts to cheer the Prince when Douglas reappears and engages Falstaff, who falls as if slain. Douglas leaves, and Prince Hal kills Hotspur. Lauding his fallen enemy, Prince Hal laments that such a noble spirit has perished in such an ignominious cause. In the midst of his eulogy, Prince Hal sees Falstaff on the ground, deplores his fat friend's death, and dashes off.

Rising, Falstaff defends his pretext of dying to save his life. Looking at Hotspur's body, he wonders for a moment if the valiant warrior is also feigning death. To be on the safe side, he stabs Hotspur's body in the thigh and then lifts the corpse to his back just as Prince Hal and Prince John come into view. Hal has reported Falstaff's death to his brother, and both are amazed to find the old knight alive. Alert to every opportunity, Falstaff claims a reward for having slain Hotspur. Prince Hal observes that he, himself, killed Percy, but Falstaff says that he slew Hotspur after they both revived and "fought a long hour by Shrewsbury clock." Prince John is skeptical, but Hal assures Falstaff that he will support his barefaced lie. The Princes depart to assess their victory, and Falstaff, vowing to "purge, and leave sack, and live cleanly," follows with Hotspur's body.

V,v. Another Part of the Field

Before his commanders, King Henry condemns Worcester for his treacherous failure to bear "true intelligence" between the two armies. Worcester's only reply is that he acted in self-interest, and the King orders the execution of Worcester and Vernon. Prince Hal reports that his followers have captured the mighty Douglas, who fell from a hill in his flight. With the King's permission Hal directs Prince John to free Douglas without ransom in recognition of his valor. The king orders Prince John and Westmoreland to move toward York in order to engage Northumberland and Archbishop Scroop, while he and Prince Hal go to Wales to encounter Glendower and Mortimer.

HENRY IV (PART TWO) [1597–1598]

CHARACTERS

RUMOUR, the Presenter.

KING HENRY THE FOURTH.

PRINCE HENRY, afterwards crowned KING HENRY THE FIFTH.

PRINCE JOHN OF LANCASTER, HUMPHREY OF GLOUCESTER, THOMAS OF CLARENCE, — sons to *Henry IV* and brethren to *Henry V.*

EARL OF NORTHUMBERLAND, RICHARD SCROOP, Archbishop of York, LORD MOWBRAY, LORD HASTINGS, LORD BARDOLPH, SIR JOHN COLEVILLE, — opposites against *King Henry IV.*

TRAVERS, MORTON, — retainers of *Northumberland,*

EARL OF WARWICK, EARL OF WESTMORELAND, EARL OF SURREY, EARL OF KENT,[1] GOWER, HARCOURT, BLUNT, — of the *King's* party.

LORD CHIEF JUSTICE.

Servant to the *Lord Chief Justice.*

SIR JOHN FALSTAFF, EDWARD POINS, BARDOLPH, PISTOL, PETO, Page [to *Falstaff*], — irregular humourists.

[ROBERT] SHALLOW, SILENCE, — country Justices.

DAVY, servant to *Shallow.*

FANG, SNARE, — two Sergeants.

[1] Some editors omit Kent, who along with Surrey and Blunt, has no speaking part.

[RALPH] MOULDY, country soldiers.
[SIMON] SHADOW, country soldiers.
[THOMAS] WART, country soldiers.
[FRANCIS] FEEBLE, country soldiers.
[PETER] BULLCALF, country soldiers.

FRANCIS, a drawer.

LADY NORTHUMBERLAND.

LADY PERCY [*Hotspur's* Widow].

HOSTESS QUICKLY, of the Boar's Head, Eastcheap.

DOLL TEARSHEET.

EPILOGUE [a Dancer].

Lords, Attendants; Porter, Drawers; Beadles, Grooms, Servants.

Scene: *England*

Induction. Warkworth. In Front of Northumberland's Castle

Rumour,[1] wearing a coat "painted full of tongues," explains how she stuffs "the ears of men with false reports." She has appeared to spread the untrue word that Hotspur has killed Prince Hal and that Douglas has slain King Henry IV. Other messengers, following her, will confirm the belief that the victory at Shrewsbury was a defeat for the royal army.

I,i. Warkworth. In Front of Northumberland's Castle

Lord Bardolph sends the Porter to fetch the Earl of Northumberland, who appears immediately. In reply to the Earl's eager inquiry, Lord Bardolph tells of the mortal wounding of King Henry, the death of Prince Hal, heavy losses to the King's forces, and the retreat of the royalist survivors from Shrewsbury. Under Northumberland's questioning, Lord Bardolph admits that his news is hearsay. At this moment Travers comes up. He, too, has heard of a rebel victory, but he has also learned from another observer that Hotspur (Northumberland's son, Henry Percy) has fallen and the rebellion has failed. While Lord Bardolph argues against accepting these adverse reports, Morton arrives with his account as an eyewitness. Morton faithfully relates that Prince Hal has killed Hotspur, that the Earl of Worcester (Northumberland's brother) and Douglas are

[1] Some editors regard this character as masculine; others treat Rumour as feminine. Sometimes called Fame as well as Rumour, the character derives from the personified abstractions of the morality plays and early interludes. Inasmuch as the role comes ultimately from Fama (Virgil's *Aeneid*), the feminine interpretation appears reasonable.

prisoners, and that a force under Prince John of Lancaster and the Earl of Westmoreland is advancing against Northumberland. Grieving for his son and smarting under his party's defeat, Northumberland flings his crutch aside, declares his strength renewed, and resolves to take the field to gain revenge. Lord Bardolph, Travers, and Morton try to dissuade the ailing Earl from risking himself and his followers in such rash action. Morton advises Northumberland that Scroop, Archbishop of York, is reorganizing the rebellion and attracting many adherents. The Earl agrees that they should move more slowly and contact potential allies.

I,ii. London. A Street

Falstaff, suffering from gout, has had a urinalysis and asks his Page for the doctor's diagnosis. The boy answers that the doctor said the specimen was healthy enough but that the man to whom it belonged had numerous diseases. Priding himself on his ability to induce laughter, Falstaff says, "I am not only witty in myself, but the cause that wit is in other men." The fat knight loses some of his gaiety when the Page tells him that his tradesman will not supply him with satin on credit. Falstaff then inquires for Bardolph, who has gone to Smithfield to purchase Falstaff a horse.

At this moment the Page announces the approach of the Lord Chief Justice, accompanied by his servant. Falstaff tries to avoid the Justice, but the official directs his servant to detain Sir John. Persistently, the Chief Justice tries to rebuke Falstaff, who repeatedly turns the conversation to other topics, including King Henry's illness. Finally the Justice says that Falstaff's valor at Shrewsbury has mitigated his complicity in the Gadshill robbery, but he warns the old knight against continuing to mislead the Crown Prince. After a long chat in which Falstaff alludes to Prince Hal's rudeness in giving the Chief Justice a box on the ear and the Justice refers to the King's separating of Falstaff from the Prince and to Falstaff's plan to join the forces of Prince John of Lancaster, Falstaff asks the Justice to lend him a thousand pounds with which to outfit himself. The Chief Justice refuses to loan him a penny and leaves. Learning from his Page that his purse contains only seven groats and twopence, Falstaff sends the boy with letters to Prince John, Prince Hal, the Earl of Westmoreland, and old "Mistress Ursula," whom he has repeatedly "sworn to marry." Cursing his gout and his pox, Falstaff limps away.

I,iii. York. The Archbishop's Palace

The Archbishop, Mowbray, Hastings, and Lord Bardolph are discussing the prospects of renewing the rebellion against Henry IV. Although they command a force of twenty-five thousand men, they agree that they must have Northumberland's support and leadership to assure success. Hastings argues that they will have to meet only a third of King Henry's total army, since he is also campaigning against the French and against Glendower. Furthermore, Hastings is certain that King Henry and Prince Hal will take the field against the Welsh and that Prince John and Westmoreland will oppose the rebels. The Archbishop urges that they revenge Richard II against Henry IV at once; Mowbray and Hastings concur.

II,i. London. A Street

Fang and Snare prepare to arrest Falstaff on a charge of debt brought by Mistress Quickly for the hundred marks he owes her. When Bardolph and Falstaff appear, the old knight defies Fang's attempt to arrest him. A brawl ensues as the Lord Chief Justice and his men come on the scene. In front of the Justice, Mistress Quickly accuses Falstaff of breach of promise and of bankrupting her. Recognizing Falstaff's talent for twisting truth to his advantage, the Justice tells him to satisfy the Hostess before he leaves on the campaign.

Gower arrives with a letter for the Chief Justice, and Falstaff cleverly placates Mistress Quickly and elicits her promise to lend him an additional twenty nobles. Sending Bardolph with the Hostess and the Sergeants, Falstaff learns from Gower of the disposition of the royalist troops. He invites Gower to dinner, but the Justice reminds Falstaff that he should be recruiting soldiers.

II,ii. London. Another Street [1]

After joking with Poins, Prince Hal confesses that he is in sober spirits because of his father's illness. Bardolph and Falstaff's Page arrive with Falstaff's letter to Prince Hal. To the accompaniment of much banter, the Prince and Poins read the letter. In it Falstaff warns Prince Hal that Poins is presuming on his friendship and is proclaiming that the Prince will marry his sister Nell. Learning from

[1] Professor J. Dover Wilson transfers this scene to "A room in the Prince's house."

Bardolph that Falstaff plans to sup at the Boar's Head with Mistress Quickly and Doll Tearsheet, a prostitute, Prince Hal suggests that Poins and he spy on Falstaff and his companions at supper. Bribing Bardolph and the Page not to reveal the scheme to Falstaff, Poins and the Prince resolve to disguise themselves as drawers in "leathern jerkins and aprons" and wait on Sir John at the Boar's Head.

II,iii. Warkworth. In Front of the Castle

Northumberland's wife and daughter-in-law are pleading with the old Earl not to take the field with the other rebels. He insists that his honor demands his participation. Lady Percy (Hotspur's widow) reminds him that he lost "two honours," his own and Hotspur's, when he remained at home and did not fight at Shrewsbury. She argues that he should not dishonor Hotspur's spirit by showing more faithfulness to others than he did to his own son; besides, Mowbray and the Archbishop have a powerful army. Northumberland says that he must seek danger before it finds him "worse provided." His wife urges him to "fly to Scotland," and Lady Percy suggests that he delay until the rebels gain some initial successes. Yielding to their appeals, the Earl decides to go to Scotland and wait there until "time and vantage" crave his company.

II,iv. London. The Boar's Head Tavern in Eastcheap

Two Drawers [1] are chatting about the shriveled apples one has brought for Falstaff and about Sneak's musicians to provide entertainment for Doll Tearsheet. One of them reminds the other of Bardolph's message that they are secretly to lend their clothes to the Prince and Poins. Mistress Quickly and Doll come in, the latter somewhat tipsy. Falstaff enters singing, tells the Drawer (Francis) to empty the chamber pot, and starts bickering with Doll. Mistress Quickly interposes to stop their salacious wrangling, and Doll offers to be friends with Sir John since he is "going to the wars." Francis returns with news that Ancient [2] Pistol wishes to speak with Falstaff. Despite the Hostess's and Doll's protests that Pistol not be admitted because he is a "swaggering rascal," Falstaff orders Francis to call him up.

Entering with Bardolph and the Page, Pistol immediately becomes involved in a scurrilous argument with Doll. Falstaff and the Hostess

[1] Many editors designate one of these Drawers as "Francis."

[2] "Ancient" was another form of "ensign," meaning standard-bearer, formerly a military rank.

try to calm the excited Doll and brawling Pistol. When Pistol snatches up his sword and resists Bardolph's attempt to usher him out, Falstaff draws and drives the Ancient out accompanied by Bardolph. In a moment Bardolph returns and says that the drunken Pistol has received a wound in the shoulder. Doll lavishes amorous attention on Falstaff, and the Page announces the arrival of the Musicians. Closely behind the entertainers come Prince Hal and Poins disguised as Drawers.

Doll questions Falstaff about the character of Prince Hal and Poins, and her fat admirer describes them in derogatory fashion while the two "victims" exchange caustic comments on Falstaff and Doll. At last the Prince and Poins reveal their true identity. Hostess Quickly welcomes Prince Hal warmly, as does Falstaff, who at the same time repudiates Doll for her "light flesh and corrupt blood." The Prince scolds Falstaff for abusing and dispraising him in the presence of "this honest, virtuous, civil gentlewoman," but the old knight argues that he has done this "that the wicked might not fall in love with him." As the chaffing increases, Peto bursts in with word that the King has arrived at Westminster, that numerous messengers have come with news from the North, and that a dozen captains are searching the taverns for Falstaff. Abruptly reminded of his public responsibilties, the Prince calls for his cloak and sword and bidding Falstaff good night, hastens away with Poins, Peto, and Bardolph. Immediately Bardolph comes back to advise Falstaff that the captains are waiting at the door for him. The two men go into another room, and Bardolph calls to the Hostess to send the weeping Doll to Falstaff.

III,i. Westminster. The Palace

It is about one o'clock in the morning, and King Henry, clad in his dressing gown, orders his Page to carry certain letters to the Earls of Warwick and Surrey and call them to him. Alone, Henry laments his sleeplessness whereas many thousands of his poorest subjects are sleeping peacefully. "Uneasy lies the head that wears a crown," he remarks. Warwick and Surrey enter. They have read the letters and understand the King's concern for the security of his kingdom, but Warwick assures his master that "Northumberland will soon be cool'd." Recalling his deposing of Richard II and the first Percy Rebellion, King Henry remembers Richard's prophecy that Northumberland would assist Bolingbroke to the throne and then turn against him. Warwick interprets Richard's prediction as a safe guess and argues that the rumor estimating the rebel forces to be "fifty thousand strong" is a gross exaggeration. Warwick believes that the King has made adequate military preparations; he has received proof of Glendower's death; and he begs the King to go to bed since his fortnight's illness has weakened him. Accepting Warwick's advice, King Henry remarks that, once he has quelled the civil war, he will plan a pilgrimage to the Holy Land.

III,ii. Gloucestershire. In Front of Justice Shallow's House

Justice Shallow and Justice Silence meet. After they exchange greetings and inquiries about various members of their families, Shallow reminisces on his madcap student days in Clement's Inn. One of his roistering companions was the boy Jack Falstaff, then page to Thomas Mowbray, Duke of Norfolk, now Sir John Falstaff, who is soon to arrive on his mission of recruiting soldiers. Interspersing his recollections of former friends, most of whom have died, with inquiries about the market prices for livestock, Shallow greets Bardolph, who arrives with a companion. Bardolph brings formal greetings from Falstaff to Shallow. While they talk, Falstaff himself joins them.

The former cronies salute each other, and Falstaff asks if Shallow and Silence have found suitable men whom he may conscript into military service. Shallow introduces Mouldy, Shadow, Wart, Feeble, and Bullcalf, all of whom have been standing in the background. After reviewing the rustics, Falstaff agrees to have a drink with Shallow but declines his invitation to dinner. Again they fall to reminiscing about their lecherous escapades more than fifty years before. When Falstaff and the two Justices have gone, Bullcalf and Mouldy bribe Bardolph to arrange for their release from military service. Francis Feeble, however, declares "A man can die but once; we owe God a death," and says that no man is too good to serve his prince.

Upon the Justices' and Falstaff's return, Bardolph, who has retained one pound for himself, tells his superior that Mouldy and Bullcalf have paid three pounds for their freedom. Falstaff insists that Shallow shall determine the four men who will go to war, but when the Justice designates Mouldy, Bullcalf, Feeble, and Shadow, Falstaff immediately says that he selects recruits for "the spirit" rather than for "the limb, the thews, the stature, bulk, and big assemblance of a man." Falstaff then picks Wart, Shadow, and Feeble, the three scrawniest and runtiest of the lot. Shallow, expressing his wish to accompany Falstaff to court after the war is over, leaves with Silence, and Falstaff sends Bardolph ahead with the country soldiers. Alone, Falstaff comments on Shallow's romantic and exaggerated reminiscences, marvels at the Justice's prosperity as a country squire, and resolves to exploit him when he returns from the campaign.

IV,i. Yorkshire. The Forest of Gaultree

While waiting for scouts to reconnoiter, the Archbishop of York informs Mowbray, Lord Bardolph, and Hastings of Northumberland's letters expressing good wishes to the rebels and stating his decision to go to Scotland and there await news of the rebellion. A messenger reports the proximity of thirty thousand enemy troops. Just as Mowbray is urging an immediate attack, the Earl of Westmoreland approaches as an emissary from Prince John of Lancaster.

Courteously addressing himself to the Archbishop, Westmoreland asks why he has taken the field. The Archbishop replies that he has carefully weighed the abuses of a shameful peace against the risks of war. He would prefer to present a list of grievances to the King, but audience has been denied. When Westmoreland demands a list of specific wrongs, the Archbishop mentions mistreatment of the commons and violence to his own family. Mowbray observes that all men suffer the "heavy and unequal hand" of the King. Westmoreland retorts that the King has restored Mowbray's estates, but the peer insists that Henry is a usurper who profited when Richard II stopped the combat arranged between him and Mowbray's father (see *Richard II*).

Commenting that Mowbray cannot second-guess history, Westmoreland tells the rebels that Prince John is ready to give them audience, rectify any abuses they can establish, and grant them amnesty. Mowbray suspects that expediency prompts Prince John's offer, but Westmoreland declares that the proposal "comes from mercy, not from fear," and boasts of his army's strength. Mowbray does not wish to continue the parley, but Hastings asks if Prince John has a full commission from the King empowering him to make terms. After Westmoreland says that this is true, the Archbishop hands Westmoreland a list of "general grievances" to take to Prince John. If the Prince will meet these demands, the rebels will accept peace. Westmoreland leaves for consultation with Prince John. Mowbray is suspicious of the offer and its ultimate effectiveness, but Hastings and the Archbishop maintain that Henry has expended most of his resources, is weary of continual insurrections, and despairs of suppressing all the forces arrayed against him. Mowbray yields to the judgment of his confederates just before Westmoreland returns and invites the rebel leaders to meet Prince John halfway between the two armies.

IV,ii. Another Part of Gaultree Forest

Prince John, with Westmoreland attending him, greets the rebel commanders. He chides the Archbishop for having forsaken his ecclesiastical office to bear the sword of rebellion; the Archbishop argues, however, that he is not trying to disturb the peace but to find correction for the wrongs he has listed. Mowbray and Hastings interrupt with ultimatums that they will continue the insurrection if the Prince does not agree to their terms. Unconcerned by their threats, Prince John says that he approves the conditions and promises speedily to redress the "griefs" the Archbishop has presented. Accepting Prince John's pledge, Hastings dispatches an officer to pay off the rebel troops while the Archbishop exchanges toasts with Prince John and Westmoreland. Mowbray suddenly feels "something ill," but the Archbishop and Westmoreland chaff him for his uneasiness. A shout from the rebel army announces tidings of the "word of peace." Prince John orders Westmoreland to discharge the royalist troops, and the Archbishop directs Hastings to lead the rebel soldiers in a final parade.

Westmoreland returns with word that Prince John's officers will not leave until they hear the order from their commander's own mouth. A moment later Hastings reports that the rebel forces have dispersed. Immediately Westmoreland arrests the Archbishop, Hastings, and Mowbray on the charge of high treason. Mowbray questions if the action is "just and honourable," and the Archbishop accuses Prince John of breaking faith. The Prince replies that he merely promised "redress" for the grievances whereof they complained. This he will "perform with a most Christian care." For the rebels, death is the fitting and just outcome, and he orders them to execution.

IV,iii. Another Part of Gaultree Forest

Falstaff and Sir John Coleville meet and identify each other, and Coleville surrenders himself to Falstaff. Prince John arrives with Westmoreland, Blunt, and other officers. He sends Westmoreland to reassemble the army, and asks Falstaff where he has been. With characteristic boastfulness, Falstaff delivers his prisoner to the Prince. After confirming Coleville's identity, Prince John orders Westmoreland, who has reappeared, to send Coleville to York for immediate execution. Blunt leads Coleville away under guard. Prince John then dispatches Westmoreland as messenger to the ailing Henry IV, gives Falstaff permission to return through Gloucestershire, and promises to commend Falstaff in better terms than the old knight deserves.

In a soliloquy Falstaff attributes Prince John's lack of humor to his abstemious habits and then eulogizes the sovereign virtues of "sherris sack." Prince Hal's valor, which contrasts with the "cold blood he did naturally inherit of his father," derives from his taste for strong sack. If Falstaff had a thousand sons, he would teach them "to forswear thin potations and to addict themselves to sack." Bardolph appears to report the army's discharge and dispersal, and Falstaff says that he must go through Gloucestershire to visit Justice Shallow, whose gullibility he plans to exploit.

IV,iv. Westminster. The Jerusalem Chamber

In the presence of his court, King Henry, feeble from his sickness, once again announces his intention of making a pilgrimage to the Holy Land as soon as he regains his strength and his forces have suppressed the insurrection. The Earl of Warwick optimistically predicts the King's recovery and his military success. When King Henry inquires the whereabouts of Prince Hal, Prince Humphrey of Gloucester says he thinks that Hal has gone hunting but does not know with whom. When the King learns that Thomas of Clarence is also present at court, he asks why Clarence is not with Prince Hal inasmuch as he is the Crown Prince's favorite brother. King Henry then adjures Clarence to cultivate Hal's company and trust so that he may guide and advise his brother after the King dies. Promising to comply with this request, Clarence admits that Hal is dining in London with Poins and his former roistering cronies. Grieved by this evidence that Hal has reverted to his dissolute companions and practices, the King pessimistically prophesies "rotten times" for England when the Prince succeeds to the throne. Warwick attempts to excuse Hal's conduct as a part of his self-education, but the King doubts that the Prince will ever reform.

At this moment, Westmoreland arrives with the welcome news of Prince John's complete success and the downfall of Mowbray, Hastings, and the Archbishop of York. No sooner has Westmoreland completed his report than Harcourt brings word that the Sheriff of Yorkshire has overthrown the Earl of Northumberland, Lord Bardolph, and a large army of English and Scots. Ironically, this abundance of good news so excites King Henry that he suffers an apoplectic fit. Recovering consciousness, he asks to be carried to another room.

IV,v. Westminster. Another Room

While Thomas of Clarence, Humphrey of Gloucester, and the Earl of Warwick hover about the King's bed, the King requests silence except for the soft music in an adjoining room. He also asks his attendants to place the crown upon his pillow. Prince Hal enters and seeks news of his father. Seeing that the King has fallen asleep, all withdraw except Prince Hal, who remains by his father's bed. Watching the dying King, Prince Hal comments on what the crown has cost its wearer. Deciding that King Henry has died, Prince Hal yields to grief, owns his past misdeeds, and pledges himself to repay his father with a worthy and strong defense of the crown for his own heirs. He takes the crown from the pillow, places it on his head, and leaves.

Waking suddenly, King Henry calls for Warwick, Clarence, and Gloucester. When they appear he asks why they left him alone, and they reply that Prince Hal was with him. Seeing that the crown has disappeared, King Henry jumps to the conclusion that Hal's unseemly haste to possess the crown led him to mistake his father's sleep for death. The King sends Warwick to fetch the Crown Prince and bitterly compares himself with the bees that collect wax and honey only to be murdered for their pains. Warwick re-enters with a description of Prince Henry's tears, but the King again asks why the Prince removed the crown. Prince Hal himself comes in, and the King orders the others to leave him and the Prince together.

To Prince Hal's remark that he never thought to hear his father speak again, the King retorts that the Prince's wish was father to the thought. Caustically he condemns Prince Hal for his wayward and irresponsible conduct and eagerness to succeed to the throne, and predicts that as Henry V he will neglect his duty in an excess of revelry and rioting. Unable to check his tears, Prince Hal returns the crown, swears obedience to the King, and takes a sacred oath that he thought the King was dead. With passionate fervor he maintains that he placed the crown on his head as a weighty symbol of care and responsibility and that he had no thought of joy or pride.

Convinced of Prince Hal's reformation and worthiness, King Henry forgives his son, commends him for his action, and instructs him to sit by the bed. The dying ruler recalls "By what bypaths and indirect crook'd ways" he gained the throne and the rebellion and bloodshed that have troubled his reign. He cautions Prince Hal that although rebellious leaders have suffered defeat they may again threaten the crown. To divert their energies he had planned to lead them abroad to the Holy Land, but his imminent death will prevent this. He advises Prince Hal to avoid internal strife by instigating "foreign quarrels." The King's speech becomes more difficult, and he invokes God's forgiveness for his seizure of the crown from Richard II and prays for peace during Prince Hal's reign. The Prince vows to maintain his throne against all the world, since his inheritance must be "plain and right."

Joyously welcoming Prince John, who enters with the Earl of Warwick, the King inquires the name of the place where he first lost consciousness. Warwick says, " 'Tis call'd Jerusalem, my noble lord." The King remembers a prophecy that he should die only in Jerusalem, which he vainly "suppos'd the Holy Land." He commands his attendants to carry him to "that chamber," where he will die.

V,i. Gloucestershire. Shallow's House

Justice Shallow exhorts Falstaff to remain overnight and calls for Davy, to whom he issues a series of instructions concerning management of the farm and household and preparation of the dinner he plans to serve Falstaff. Davy requests Shallow to hear a complaint of William Visor against Clement Perkes. Shallow promises to handle the matter equitably and urges Falstaff, Bardolph, and the Page to follow him inside. Shallow is cultivating Falstaff as a friend in court. The fat knight remarks to himself that he will turn Shallow into a laughingstock for Prince Hal's continual amusement.

V,ii. Westminster. The Palace

Learning of King Henry IV's death, the Lord Chief Justice tells Warwick of his fears that he will suffer from the disfavor of Henry V, who has had no love for the Justice. Prince John of Lancaster, Thomas of Clarence, and Humphrey of Gloucester approach, and Warwick and the Chief Justice express the wish that Henry V had the personality and character of his three brothers. Following an exchange of greetings and Clarence's observation that the Justice must now be lenient with Sir John Falstaff, the Justice asserts his honorable and impartial execution of duty and resigns himself to face what may come to him through the person of the new king.

Walking up with his attendants, Henry V detects his brothers' apprehensions and assures them that they are in an English court, not in a treacherous and tyrannical Turkish one.[1] Inviting them to share the burden their father's death has imposed on his sons, he promises to fill the roles of father and brother to them.

When the Lord Chief Justice says that the new King has no just cause to hate him, Henry recalls his imprisonment and other indignities at the hands of the Justice. The Justice makes a spirited defense of his actions, arguing that he did no more than discharge the responsibilities of his office in loyalty to Henry IV after Prince Hal struck him in his "very seat of judgment." Praising the Justice's conduct and character, Henry V retains him in office and accepts him as personal counselor. He seeks the Justice's advice in selecting his council and pledges to rule the nation wisely and fairly for all.

V,iii. Gloucestershire. Shallow's Orchard.[2]

Falstaff, Shallow, Silence, Davy, Bardolph, and the Page are disporting themselves with drink and song in the orchard. In the midst of their merriment, Davy announces the arrival of Pistol with news from court. Acclaiming Falstaff as "now one of the greatest men in this realm," Pistol gleefully tells the company that Prince Hal is now Henry V. Immediately Falstaff orders Bardolph to saddle the horses, promises Shallow any office he may choose, and assures Pistol that he will receive a "double-charge" of dignities. Confident that the young King is pining to see him and that the laws of England are at his command, Falstaff prepares to ride all night, and "woe to my Lord Chief Justice!"

V,iv. London. A Street

Beadles have arrested Mistress Quickly and Doll Tearsheet and are conducting the prostitute to a whipping for her offenses. Doll claims to be pregnant and says that she will miscarry. The Hostess implies that the infant is Falstaff's, but the first Beadle is quite aware of the cushions with which Doll has stuffed her apparel. Unimpressed by the women's resistance, the Beadles lead them out.

[1] For the implications of this statement see "Amurath" in the biographical index.

[2] Some editors designate the place as "Shallow's Garden."

V,v. Westminster. Near the Abbey

Grooms spread rushes on the street in front of the royal procession. After the King and his train pass, Falstaff, Shallow, Pistol, Bardolph, and the Page appear. Carefully Falstaff groups his companions so that they will make a good showing when King Henry returns. Pistol tells Falstaff of Doll's imprisonment, and the old knight promises to free her. Trumpets sound, and King Henry V marches up with the Lord Chief Justice and other members of his retinue. Impulsively, Falstaff and Pistol greet Henry V, who coldly tells the Lord Chief Justice to "speak to that vain man." The Justice rebukes Falstaff, who replies that he is addressing the King himself. Seriously, Henry V commands Falstaff to fall to his prayers, to correct his vicious habits, to abandon his gormandizing, and to prepare his spirit for the grave. Henry warns Falstaff against replying with "a fool-born jest," declares that he has forsaken his dissolute pranks and companions, and orders Falstaff and his fellows to remain at least ten miles' distance from court. Henry will allow Falstaff "competence of life" and the promise of some advancement if he and his cronies reform themselves. Delegating the Lord Chief Justice to carry out his orders, Henry departs with his escort.

Crestfallen, Falstaff says to Shallow, "I owe you a thousand pound." To Shallow's plea that Falstaff repay the debt at once, the old knight wistfully observes that the King, not wishing to favor him publicly, will send for him privately and reward him. Falstaff invites his friends to dinner, but the Lord Chief Justice instructs the officers to lead Falstaff and his companions to the Fleet prison. Prince John approves the Justice's action and comments that Henry has provided adequately for the prisoners pending their rehabilitation. Prince John then prophesies Henry V's invasion of France.

Epilogue

A dancer appeals for the audience's approval. In conclusion the Epilogue announces a forthcoming play which will continue the story with Sir John Falstaff and "fair Katherine of France." It is possible that Falstaff will die of a fever. In any event the audience must not confuse Falstaff with Sir John Oldcastle, who died a martyr and was a different man.

HENRY V [1598–1599]

CHARACTERS

CHORUS

KING HENRY THE FIFTH.

DUKE OF GLOUCESTER, DUKE OF BEDFORD, brothers to the *King*.

DUKE OF EXETER, uncle to the *King*.

DUKE OF YORK, cousin to the *King*.

EARL OF SALISBURY.

EARL OF WESTMORELAND.

EARL OF WARWICK.

ARCHBISHOP OF CANTERBURY.

BISHOP OF ELY.

EARL OF CAMBRIDGE.

LORD SCROOP.

SIR THOMAS GREY.

SIR THOMAS ERPINGHAM, GOWER, FLUELLEN, MACMORRIS, JAMY, officers in *King Henry's* army.

[JOHN] BATES, [ALEXANDER] COURT, [MICHAEL] WILLIAMS, soldiers in the same.

PISTOL.

NYM.

BARDOLPH.

BOY.

A Herald.

CHARLES THE SIXTH, King of France.

LEWIS, the Dauphin.

DUKE OF BURGUNDY.

DUKE OF ORLEANS.

DUKE OF BRITAINE.

DUKE OF BOURBON.

DUKE OF BERRI.

The Constable of France.

RAMBURES, GRANDPRÉ, BEAUMONT, French lords.

Governor of Harfleur.

MONTJOY, a French herald.

Ambassadors to the *King of England.*

ISABEL, Queen of France.

KATHERINE, daughter to *Charles* and *Isabel.*

ALICE, a lady attending *Katherine.*

HOSTESS of the Boar's Head Tavern, Eastcheap; formerly *Mistress Nell Quickly;* now married to *Pistol.*

Lords, Ladies, Officers, Soldiers, Messengers, and Attendants.

Scene: *England and France*

Prologue

Chorus enters, apologizes for the inadequacy of the theater as a place for the enactment of Henry V's conquests in France, exhorts the audience to use its imagination to enhance the production, and appeals for a favorable response to the play.

I,i. London. An Antechamber in the King's Palace

The Archbishop of Canterbury and the Bishop of Ely express great concern about a bill pending in parliament which would authorize the appropriation of all the temporal estates of the Church. Seeking to forestall this legislation, they agree that Henry V has changed from a dissolute and irresponsible prince into a pious, wise, and admirable leader. Ely wonders what Henry's attitude may be toward the proposed bill. Canterbury replies that the King "seems indifferent," but the prelate promised Henry that the Church would contribute a large sum to support an invasion of France. Canterbury hoped that this offer might win royal favor for the Church, but Henry had interrupted their conference to grant an audience to the French ambassador just as Canterbury was preparing to demonstrate the King's rightful claim to the throne of France.

I,ii. London. The Presence Chamber in the Palace

Before his court Henry tells Exeter and Westmoreland that he wishes to consult the Archbishop of Canterbury before he hears the French Ambassador. As soon as the two bishops enter, Henry asks Canterbury whether the Salic law[1] imposes any legal, ethical, or

[1] An ancient legal principle that denied women the privilege of royal succession.

religious obstacles to his claim of the French throne. The King admonishes Canterbury to make a full and completely honest answer.

In a summary of Western European history and a lengthy review of the French succession, Canterbury shows that the French monarchs themselves have violated and ignored the Salic law in their accession. Canterbury assures Henry that he may claim France "with right and conscience," and calls on the monarch to emulate the military exploits of his great-grandfather (Edward III) and his great-uncle (Edward the Black Prince). The Bishop of Ely and the Duke of Exeter and Earl of Westmoreland echo Canterbury's exhortation to launch the campaign. Henry, recalling the Scottish invasions during the reign of Edward III, hesitates to weaken England lest the Scots seize the opportunity to attack. His advisers discuss this problem until Canterbury, citing the disciplined cooperation of honeybees, suggests that Henry take one fourth of his forces to France and leave the remaining three fourths to guard England. Satisfied that he has the sanction of law and of religion as well as the support of his counselors, Henry resolves to undertake the subjugation of France and prepares to receive the French Ambassadors.

After the first Ambassador gains the King's permission to deliver his message frankly and plainly, he repudiates Henry's claim to France, contemns his youthfulness and lack of responsibility, and presents him with a large number of tennis balls that the Dauphin has sent in lieu of the French possessions. With diplomatic eloquence and considerable irony, Henry expresses his thanks for the gift and warns that the tennis balls will turn to "gunstones" and that thousands of Frenchmen will regret the Dauphin's jest that precipitates a bloody war. The King dismisses the envoys and starts organizing his expedition.

II, Prologue

Chorus describes the preparations for war and states that the French, "advis'd by good intelligence," are attempting to divert the English through intrigue and diplomacy. To this end, the French have suborned Richard Earl of Cambridge, Lord Scroop of Masham, and Sir Thomas Grey to attempt the assassination of Henry V in Southampton prior to his embarkation. Chorus promises to convey the theater audience to France and back again.

II,i. London. A Street

Lieutenant Bardolph asks Corporal Nym if he and Ancient [1] Pistol have settled their quarrel. Bardolph offers to treat them to breakfast so that they may "be all three sworn brothers to France." It emerges that Pistol has married Mistress Quickly, although she had plighted her troth to Nym. When Pistol and the Hostess approach, the blustering Pistol and Nym fall to wrangling and threatening each other, until Bardolph has to draw his own sword to keep them apart. As the brawl shows signs of beginning again, the Boy comes seeking aid for Falstaff, who is extremely ill. Commenting, "The King has kill'd his heart" (see *2 Henry IV,* V,v), Mistress Quickly (now Mistress Pistol) returns with the Boy. Pistol and Nym draw their swords over a gambling debt, and once more Bardolph has to come between them. Finally Pistol and Nym agree on a settlement and shake hands. The Hostess reappears to summon them to the bedside of Falstaff, who is dying of fever.

II,ii. Southampton. A Council Chamber

Exeter, Bedford, and Westmoreland are discussing the recently discovered conspiracy against the King's life. Bedford explains that the offenders are unaware that Henry has learned of the plot. To the blare of trumpets, King Henry, Scroop, Cambridge, and Grey, with other members of the court, enter the chamber. Addressing the traitors in gracious words, Henry elicits assurances of loyalty and confidence from each one in turn. Henry then orders Exeter to free a man arrested for drunken railing against the King. Successively, Scroop, Cambridge, and Grey advise that Henry punish the offender severely as an example; but the King, inquiring how he can punish serious crimes if he treats a drunken wretch so harshly, insists on releasing the man.

Turning to the three tratiors, Henry hands them papers which they assume to be their official appointments as commissioners to rule England in the monarch's absence. After they have read their papers they turn pale, confess their crime, and appeal for the King's mercy. Declaring that their recent harshness towards the drunken railer has suppressed any inclination he may have toward mercy, Henry denounces them for high treason against their country and their king

[1] "Ancient" was another form of "ensign," meaning standard-bearer, a military rank.

and orders their instant arrest. Exeter specifically charges each one by name.

Scroop and Grey profess themselves relieved by the discovery that has interfered with their intended crime. Cambridge denies that "the gold of France" seduced him but likewise thanks God for the plot's exposure. Stating that although he seeks no personal revenge he must protect the nation, Henry orders execution of all three men. Guards lead the traitors out of the chamber, and the King, interpreting the revelation of the conspiracy as a divine omen, calls his faithful supporters to follow him to France, placing their forces "into the hand of God."

II,iii. London. In Front of the Boar's Head Tavern, Eastcheap

Pistol, Nym, Bardolph, the Boy, and the Hostess are grieving for Falstaff, who has died. The Hostess graphically describes the old knight's death, and each of his acquaintances recalls some personal characteristic that endeared Falstaff to his friends. Nym reminds them that the army is ready to sail from Southampton. Eager to share in the booty of war, Pistol kisses his wife, urges her to take care of his effects, and invites Bardolph and Nym to kiss her good-by—an opportunity Bardolph accepts but Nym does not.

II,iv. France. The Palace of the French King

Having learned of the pending English invasion, Charles VI is issuing orders for defense of the French cities. Although the Dauphin agrees that preparedness is expedient, he does not share his father's apprehensions and characterizes Henry V as "a vain, giddy, shallow, humorous youth." The Constable of France, having heard the Ambassadors' report, cautions the Dauphin against underrating and misjudging the English king. Still contemptuous of Henry's ability, the Dauphin concedes that discretion demands adequate preparations for defense. Charles remembers the victory of Edward III and the Black Prince at Cressy and reminds his advisers that Henry is a descendant of "that victorious stock."

A messenger announces the arrival of English Ambassadors; Charles consents to see them immediately; the Dauphin urges his father to meet them firmly and aggressively. Accompanied by his retinue, the Duke of Exeter in the name of Henry V confronts Charles and demands that he surrender the crown and its possessions.

In support of this ultimatum, Exeter delivers a document setting forth Henry's claims. When Exeter says that war is the alternative to rejection, Charles promises to reply formally the next day. Turning, Exeter delivers Henry's more personal defiance and pledge to punish the Dauphin for his insolence in sending the tennis balls.

III, Prologue

Chorus asks the audience to envision the equipping and loading of Henry's ships at Southampton pier, the sailing of the "fleet majestical," and the arrival at Harfleur. The English gunners train their cannon on the city and await the return of the English Ambassadors. What will the French answer be?

III,i. France. In Front of Harfleur

Henry V, leading his commanders and followed by soldiers with scaling ladders, delivers an eloquent and stirring appeal for courage and confidence as they resume their attack on the French city.

III,ii. In Front of Harfleur

Bardolph is exhorting his somewhat reluctant and fainthearted companions to advance into battle. Fluellen appears and drives them all forward, leaving the Boy by himself. In a soliloquy, the Boy reflects on the cowardice, thievery, and rascality of Bardolph, Nym, and Pistol. His sense of manhood has rebelled against their insistence that he pick men's pockets, and he resolves to desert them and seek "some better service."

Gower tells Fluellen to report to the Duke of Gloucester, who with the Irish Captain Macmorris is digging tunnels beneath the city. While Fluellen is criticizing the Irishman's methods and knowledge of warfare, Captain Jamy walks up with Macmorris, who says that the miners have stopped their work before completing it. Fluellen tries to engage Macmorris in a discussion of military science, but the Irish captain is sensitive about having had to abandon the mining maneuver and wishes to rush into the thick of battle. Jamy would like to hear the argument; Macmorris and Fluellen grow angry with each other; Gower tries to calm the two officers; a trumpet announces that officials of Harfleur want to parley.

III,iii. In Front of the Gates of Harfleur

Meeting the Governor of Harfleur and various citizens, Henry warns that he will raze the city and destroy the inhabitants unless the town yields at once. Having received word that the Dauphin cannot aid the town's defense, the Governor surrenders unconditionally. Henry orders Exeter to occupy Harfleur and use mercy to all. Winter is approaching; the English army is suffering from sickness; and Henry plans a withdrawal on Calais.

III,iv. Rouen. The French King's Palace

Katherine of France is taking a lesson in oral English from Alice, her old Gentlewoman. By calling out French words and then identifying and pronouncing their English equivalents, Katherine learns several basic words and phrases.

III,v. Rouen. The French King's Palace

When Charles states that Henry has crossed the river Somme unopposed, the Constable, Dauphin, and Duke of Bourbon strenuously urge engaging the English quickly in order to avoid additional shame and dishonor. Charles thereupon issues a call to the most illustrious peers and knights of France to collect their troops, oppose Henry, and bring the English King as a prisoner to the French court. Yearning for a good fight, the Constable fears that Henry will lose heart and sue for terms when he sees himself outnumbered by the forces of France. Charles orders Montjoy the herald to find out what ransom Henry will pay for peace and commands the Dauphin to remain in Rouen until the Constable returns with "word of England's fall."

III,vi. The English Camp in Picardy

Fluellen tells Gower of the Duke of Exeter's and Ancient Pistol's valiant defense of the bridge. No sooner has Fluellen completed his account than Pistol himself appears and begs the Welsh captain to intercede for Bardolph, whom Exeter has sentenced to hang for stealing a small item from a church. Fluellen, however, applauds Exeter's strict discipline and refuses to interfere. Indignantly, Pistol curses Fluellen and leaves. Gower and Fluellen agree that Pistol is an impostor, and the Welshman says that he will keep a close eye on the Ancient.

With a drum and flags, Henry and Gloucester lead a number of poor soldiers through the camp. Fluellen reports that the Duke of Exeter is successfully holding the bridge. French casualties have been heavy. Exeter's only loss in manpower is Bardolph, who "is like to be executed for robbing a church." Showing no recognition of his onetime crony, Henry sanctions the execution and gives specific orders that the English troops must not pillage, must pay for everything they take, and must treat the French people courteously.

A flourish of trumpets announces Montjoy's arrival. In direct language the herald relays Charles's message to Henry. France has roused itself; England will regret its folly in invading France. The French King judges Henry incapable of paying a suitable ransom or of making fit reparations for the damage and disgrace he has inflicted on France. Waiting until Montjoy finishes his message, Henry confesses that although there was a time when he judged one English soldier the equal of three Frenchmen, his army is now weakened by sickness. Nevertheless, he wants to march on Calais. If Charles obstructs the way, the French will have to answer the consequences. Henry does not seek a battle with his army in a weakened condition, but he will not shun one. Montjoy, having received a generous gift from Henry, departs. Gloucester hopes that the French will not join battle, but Henry observes, "We are in God's hand, . . . not in theirs."

III,vii. The French Camp near Agincourt

Waiting impatiently for daylight, the French commanders argue about the excellence of their equipment, horses, and women. After boasting of his future feats against the English, the Dauphin goes to arm himself. In mocking fashion, the remaining leaders express doubts concerning the Dauphin's courage and competence as a soldier.

A messenger enters and reports that the English have advanced within fifteen hundred paces of the French camp. Ironically professing sorrow for Henry V, the French officers joke about the obstinate foolishness of the English in pushing their way toward certain disaster. Noting that it is two o'clock in the morning, the Duke of Orleans prophesies that each one of them will capture a hundred English by ten.

IV, Prologue

Chorus vividly describes activity in the opposing camps on the eve of the Battle of Agincourt. Sentinels speak in low tones; flickering flames throw shadows across the soldiers' faces; horses neigh in the dark; armorers make last-minute repairs. The French, overconfident, shoot dice for the English prisoners they expect to capture. The English, outnumbered, "Sit patiently and inly ruminate/The morning's danger." Henry V visits his troops, greeting them and calling "them brothers, friends, and countrymen." Thus does "A little touch of Harry in the night" encourage every fearful and anxious soldier. Again Chorus apologizes for depicting such great events in the limited area of the theater.

IV,i. France. The English Camp at Agincourt

Henry confesses to his two brothers, Bedford and Gloucester, that the English are in great danger, but he expresses hope. When Sir Thomas Erpingham approaches, Henry says that the old knight deserves a good soft pillow rather than the "turf of France," but Erpingham insists that he prefers to share the fortunes of his King. Henry borrows Sir Thomas's cloak as a disguise, says that he wishes to be alone, and dismisses his comrades.

Pistol appears and challenges Henry, who identifies himself as a noncommissioned officer. After Pistol professes his affection for the King, Henry V says that his name is "Harry le Roy," which Pistol takes to be a Cornish name. Henry tells him that he is a Welshman,[1] but when he adds that he is a friend and kinsman of Fluellen, Pistol insults him and leaves as Gower and Fluellen arrive.

Assuming a knowledge of ancient history, Fluellen begs Gower to follow the Romans' example and speak lower. Gower justifies himself on the grounds that the French are noisy, but Fluellen insists that this does not excuse any slackening of sound military practice. The two captains pass on, and Henry praises Fluellen's admirable caution and valor.

Three English soldiers (Bates, Court, and Williams) walk up and ask the King to identify himself. Concealing his true identity, Henry says that he serves under Sir Thomas Erpingham, who holds a pessimistic view of the forthcoming battle. Bates asks if Sir Thomas has indicated this opinion to the King, but Henry explains that this would be inappropriate. The King is "but a man"; he experiences the same sensations all other men do; at the same time his office demands that he conceal all fear from his army. Hence it is essential that no one add to the King's fears or apprehensions. Bates observes that, whatever outward courage Henry may show, he believes that the King would rather be in the Thames up to his neck than in France preparing for battle. Henry, incognito, assures Bates that the King is exactly where he prefers to be. Bates frankly remarks,

[1] Henry V was born in Wales.

"Would he were here alone." Henry refuses to accept this as literal opinion and says that he himself is contented to be with the King, "his cause being just and his quarrel honourable."

At this point, Williams interrupts, saying, "That's more than we know." Bates insists that judging the reasons for a war is beyond the responsibility of ordinary soldiers and citizens, who must content themselves with serving the King. Williams, however, holds that the King must bear a spiritual responsibility for all who die, many of whom go to their deaths unprepared. Eloquently, Henry defines the relationship between the monarch and his subjects in wartime. "Every subject's duty is the King's, but every subject's soul is his own," he argues.

Williams agrees that every man must answer for his personal sins, and Bates vows to fight "lustily." Henry tells them that he has heard the King declare that he will never surrender, come what may. Cynically Williams replies that, although this is good pre-battle propaganda, the King may change his mind after his soldiers' throats are cut. When Williams persists in doubting the King's sincerity, Henry becomes impatient and challenges Williams to back up his charge at a later date. Exchanging gages, they agree that Williams will give his rival a box on the ear when he finds him wearing the glove. Bates orders the two men to be friends and direct their attention to the French, and the soldiers leave.

Alone, Henry reflects on his royal office, on the worries and burdens pertaining to it, and on the unawareness of ordinary citizens regarding the sleeplessness of their ruler. Sir Thomas Erpingham, finding the King, tells Henry that his nobles are searching for him. Henry commands Erpingham to bring his aides to his tent. Once more by himself, Henry prays that the Almighty will give his troops courage in the face of overwhelming opposition and will not punish them for Henry IV's usurpation of Richard II, for whose death Henry V constantly does penance.[1] Gloucester calls Henry to rejoin his comrades.

IV,ii. The French Camp

Orleans, the Dauphin, Rambures, and Beaumont gaily prepare to mount their chargers. The Constable joins them, and a messenger reports that the English have grouped themselves for battle. With

[1] Henry states that he has given Richard's body proper burial, that he contributes generously to philanthropic causes, and that he has endowed two chantries where masses are performed for Richard's soul.

high confidence the Constable urges his fellow officers to gallop forth and terrify the English with the cavalry charge. Grandpré arrives with a description of the poor mounts and disreputable appearance of the English forces. Relishing their anticipated victory, the Frenchmen depart for battle.

IV,iii. The English Camp

Henry's commanders await the return of the King, who has gone to reconnoiter the French position. Westmoreland estimates the French army at sixty thousand men; Exeter numbers the English at one fifth this total.[1] Salisbury comments that the odds are "fearful" and takes a fond farewell of his companions.

Westmoreland wishes that "But one ten thousand" of the idle men in England could be in France. Henry, who has just returned, tells Westmoreland that they need no greater force because, if they are "mark'd to die," they have enough already. If they are destined to live, then each man will gain "the greater share of honour." More than this, Henry will release any man who "hath no stomach for this fight" and arrange his return to England. Henry prophesies, however, that anyone who survives the impending battle will take lifelong pride and satisfaction in belonging to the brotherhood that fought so gloriously together "upon Saint Crispin's day."

Salisbury returns to announce that the French army is in battle position. Westmoreland, his spirits revived, wishes that he and Henry alone could face the enemy; and Henry says that this optimism is the equivalent of five thousand men. A trumpet signals the arrival of Montjoy, who delivers the Constable's last appeal to Henry to avoid bloodshed and defeat by negotiating his ransom.[2] Defiantly, Henry refuses to capitulate and sends Montjoy back. The Duke of York (see Aumerle in *Richard II*) seeks and receives permission to lead the English attack.

IV,iv. The Battlefield

Pistol compels a French soldier to yield. With the help of the Boy as interpreter, the swaggering Pistol agrees to spare the Frenchman's life upon his promise to pay two hundred crowns ransom. Voicing his

[1] Historians differ in their estimates of the two armies. An average gives the French between 40,000 and 60,000 troops of all ranks, and the English 5,000 to 10,000.

[2] In actual history Henry, aware of his dangerous position, tried to arrange a settlement, but the French rejected it.

abject gratitude to "the most brave, valorous, and thrice-worthy signieur of England," the Frenchman follows Pistol from the scene. The Boy comments that Bardolph and Nym, both of whom have been hanged, had ten times the courage of "this roaring devil" (Pistol). Then the Boy starts to join the lackeys who are guarding the otherwise defenseless English camp.

IV,v. Another Part of the Battlefield

Amazed at the resistance and ferocity of the English, whom they have despised, the French commanders bewail their disgraceful defeat and review their position. The Dauphin suggests that they commit suicide; Bourbon advises that they return to the melee and die in honor; the Constable urges that they sacrifice their lives en masse; Orleans believes that if the French could restore discipline they could still "smother up the English" with sheer numbers. Bourbon recklessly starts back into the fray.

IV,vi. Another Part of the Battlefield

The Duke of Exeter reports to King Henry the valiant and noble deaths of the Earl of Suffolk and the Duke of York. An alarm cuts short the grieving of Exeter and the King, and Henry orders the immediate execution of the French prisoners.[1]

IV,vii. Another Part of the Battlefield

Fluellen angrily criticizes the French for violating the laws of war by killing the pages and servants guarding the camp. Gower explains that the soldiers who committed the atrocity were running from the fight and that Henry has commanded the slaughter of all French captives in reprisal. Fluellen accounts for Henry's nobility by the fact that he was born at Monmouth, in Wales; he goes on to compare Henry with Alexander the Great, and Monmouth with Macedon; and he particularly approves of Henry's rejection of Sir John Falstaff. Enraged by the needless slaying of the camp guards, Henry appears with his aides and commands the Herald to order any surviving Frenchmen to rejoin battle or leave the field.

[1] Even French historians agree that this harsh order was necessary and justified, lest the prisoners escape or counterattack. Kittredge notes that in the play Henry does not implement the command until he learns of the French massacre of the lackeys and boys guarding the camp (IV,vii).

Montjoy approaches, and Henry ironically inquires if he has come to repeat Charles VI's demand for ransom. Montjoy humbly requests permission only for the survivors to identify and bury their slain comrades. Henry expresses concern about the French horsemen still riding over the field, but Montjoy concedes that Henry has won the battle. Praising God for the victory, King Henry names the scene "the field of Agincourt." Fluellen explains the Welsh derivation of the leek he wears in his cap, recalls that Henry has Welsh blood, and professes his loyalty to the King. Henry thanks Fluellen and sends Heralds with Montjoy to record the casualties on both sides.

At this moment, Exeter brings Williams before the King. Henry asks Williams why he is wearing the glove in his cap, and the soldier explains the exchange of gages on the night before the battle. In reply to the King's question, Fluellen states that Williams must, on his honor, keep the oath he has sworn to strike whomever he finds wearing the other glove. Henry tells Williams to keep his vow and orders him to summon Gower, in whose company Williams serves.

As soon as Williams leaves, Henry gives his gage to Fluellen, stating that he seized it from Alençon's helmet and that anyone who challenges it is an enemy to Henry himself. Henry then requests Fluellen to fetch Gower to the royal tent. The Welshman departs, and Henry sends Warwick and Gloucester to make certain that no harm comes of Fluellen's encounter with Williams.[1]

IV,viii. In Front of King Henry's Pavilion

Williams is conducting Gower toward the King's tent. When Fluellen follows on their heels, Williams recognizes the glove on the Welshman's cap and immediately strikes the peppery captain. Outraged, Fluellen brands Williams a traitor and friend of the Duke Alençon. He repeats his charge to Warwick and Gloucester, who arrive and inquire into the quarrel.

When the King and Exeter join the group, Williams and Gower repeat their respective stories. King Henry admits that he was the one who exchanged gages with Williams. Maintaining his loyalty, the soldier insists that he did not recognize the King incognito and that if he had done so he would not have quarreled with him. Filling the glove with gold coins, Henry returns it to Williams and directs him

[1] In transferring the challenge to Fluellen, Henry is not guilty of cowardice; he rather protects the blunt and honest Williams from striking his king, an act that would constitute treason.

to keep the gage as a symbol of his honor. Henry also orders Fluellen to accept Williams as a friend. Admiring the soldier's independent spirit and courage, Fluellen hands him a shilling which Williams truculently declines. Patiently Fluellen says that Williams can use it to mend his shoes; furthermore, the coin is not counterfeit.

At this point an English herald hands the King a detailed list of French casualties. After Exeter comments on the more than fifteen hundred prisoners of war, Henry identifies the most prominent of the ten thousand Frenchmen who died. In sharp contrast to these figures, Henry learns from another list that the English have lost the Duke of York, the Earl of Suffolk, Sir Richard Ketley, Davy Gam, Esquire, and twenty-five common soldiers.[1] Reverently, King Henry orders on pain of death that no one boast of the remarkable victory "or take that praise from God/Which is his only." Henry consents, however, to Fluellen's request that the number of casualties be published, but with the acknowledgment "That God fought for us." Henry arranges for proper funeral services and burial of the dead, and for the return of the army to Calais and then to England.

V, Prologue

Chorus invites the audience to imagine Henry's recrossing of the English Channel and triumphant procession into London. Although Henry modestly desires to give all credit for his victory to God, the Mayor and citizens go forth to welcome their King. After many negotiations Henry returns to France.

V,i. France. The English Camp

When Gower asks Fluellen why he wears the leek in his cap after Saint David's Day (March 1), the Welshman explains that he retains it as a taunt to Pistol, who brought Fluellen bread and salt and suggested that he eat the leek. Pistol appears and trades insults with Fluellen. Striking Pistol, Fluellen compels him to eat the leek, skin and all. Giving Pistol a groat with which to purchase treatment for his broken pate, Fluellen leaves, unmoved by Pistol's threats of revenge. Gower is similarly unexcited by Pistol's blustering and advises him to have greater respect for Welshmen and to mend his

[1] Shakespeare found these figures in his source material; J. Dover Wilson notes that, although they may not be correct, they are not as exaggerated as one might suppose. Historians vary in their estimates.

manners. Alone, Pistol reflects on the news that his Nell (Mistress Quickly, his wife) has died of venereal disease; now old and weary, he will go back to England and live by pandering and thievery.

V,ii. France. The French King's Palace

King Henry, accompanied by his brothers and advisers, greets the King and Queen of France, Princess Katherine, and their retinue. Cordiality and peace have replaced recent defiance and hostility. The Duke of Burgundy pledges his duty to both monarchs, reminds the Kings that he has labored zealously to arrange their meeting, and appeals for lasting amity between France and England. Briefly Henry states that if France wishes peace she must agree to the terms he has already proposed. Saying that he has only hastily glanced at the articles of the treaty, King Charles requests another opportunity to study the document in detail. Henry delegates five of his counselors to represent him at the conference and suggests that Queen Isabel add a woman's voice to the diplomatic discussion. She agrees, and all leave except Henry, Katherine, and Alice.

Apologizing for his rough and military speech, Henry avows his love for Katherine, beseeching her to become his queen. The Princess replies in French. With Alice's occasional assistance as interpreter and with Henry's and Katherine's infrequent ventures into each other's language, they pursue their courtship. At last Katherine consents to marry Henry if her father approves. Joyfully, Henry starts to kiss her hand. Coyly, Katherine tries to forestall him, whereupon he declares that he will kiss her lips. When she objects that such intimacy before marriage is not the custom of France, Henry says that "nice customs curtsy to great kings" and kisses her just as the French court and English lords return.

After a good-natured exchange between Henry and Burgundy about Henry's proposal to Katherine, the English representatives report that King Charles has consented to the marriage and to all important articles except the full title with which he should address Henry. At this point Charles agrees to designate and recognize Henry as his "dearest son, King of England, and heir of France." In full concord the two rulers endorse the treaty, and Henry kisses Katherine as his "sovereign queen." Queen Isabel invokes divine blessing on the marriage with the hope that it will be a symbol of the relationship between all Englishmen and all Frenchmen. King Henry orders preparations for the wedding, at which time he will receive oaths of loyalty from Burgundy and "all the peers."

Epiloque

Chorus summarizes how

> . . . with rough and all-unable pen,
> Our bending author hath pursu'd the story,
> In little room confining mighty men,

of Henry's achievements in France. Unhappily, incompetent administrators in the reign of Henry VI lost France and impoverished England, "Which oft our stage hath shown." [1]

[1] A reference to the three parts of *Henry VI,* which Shakespeare wrote before he composed the two parts of *Henry IV* and *Henry V*.

HENRY VI (PART ONE) [1589–1590]

CHARACTERS

KING HENRY THE SIXTH.

DUKE OF GLOUCESTER, uncle to the *King,* and Protector.

DUKE OF BEDFORD, uncle to the *King,* and Regent of France.

THOMAS BEAUFORT, Duke of Exeter, great-uncle to the *King.*

HENRY BEAUFORT, great-uncle to the *King,* Bishop of Winchester, afterwards Cardinal.

JOHN BEAUFORT, Earl of Somerset, afterwards Duke.

RICHARD PLANTAGENET, son of Richard late Earl of Cambridge, afterwards Duke of York.

EARL OF WARWICK.

EARL OF SALISBURY.

EARL OF SUFFOLK.

LORD TALBOT, afterwards Earl of Shrewsbury.

JOHN TALBOT, his son.

EDMUND MORTIMER, Earl of March.

SIR JOHN FASTOLFE.[1]

SIR WILLIAM LUCY.

SIR WILLIAM GLANSDALE.

SIR THOMAS GARGRAVE.

MAYOR OF LONDON.

WOODVILE, Lieutenant of the Tower.

VERNON, of the White Rose or York faction.

BASSET, of the Red Rose or Lancaster faction.

A Lawyer.

Mortimer's Keepers.

CHARLES, Dauphin, and afterwards King, of France.

REIGNIER, Duke of Anjou, and titular King of Naples.

DUKE OF BURGUNDY.

DUKE OF ALENÇON.

BASTARD OF ORLEANS.

GOVERNOR OF PARIS.

Master Gunner of Orleans, and his Son.

General of the French forces in Bordeaux.

[1] Some editors prefer to designate this character as Sir John Falstaff.

A French Sergeant.

A Porter.

An old Shepherd, father to *Joan la Pucelle.*

MARGARET, daughter to *Reignier,* afterwards married to *King Henry.*

COUNTESS OF AUVERGNE.

JOAN LA PUCELLE, commonly called *Joan of Arc.*[1]

Lords, Warders of the Tower, Heralds, Ambassadors, Officers, Soldiers, English and French Attendants.

Fiends appearing to *Joan la Pucelle.*

Scene: *England and France*

I,i. Westminster Abbey

To the cadence of a "Dead March," members of the court and attendants escort the funeral of Henry V. The Dukes of Bedford and Gloucester praise the character and achievements of their late brother. The Duke of Exeter also mourns the death of Henry V but suggests that "the subtle-witted French/Conjurers and sorcerers . . . By magic verses have contriv'd his end." Winchester recalls that Henry V as the Almighty's champion overcame his enemies, but Gloucester retorts that the prayers of the church led to Henry's untimely death. In the ensuing quarrel, Winchester and Gloucester accuse each other of attempting to dominate the boy king, Henry VI. Winchester intimates that Gloucester is henpecked by his proud wife, and Gloucester charges Winchester with worldliness and vindictiveness. Bedford interposes and commands the two rivals to "cease these jars" and to pray together for the blessing and guidance of the spirit of Henry V.

At this moment a messenger brings news of a French revolt and the loss of important English possessions in France. While Bedford and Gloucester voice their dismay, Exeter inquires if treachery led to the disaster. The messenger attributes the catastrophe to a lack of manpower and funds and to intrigue and dissension in England. Exeter is deeply disturbed, and Bedford as Regent of France resolves to discard his mourning clothes, don armor, and fight to recover the lost territories. A second messenger arrives with word that Charles the Dauphin has been crowned King of France and is

[1] Andrew S. Cairncross in the New Arden Shakespeare edition alters the name to *Joan of Aire.*

attracting strong support. Exeter seems pessimistic, but Bedford and Gloucester prepare for the campaign in France. A third messenger enters to report the retreat of Lord Talbot from the siege of Orleans, his subsequent defeat, and his wounding by "A base Walloon." Betrayed by Sir John Fastolfe's cowardice, Talbot was captured along with Lord Scales and Lord Hungerford. Determined to avenge Talbot's defeat and ransom him from the French, Bedford leaves to keep Saint George's feast in France. Exeter exhorts his nephews to remember their oaths to Henry V, and Gloucester departs for the Tower to review the artillery and munition and to crown Henry VI. Exeter, as special guardian to the young monarch, plans to go to Eltham to insure the King's safety. Alone and envious of the other peers, Winchester states his intention of kidnaping the King and through him sitting "at the chiefest stern of public weal."

I,ii. France. In Front of Orleans

Contemptuously deriding the strength and capacity of their foes, Charles, Alençon, and Reignier decide to attack the English besiegers and free Orleans. Accustomed to fear the valiant exploits of the captured Talbot, they underrate the abilities as a commander of "mad-brain'd Salisbury." They sound the alarm and proceed into battle. In a short time they return, having been defeated with heavy losses. Marveling at the ferocity and determination of the English, the three French leaders agree to abandon the city. At this instant the Bastard of Orleans meets them and tells them of the presence of a "holy maid" who has had a heavenly vision ordaining her "to raise this tedious siege" and drive the English out of France. Thinking to test Joan's powers, Charles commands Reignier to pose as the Dauphin and to question her when she appears.

Accompanying the Bastard before the French commanders, Joan la Pucelle immediately addresses Reignier by his correct name, orders the real Dauphin to converse with her, and commands his companions to give them privacy for their conference. Briefly Joan identifies herself as a shepherd's daughter, uneducated in any kind of art, but endowed by "Heaven and our Lady" to liberate France. To prove her statements, Joan challenges Charles to engage her in hand-to-hand combat. After a short struggle, Joan overcomes the Dauphin, and he owns his admiration and love for her. Joan declares that she must not "yield to any rites of love" until she has discharged her divine commission.

Finally, Alençon and Reignier, impatient with the long conference and curious about it, interrupt to learn the Dauphin's instructions regarding the city of Orleans. Joan commands them to "Fight till the last gasp," and Charles endorses her order. Joan promises an immediate raising of the siege. Charles extols Joan's inspiration and character, and the French leaders repose faith in her.

I,iii. London. In Front of the Tower Gates

Suspecting dishonesty in administration, the Duke of Gloucester arrives to inspect the Tower and calls on the Warders to admit him. To Gloucester's amazement and anger, the officials refuse to let him in, even though he is Lord Protector. Gloucester directs his men to break through the gates when Woodvile, Lieutenant of the Tower, opposes him. Woodvile says that the Cardinal of Winchester has forbidden Gloucester or any of his people to enter the Tower. Enraged, Gloucester orders Woodvile to open the gates, and Gloucester's Servingmen threaten to force their master's entrance.

At this moment, the Cardinal of Winchester and his Men appear and block Gloucester's entry. Taunting each other, the kinsmen quarrel until Gloucester's Men drive off the Cardinal's. In the midst of the melee the Mayor of London and his Officers come up. The Mayor orders both sides to keep the peace, but the fracas flares again. At the Mayor's command an officer reads a proclamation directing all men to disarm, disband, and return to their "several dwelling places . . . upon pain of death." Exchanging threats, Gloucester and Winchester submit to the order and leave. The Mayor, a man of peace, deplores the wrangling of the nobility.

I,iv. Orleans, in France

Having learned of an English plan to reconnoiter the city through a secret grating, the Master Gunner has placed a "piece of ordnance" to fire upon the enemy. The Gunner orders his son (the Boy) to keep watch and bring word if the English appear. A moment after the Gunner leaves, the Boy says that he will not trouble his father if he sights the enemy.

Salisbury and Talbot, accompanied by Glansdale and Gargrave, appear on the turrets. In reply to Salisbury's question, Talbot explains that he has been exchanged for Lord Ponton de Santrailles and goes on to condemn Fastolfe, through whose treachery he was captured. While Talbot is describing the close guard his captors exercised over him and the ridicule they heaped upon him, Salisbury interrupts to confer with his companions on the best method of attacking Orleans. While they are reconnoitering, the Gunner's Boy returns to his post with a linstock. An instant later guns fire, mortally wounding Salisbury and Gargrave. While Talbot laments the loss of his comrades, there is a commotion and a messenger reports the arrival of Joan and the Dauphin to lift the siege of Orleans. Vowing to avenge his friends' deaths, Talbot orders his attendants to carry Salisbury to his tent and prepares to face the French.

I,v. In Front of Orleans

Talbot chases the Dauphin from the field but bewails the fact that his English troops cannot withstand "A woman clad in armour." Joan appears and engages Talbot in combat. At the height of their struggle Joan withdraws to replenish the city's supplies. Greatly perplexed, Talbot cannot decide how to oppose Joan, who defeats the English with fear rather than with force. A series of skirmishes results in Joan's entry into Orleans, and Talbot, overcome with shame, wishes that he could die with Salisbury.

I,vi. Orleans

Having entered Orleans, Joan greets the French commanders. The Dauphin, Alençon, and Reignier heap praises on their new champion. Charles, giving Joan credit for the victory and offering to share his crown with her, vows to erect a stately monument to her and prophesies that "Joan la Pucelle shall be France's saint." [1]

II,i. Orleans

A French sergeant posts two sentinels to guard the walls of the city. Talbot, Bedford, Burgundy, and their forces approach with scaling ladders. Talbot advises an immediate assault on Orleans to take advantage of the Frenchmen's false sense of security after their carousing and banqueting. Bedford sarcastically criticizes Charles's cowardly alliance "with witches and the help of hell." Burgundy makes a coarse joke about Joan, and the three leaders separate to scale the walls.

Summoned by the Sentinel, the Bastard of Orleans, Alençon, and Reignier go half-dressed into battle. Charles and Joan join their confederates. Charles suspects treachery, but Joan blames the carelessness of the watch in not giving an alarm. When the French commanders start to quarrel about whose laxness has permitted the

[1] A striking prophecy! Joan was beatified in 1909 and canonized in 1920.

English advance, Joan silences them and prepares to counterattack. An English soldier disperses them by crying, "A Talbot!"

II,ii. Orleans. Inside the Town

Bedford stops his men's pursuit of the French. Talbot, having avenged Salisbury's death, directs the preparation of a tomb to commemorate the Earl's exploits. When Talbot voices surprise at not having encountered the Dauphin or Joan of Arc, Bedford repeats a rumor that the Dauphin and La Pucelle have fled the city. Burgundy says that he saw them "swiftly running,/Like to a pair of loving turtledoves/That could not live asunder day or night." A messenger arrives with the Countess of Auvergne's invitation for Talbot to visit her in order that she may "boast she hath beheld the man/Whose glory fills the world with loud report." Burgundy urges Talbot not to despise the Countess's gentle suit. Resolving to "prove this lady's courtesy," Talbot asks his comrades to accompany him, but they decline. After whispering instructions to one of his officers, Talbot leaves to meet the Countess.

II,iii. Auvergne. The Castle of the Countess

Having formulated a plan to capture Talbot, the Countess gives last-minute instructions to her Porter as a messenger ushers the English general into her presence. Expecting to see "some Hercules,/A second Hector," the Countess is amazed at Talbot's small and unimpressive appearance. When she calls him "a child, a silly dwarf" and a "weak and writhled shrimp," he starts to leave. Convinced that he is actually the dreaded Talbot and reassured by the arrival of the Porter, who has locked the doors, the Countess tells her guest that she has lured him into her castle to imprison him. Laughing at the Countess, Talbot replies that she has captured his shadow but not his substance. Winding his horn, he calls his soldiers, whom he introduces to his hostess as his true substance. The Countess apologizes for her presumption, acknowledges his superiority, and invites him to a feast.

II,iv. London. The Temple Garden [1]

Richard Plantagenet and the Earl (afterwards Duke) of Somerset and their supporters have left the Temple Hall to continue their

[1] The Temple was one of the Inns of Court belonging to the four legal societies which trained students for law practice.

dispute in the garden. Suffolk and Warwick, disclaiming expert legal knowledge, refuse to state an opinion on the argument. Exasperated by the lords' unwillingness to take sides, Richard invites those who support his position to pluck a white rose with him. In corresponding fashion Somerset requests those who agree with him to pluck a red rose.[1] After Warwick has selected a white rose and Suffolk a red one, Vernon proposes that all agree to abide by the preference of the majority. When Richard and Somerset subscribe to this in principle, Vernon and an unnamed Lawyer pluck white roses with Plantagenet. Ignoring his previous commitment to accept the majority opinion, Somerset maintains his views. The quarrel grows more heated when Warwick argues for Richard's royal descent and Somerset objects that Richard is the son of a condemned and executed traitor. Somerset and Suffolk leave in angry defiance. Richard chafes with vexation, and Warwick, pledging loyalty to him, predicts that Parliament will elevate Richard to the Duchy of York and that the present quarrel will lead to war between the Houses of Lancaster and York. After thanking Warwick, Vernon, and the Lawyer for their support, Richard invites them to dinner.

II,v. The Tower of London

Jailers carry Edmund Mortimer forth in a chair. Weak, near death, and heavy with grief, Mortimer asks if his nephew will visit him. The Jailer says that Richard has promised to come. Having been imprisoned since the accession of Henry V, Mortimer hopes for Richard's better success. Richard enters and after embracing Mortimer informs him of the recent quarrel with Somerset. At Richard's request, Mortimer reviews the genealogical steps through which the Yorkists claim the throne. Designating Richard as his heir and cautioning him to be discreet and politic in challenging the House of Lancaster, Mortimer requests a suitable funeral and dies. Resolving to lock Mortimer's counsel in his heart, Richard commands the Jailers to remove the body and starts for Parliament to regain his rightful title.

III,i. London. The Parliament House

After the King and several peers have entered the hall, Gloucester attempts to submit a bill, only to have Winchester snatch it from his

[1] In this non-historical scene Shakespeare dramatizes the choice of emblems by the House of York (white) and the House of Lancaster (red), rivals in the Wars of the Roses.

hand and tear it in pieces. Although Gloucester would have preferred to read his charges against Winchester, he proceeds verbatim to accuse his uncle of gross corruption, treachery, and plotting against his life. Winchester denies the indictment, citing his poverty as evidence of honesty, and impugns Gloucester for overweening ambition and thirst for political power. Recalling Winchester's illegitimate birth, Gloucester labels him a "saucy priest." Winchester describes his nephew as "unreverent" and threatens to appeal to the Pope. Warwick sides with Gloucester, and Somerset with Winchester, but Richard Plantagenet prudently conceals his prejudice against the Cardinal. Deploring civil strife and its perils to the state, King Henry pleads with Gloucester and Winchester to join their hearts "in love and amity."

Sounds of rioting interrupt the King, and the Mayor of London appears and reports that Winchester's and Gloucester's Men, forbidden "to carry any weapon," have begun stoning one another, damaging property, and disturbing the peace. Members of the two factions enter skirmishing. At the King's command, Gloucester orders his Men to cease fighting. Winchester at first refuses to intervene unless Gloucester submits to him. After Gloucester offers his hand and the King and Warwick add their pleas for reconciliation, Winchester reluctantly consents to shake hands with his nephew. The truce is an uneasy one, but the King welcomes it joyfully and dismisses the contending Servingmen, who leave to attend to their wounds and bruises.

Immediately Warwick petitions the King to restore Richard Plantagenet to his father's forfeited titles. After Gloucester and Winchester concur in this request, the King assigns Richard the whole inheritance "That doth belong unto the house of York" and creates him Duke of York. All except Somerset hail the new duke. Immediately Gloucester advises Henry to embark for France and his coronation in Paris. The King and his court depart, leaving Exeter alone. Recognizing dissension among the peers as a canker that will weaken and divide England, Exeter recalls a prophecy that Henry V would win all and that Henry VI would lose all. He hopes that he may die before "that hapless time."

III,ii. France. In Front of Rouen

Joan of Arc and four soldiers, disguised as peasants, deceive the Watchmen and gain admission to Rouen. No sooner have they entered the town than Charles and his leaders arrive to await Joan's signal from the tower that she has succeeded. Joan emerges on top of the wall with a flaming torch, and the French commanders lead their forces into the city.

Forced to abandon Rouen, Talbot curses the treachery of "Pucelle, that witch, that damned sorceress." After a number of skirmishes, Joan and her fellow leaders emerge on the walls to taunt Talbot and his colleagues, who have reappeared below. Exchanging insults with the enemy, Talbot with Burgundy's assistance launches a new attack on the city. Bedford, dying and confined to a litter, obstinately refuses to leave the scene, preferring to remain and inspire the English with his presence.

During a succession of sallies, Sir John Fastolfe deserts, and Bedford dies in peace after watching the flight of Joan, Charles, and Alençon. Talbot and Burgundy return, complimenting each other on their victory. Talbot arranges for the occupation of Rouen and the burial of Bedford and plans to meet King Henry VI in Paris.

III,iii. Plains near Rouen

Joan assures her companions that Talbot's success is temporary. After they have stated their confidence in her, she tells them of her plan to lure Burgundy from the English. While they confer, Talbot and his army march past in the distance. As Burgundy approaches, Joan arranges a parley with him. Describing the "pining malady of France," Joan appeals to Burgundy's patriotism and exhorts him to ally himself with her in repelling the English invaders. In an aside, Burgundy comments on the bewitching power Joan exercises over him. She continues to argue that he will receive no lasting benefit or favor from the English if they gain control of France. Overcome by Joan's persuasiveness, Burgundy deserts Talbot and embraces the French lords as allies.

III,iv. Paris. The Palace

Before King Henry and his assembled lords, Talbot recites his impressive successes in France and tenders them to the monarch. He reasserts his loyalty and ascribes his victory to God and the King. Henry praises Talbot and in recognition of his service creates him Earl of Shrewsbury. When the King and the majority of the peers have departed, Vernon and Basset begin to quarrel over the dissension between York and Lancaster. Vernon strikes Basset, and the two vow to settle their dispute at a later date under arms.

IV,i. Paris. The Palace

At Gloucester's behest, Winchester sets the crown on the head of Henry VI, and the Governor of Paris kneels before the ruler and then retires. Sir John Fastolfe arrives with a letter from the Duke of Burgundy. Enraged by the sight of a coward and deserter, Talbot rips the Garter [1] from Fastolfe's leg and describes his perfidy to the court. Having listened attentively to Talbot's denunciation, Henry deprives Fastolfe of his title and banishes him on pain of death. The King then asks Gloucester to read the letter in which Burgundy states his decision to join the cause of Charles. Vexed by this act, Henry directs Talbot to punish Burgundy for his treason. Talbot willingly accepts the commission and departs.

Vernon and Basset enter and appeal to the King for permission to fight a duel. On command each gives his explanation of the quarrel, which is a continuation of the argument between York and Somerset, who thereupon start taunting each other in the King's presence. Both request sanction to settle the issue by combat. Gloucester rebukes the lords for troubling and disturbing the King, and Exeter urges them to be friends. Henry, warning the lords against encouraging the French through their disagreement, appeals to the would-be combatants to forget their contention. Attempting to resolve the matter, Henry puts on a red rose to signify his preference for Somerset, appoints York regent in France, and calls on Somerset to unite his forces with those of his rival. Summoning Gloucester to accompany him to Calais and thence to England, Henry directs York and Somerset to attack Charles, Alençon, and their French allies.

On the departure of the King, Warwick attempts to calm York's irritation over Henry's approval of Somerset. They leave, and Exeter again prophesies that such envy and jealousy will breed confusion for the young King.

IV,ii. France. In Front of Bordeaux

Talbot calls on the commander of Bordeaux to surrender the city. Certain of the Dauphin's support, the French officer defies Talbot and refuses to yield. In the distance drums signal the approach of Charles's army. Knowing himself outnumbered, Talbot invokes the aid of God and Saint George and prepares to engage the enemy.

[1] Emblem of the Order of the Garter, one of the most esteemed honors of English chivalry.

IV,iii. Plains in Gascony

A messenger reports to the Duke of York that the French armies are converging on Bordeaux to fight with Talbot. York curses Somerset for delay in sending the reinforcements necessary to relieve Talbot. Sir William Lucy appears with a special plea to York to hasten to Talbot's assistance. York continues to blame the "vile traitor Somerset" for perverse procrastination, and Lucy describes the imminent reunion of Talbot and his son, who have not met for seven years. Emphasizing his inability to aid Talbot, York leaves with his soldiers. Lucy comments that the rivalry and sedition of Henry VI's commanders are losing the territories that Henry V had conquered.

IV,iv. Other Plains in Gascony

Somerset is explaining to one of Talbot's officers that the Duke of York rashly ordered Talbot into a position from which he cannot escape. Sir William Lucy arrives with a frantic appeal to Somerset to march toward Bordeaux in support of Talbot. Somerset replies that York placed Talbot in his present predicament and that York may aid him. When Lucy says that York blames Somerset for the impending disaster, Somerset retorts that York is lying and could aid Talbot if he wished to do so. Lucy argues that "The fraud of England, not the force of France" has entrapped Talbot, and Somerset finally consents to send a detachment of cavalry. Lucy comments that the rescue is too late and that Talbot's defeat and death will be Somerset's shame.

IV,v. The English Camp near Bordeaux

Talbot welcomes his son John but directs him to flee certain death in the forthcoming battle. Scorning such a dishonorable action, John Talbot overcomes his father's many arguments and at last wins consent to fight by his side.

IV,vi. A Field of Battle

Encouraging his soldiers and denouncing the Duke of York for having broken his pledged word to support him, Talbot rescues John from the French, who are pressing their attack. Again Talbot implores his son to flee and save his life, but John restates his determination to remain with his father. Together they continue the struggle.

IV,vii. Another Part of the Field

A servant leads Talbot, near death from his wounds, across the field. While the old general is inquiring about his son, soldiers appear with John's body. Eulogizing his son's valor, Talbot orders the men to lay the body in his arms and dies.

While Charles, Joan, Orleans, and Burgundy are commenting on young Talbot's remarkable exploits, they discover the bodies of the two Talbots. The Bastard of Orleans suggests that they mutilate the corpses, but Charles rejects the idea as Sir William Lucy approaches under truce with a French herald. In high-flown and tedious style Lucy asks the whereabouts of Lord Talbot. Contemptuously, Joan points to the ground. Vowing to avenge the deaths of Talbot and his son, Lucy secures permission to remove the bodies for proper burial. Charles, optimistic now that Talbot is dead, announces an advance on Paris.

V,i. London. The Palace

King Henry has received letters from the Pope, the Emperor, and the Earl of Armagnac imploring him to make peace with France. Gloucester urges his nephew to comply and also to accept the daughter of the Earl of Armagnac as his bride. Although Henry hesitates to marry because of his youth and his inclination to study, he agrees to follow his advisers' counsel.

Winchester, wearing a cardinal's cap, enters with the Ambassadors and the Papal Legate. Exeter recalls the prophecy of Henry V that if Winchester ever became a cardinal he would rival the king in authority. Henry informs the envoys that he will "draw conditions of a friendly peace" and transmit them to France by Winchester. Gloucester announces that Henry has agreed to make the daughter of Armagnac his queen, and the King sends her a jewel as a pledge of his love. When all have withdrawn except Winchester and the Papal Legate, Winchester says that he will send the Pope the sum of money he has promised for his elevation to the cardinalship. To himself, Winchester vows that he will now force Humphrey of Gloucester to submit or "sack this country with a mutiny."

V,ii. France. Plains in Anjou

While Charles, Joan, and Alençon discuss their plans to occupy Paris, a scout reports that the English army has regrouped itself and is preparing for battle. Burgundy hopes that Talbot's ghost will not be present, but Joan scorns fear and promises victory.

V,iii. France. In Front of Angiers

Seeing that the Duke of York is prevailing and that the Frenchmen flee, Joan invokes "familiar spirits" to come to her assistance. Fiends appear, but they remain silent, hang their heads, then shake them, and depart. Joan realizes that her spiritual power has forsaken her and that her "ancient incantations" are too weak to save France from defeat. After the Duke of York overcomes Burgundy in hand-to-hand combat, the French flee, leaving Joan in York's custody. She scornfully defies her captor, but York calls her a witch and enchantress, implies that he will send her to the stake, and leaves with her.

Immediately Suffolk appears with his captive, Margaret, the daughter of Reignier. Overwhelmed by her beauty, he starts to set her free, but her charms induce him to keep her and declare his love for her. She asks what ransom she must pay for her release, but Suffolk, who already has a wife, talks to himself while he racks his brain for a plan whereby he can win Margaret. At last he decides to arrange her marriage to Henry VI despite the many diplomatic obstacles he foresees. Hurriedly, Suffolk proposes the royal marriage to Margaret, who consents if her father approves.

Summoning Reignier from the walls, Suffolk seeks his consent to Margaret's marriage with Henry. Quickly Reignier endorses the match on condition that he retain peaceful title to Maine and Anjou. Suffolk concludes the arrangements and prepares to leave for England. Before he goes, he kisses Margaret and privately wishes that he could enjoy her favors.

V,iv. The Duke of York's Camp in Anjou

York orders Joan conducted to the stake. The Old Shepherd, Joan's father, bemoans his daughter's fate and declares that he will die with her. Contemptuously, Joan disowns her father and claims gentler blood than his. Frustrated and infuriated by Joan's continued rejection of him, the Shepherd curses her, declares that she deserves burning because hanging is too good for her, and leaves.

When York orders her removal, Joan recalls her royal ancestry, her divine inspiration, and her chasteness of thought and deed. Deaf to her pleas, York repeats his command to take her away. Warwick interposes to demand additional fagots and pitch "so her torture may be shortened." On hearing this, Joan suddenly repudiates her avowals of chastity and declares that she is pregnant with Alençon's child.[1] In confusion she withdraws this statement and says that Reignier is the father of her unborn infant. Unmoved by her frantic assertions, Warwick and York remind Joan that she described herself as an untainted virgin, and York sends her to death.

No sooner have guards led Joan away than Winchester arrives with news of the peace concluded between England and France. Bitterly York laments the loss of so many lives in the recent war and the surrender of much territory. Pessimistically, he foresees the "utter loss of all the realm of France." Warwick assures him that the treaty will give little advantage to the French.

At this point Charles arrives with his allies to learn the conditions of the peace. Winchester proclaims that Charles may occupy the throne of France so long as he submits himself as a viceroy of Henry VI and pays tribute to him. Alençon pronounces the offer "absurd and reasonless," and Charles replies that since he possesses "more than half the Gallian territories" he prefers holding full title to these rather than being merely the sub-ruler of all of France. York threatens to continue the wars if Charles does not accept the terms Winchester has described. Reignier advises Charles to agree; Alençon urges that it is politic for Charles to consent to a truce that he may later break when he finds it convenient to do so. In the face of these opinions, Charles and the French lords swear allegiance to Henry with tokens of their fealty, and York confirms the peace.

V,v. London. The Palace

Swayed by Suffolk's eloquent description of Margaret's charms, King Henry seeks Gloucester's consent to the proposed marriage. Gloucester as Protector reminds the King that he is betrothed to the Earl of Aramagnac's daughter and asks how the monarch can honorably "dispense with that contract." Suffolk argues that since Armagnac is a poor earl, Henry may violate his agreement with impunity. Gloucester retorts that although Reignier excels in glorious titles he is actually no better than an earl. Exeter comments that Armagnac will provide his daughter with a more liberal dowry than Margaret can bring, but Suffolk pleads that the King should marry for love and not for wealth. Peremptorily, Henry declares his inten-

[1] An old principle of Roman law prohibited the execution of a woman while she was pregnant.

tion of making Margaret his queen and instructs Suffolk to speed to France in order to conclude the arrangements. To subsidize the marriage, Henry levies a heavy tax on all England. Henry then appeals for Gloucester's forgiveness for his sudden decision and retires. Expressing his misgivings, Gloucester joins Exeter and departs.

Left to himself, Suffolk prepares to return to France in the manner Paris once journeyed to Greece "With hope to find the like event in love/But prosper better than the Troyan did." He adds,

> Margaret shall now be Queen, and rule the King;
> But I will rule both her, the King, and realm.

HENRY VI (PART TWO) [1590–1591]

CHARACTERS

KING HENRY THE SIXTH.

HUMPHREY, Duke of Gloucester, his uncle.

CARDINAL BEAUFORT, Bishop of Winchester, great-uncle to the *King*.

RICHARD PLANTAGENET, Duke of York.

EDWARD and RICHARD, his sons.

DUKE OF SOMERSET.

DUKE OF SUFFOLK.

DUKE OF BUCKINGHAM.

LORD CLIFFORD.

YOUNG CLIFFORD, his son.

EARL OF SALISBURY.

EARL OF WARWICK.

LORD SCALES.

LORD SAY.

SIR HUMPHREY STAFFORD.

WILLIAM STAFFORD, his brother.

SIR JOHN STANLEY.

VAUX.

MATTHEW GOFFE.

A Lieutenant, a Shipmaster, a Master's Mate, and WALTER WHITMORE.

Two Gentlemen, prisoners with *Suffolk*.

JOHN HUME and JOHN SOUTHWELL, two priests.

ROGER BOLINGBROKE, a conjurer.

A Spirit.

THOMAS HORNER, an armorer.

PETER [THUMP], his man.

Clerk of Chatham.

Mayor of Saint Albans.

SAUNDER SIMPCOX, an impostor.

ALEXANDER IDEN, a Kentish gentleman.

JACK CADE, a rebel.

GEORGE BEVIS, JOHN HOLLAND, DICK the butcher, SMITH the weaver, MICHAEL, etc., his followers.

Two Murderers.

MARGARET, Queen to *King Henry*.

ELEANOR, Duchess of Gloucester.

MARGERY JOURDAIN, a witch.

Wife to *Simpcox.*

Lords, Ladies, and Attendants; Petitioners, Aldermen, a Herald, a Beadle, a Sheriff, Officers, Citizens, Prentices, Falconers, Guards, Soldiers, Messengers, etc.

Scene: *England*

I,i. London. The Palace

Suffolk describes his recent marriage to Margaret as procurator of Henry VI and presents her to the King, who kisses her and praises her beauty. After the court cheers the new Queen, Suffolk hands Gloucester a copy of the marriage contract whereby Reignier gains title to Maine and Anjou. Gloucester drops the paper and says that he can read no farther. Winchester picks up the document and reveals that Suffolk has agreed for Henry to bear the cost of the wedding and to accept Margaret without a dowry.

Enchanted with his bride, King Henry commends Suffolk and promotes him to a dukedom. After relieving the Duke of York of the regency of France for eighteen months and thanking all his peers, the King goes with Margaret and Suffolk to prepare for the Queen's coronation.

Sadly recalling Henry V's exploits, the recent sacrifices in France and Normandy, and Henry VI's coronation in Paris, Humphrey of Gloucester denounces the marriage as a shameful alliance destined to undo all that English arms and diplomacy have achieved. Winchester observes that England still controls France, but Gloucester sees that Suffolk, "the new-made duke that rules the roast," has tragically weakened England's power by ceding Anjou and Maine to Reignier, Margaret's father. Salisbury, Warwick, and the Duke of York unanimously condemn Suffolk for arranging the match. Gloucester also criticizes Suffolk for his lavish expenses and for the exorbitant taxes they have necessitated.

Winchester chides Gloucester for opposing the King's pleasure, but Humphrey retorts that the Cardinal dislikes his presence rather than what he has said. Trying to avoid a resumption of his private quarrel with Winchester, Gloucester leaves. Winchester declares that Gloucester is an ambitious man who as Protector and heir apparent [1] to the crown seeks to mislead the common people and his fellow peers

[1] Today Gloucester would be called heir presumptive.

with "smoothing words" and "flattering gloss." Buckingham adds that the King is of age to govern in his own right and suggests to Somerset that they join Suffolk in removing Gloucester from the protectorship. Winchester says, "This weighty business will not brook delay," and departs to find Suffolk. Somerset cautions Buckingham that when Gloucester is displaced, Winchester will become a haughty and intolerable protector. Buckingham, however, believes that he or Somerset can secure the appointment.

"Pride went before, ambition follows him," Salisbury drily observes as Somerset follows Buckingham from the hall. Praising the nobility of Gloucester and condemning the worldly, haughty, and unmannerly qualities of Winchester, Salisbury exhorts Warwick and York to join him in supporting "the good Duke Humphrey" against the schemes of his rivals. The three men agree, Warwick stating his determination to recapture Maine from the French.

Alone, York soliloquizes on the lessening of England's power in France. Regarding himself as the rightful heir to the kingdom and all of its territories, York cannot blame those who have squandered what was not really theirs. Ambitiously and hypocritically, he resolves to "take the Nevils' [Salisbury's and Warwick's] parts,/And make a show of love to proud Duke Humphrey" until opportunity allows him to seize the throne. He will bide his time until Henry's "surfeiting in joys of love" and Humphrey's dissension with the peers permit him successfully to "grapple with the house of Lancaster."

I,ii. London. The Duke of Gloucester's House

Eleanor, Duchess of Gloucester, seeks the causes of her husband's sober preoccupation. Supposing that he hopes to ascend the throne, she says that she will help him achieve this goal. Swiftly Humphrey commands her to quell her ambitious thoughts and asserts his loyalty to King Henry. He adds that a recent dream has saddened him because it seemed to forecast his removal from the protectorship by Winchester and the appointment of Somerset and Suffolk to the office. Eleanor discounts his interpretation but tells of her own dream in which Henry and Margaret crown her Queen of England in Westminster cathedral. Angrily Humphrey rebukes Eleanor for her treacherous and presumptuous ambition, which he says will disgrace himself and her. Petulantly, Eleanor remarks that henceforth she will keep her dreams to herself. Humphrey's anger passes, and a messenger summons him to accompany the King and Queen on a hawking party to Saint Albans. He leaves, Eleanor promising to follow.

Left to herself, Eleanor confesses her unhappiness at being second woman in the kingdom. If she were in Humphrey's position she would ruthlessly seize the throne. Being a woman, she will do all she can to promote Humphrey and herself.[1] She calls Hume, who enters and greets her as "your Royal Majesty." He assures Eleanor that through his advice and the grace of God her title "shall be multiplied" from "Grace," the appropriate form of address for a duchess. When Hume adds that he has arranged a seance with Margery Jourdain ("the cunning witch") and Roger Bolingbroke ("the conjurer") at which time they will raise a spirit to answer whatever questions Eleanor propounds, she rewards him and departs for Saint Albans. Hume then reveals to the audience that, although he is accepting payment from the Duchess, he is in the employment of Winchester, who with Suffolk has hired him to betray Eleanor.

I,iii. London. The Palace

Three or four petitioners, including Peter, are waiting to see the Protector, Humphrey Duke of Gloucester. When Suffolk and the Queen enter, one of the petitioners mistakes Suffolk for Gloucester. Examining the petitions, Suffolk and the Queen find one that sues for the remedy of personal grievances committed by one of Winchester's servants; another seeks redress against the Duke of Suffolk; a third is Peter's charge that his master, Thomas Horner, supports York's claim to the throne. Suffolk orders Peter held for the arrival of Horner. The Queen tears up the other petitions and summarily dismisses the "base cullions" who submitted them. To Suffolk, the Queen complains of Duke Humphrey's management of the kingdom and of Henry's neglect of her because of his absorption in religious studies. She confesses that she thought Henry would resemble Suffolk, and she wishes that the College of Cardinals would elect Henry pope and take him to Rome. Suffolk tries to calm her, but Margaret says that several peers hold more individual power than the King has. Suffolk drily notes that the Nevils "are no simple peers" and are as strong as the five others she has named. Margaret then admits that Eleanor's pride and haughty bearing vex her more than anything else. Suffolk tells the Queen that he has laid a trap for the Duchess and

[1] The reader would find it interesting to compare Eleanor's role in this scene with that of Lady Macbeth.

that they must join Winchester's party until Humphrey and York fall into disgrace.

A trumpet signals the arrival of King Henry, his courtiers, and attendants. When Henry says that he cannot decide whether York or Somerset should be Regent of France, a violent quarrel among the lords ensues. The Queen declares that the King prefers Somerset, whereupon Gloucester rebukes her by stating that Henry is old enough to make his own decisions. If this be true, she says, then Gloucester should resign the protectorship. Humphrey says that he will give up the post at the King's pleasure. At this Suffolk accuses Gloucester of insolent incompetence; Winchester charges him with extortion; Somerset says that he has misappropriated public funds for his own use; Buckingham adds the charge of cruelty in executing justice; the Queen says that he is guilty of selling public offices in France. Humphrey leaves; the Queen drops her fan and then boxes Eleanor on the ear for failing to pick it up. The two women quarrel, and Eleanor departs, vowing vengeance on Margaret for such an insult. Buckingham quietly remarks to Winchester that he will follow Eleanor, who is now provoked enough to rush to her own destruction.

Humphrey, having brought his temper under control by walking outside, returns, defies the peers to prove their "spiteful false accusations," and advises the King that York is best fitted for the Regency of France. When Suffolk objects, York cynically agrees that he is not qualified because he cannot flatter Suffolk and because Somerset will undermine his efforts as he did in the French wars (see *1 Henry VI,* IV, iii and iv). This produces an angry exchange between Warwick, who corroborates York, and Suffolk, who sponsors Somerset.

At this moment, Horner and Peter appear to settle their complaint. Horner vehemently denies Peter's testimony that he described York as rightful heir to the crown and says that the apprentice is trying to get even with him by bringing a false accusation. York demands Peter's execution. Gloucester advises the King to appoint Somerset Regent of France and to set a day when Horner and Peter may settle their dispute in single combat. King Henry commits Horner and Peter to prison until the last of the month and goes to see Somerset depart for France.

I,iv. London. The Duke of Gloucester's Garden

At Hume's direction, Bolingbroke, Margery Jourdain, and Southwell prepare to demonstrate their occult powers. Eleanor, escorted by

Hume, appears above. As Bolingbroke and Southwell conjure, "It thunders and lightens terribly" and a Spirit rises. While Bolingbroke reads the Duchess's questions, Southwell writes down the Spirit's answers: (1) that the duke who will depose Henry VI still lives but will in turn die a violent death; (2) that Suffolk will die "by water"; (3) and that Somerset should "shun castles." Bolingbroke discharges the Spirit, which vanishes as York and Buckingham and their guard break in to arrest Eleanor and her practitioners of black magic. The guards march the prisoners off, and York commends Buckingham for having executed the plot so efficiently. Reading the copy Southwell has made of the answers, York dismisses them as being difficult to interpret, and Buckingham sets out for Saint Albans to report the incident to Henry and Gloucester. Before he leaves, York sends an invitation to Salisbury and Warwick to sup with him the following night.

II,i. Saint Albans

Pleased with the hawking, the Queen says that she has not enjoyed better sport for a long time. King Henry views the falcon's flight as evidence of divine power; Suffolk observes that Gloucester's hawks soar as high as their master's ambition; Winchester jibes at Gloucester, and the two kinsmen resume their bickering. Suffolk and the Queen add their taunts to Winchester's. King Henry vainly tries to restore peace while Winchester and Gloucester continue to wrangle in asides until each challenges the other to personal combat. Weary of the quarrel, King Henry again urges them to compose themselves as a citizen of Saint Albans appears crying, "A miracle!"

Under Suffolk's questioning, the citizen explains that within the last half hour a man "that ne'er saw in his life before" has received his sight. King Henry praises the Almighty for this proof of divine grace. A procession including the Mayor of Saint Albans, Simpcox (in a litter) and his wife, and several townsmen, approaches. To inquiries by Winchester, Suffolk, and the King, Simpcox relates how by following the instructions of good Saint Alban he has visited the shrine and gained his sight. His inability to walk he attributes to a fall from a plum tree. On all points Simpcox's wife supports her husband, and King Henry is greatly impressed with this manifestation of God's goodness. Gloucester, however, is skeptical. He cannot believe that a man blind from birth would climb a tree. Pretending to doubt that Simpcox can really see, Gloucester asks him to identify colors. When Simpcox correctly designates red and black, Gloucester exposes him as a lying knave and impostor and orders that he be whipped. Humphrey tells Simpcox that he may avoid the whipping by jumping over the stool and running away, but the poor man insists that he is physically unable to stand alone. When a Beadle hits Simpcox once with his whip, the man leaps to his feet and scampers off. The citizens again cry, "A miracle!" King Henry marvels that the Almighty permits such things to happen. The Queen laughs. Simpcox's wife pleads that she and her husband perpetrated the hoax because of poverty. Gloucester orders that the couple be whipped through every market town to Berwick. The Cardinal of Winchester and Suffolk sarcastically praise Gloucester for having worked a miracle.

Before the quarrel becomes more intense, Buckingham arrives and relates to the King how Eleanor has been practicing witchcraft against the monarch and the state. Disheartened by this news, Gloucester has no desire to contend further with the Cardinal. When the Queen taunts him, Humphrey affirms his loyalty, says that he cannot explain Eleanor's actions, and adds that if the Duchess is guilty he will banish her from his company and let the law take its course. The King declares that he will spend the night at Saint Albans and return to London the next day to review the Duchess's offenses.

II,ii. London. The Duke of York's Garden

After dinner the Duke of York explains to Salisbury and Warwick his claim to the throne. Persuaded of the legality of his case, the Nevils kneel and acknowledge him as their rightful sovereign. York thanks them but cautions them that he is not king until he is crowned and the Lancastrian incumbent is removed. He advises his new supporters to tolerate the insolence of Suffolk, Cardinal Winchester, and the others until they have "snar'd the shepherd of the flock . . . the good Duke Humphrey." In doing this they will bring about their own downfall, and then York will seize the crown. Warwick prophesies that he will make York a king, and York promises to make the Earl of Warwick "The greatest man in England but the King."

II,iii. London. A Hall of Justice

King Henry pronounces justice on Eleanor and her accomplices, all of whom have been found guilty. He sentences Margery Jourdain to be burned; he sends Bolingbroke, Hume, and Southwell to the gallows; he condemns Eleanor to do three days' public penance and then to live in exile on the Isle of Man in the custody of Sir John Stanley. Eleanor welcomes her fate, and Gloucester says that he cannot justify anyone whom the law has found guilty; but when Eleanor departs under guard, tears come to his eyes and he asks the King's permission to go. Demanding Humphrey's staff of office, Henry puts himself under the protectorship and guidance of God and tells his uncle to leave in peace. Willingly, Gloucester surrenders his staff and bids the King farewell.

Margaret and Suffolk gloat over the downfall of the Duke and Duchess of Gloucester, but York reminds Henry that this is the day appointed for the trial by combat between Horner and Peter. The King commands the lists made ready. Horner, the Armorer, enters at one door, accompanied by his neighbors. All of them are drinking, and Horner is drunk. At the other door Peter enters with a number of apprentices who are drinking to him. Horner, maintaining his innocence, goads the reluctant Peter into combat. Peter slays Horner, who dies confessing his treason. York cynically advises Peter to thank God and the strong wine that incapacitated his rival. King Henry regards the outcome as ample proof of Horner's guilt and prepares to reward Peter for his truth and innocence.

II,iv. London. A Street

In mourning, the Duke of Gloucester and his servants await the arrival of Eleanor, who is supposed to pass as she does her penance. When she appears "barefoot in a white sheet" and holding a taper, one of the servants proposes that they rescue her from the Sheriff and Sir John Stanley. Gloucester, however, commands his Men not to stir. Shamed by the sneers of the crowd, Eleanor urges Humphrey to curse their mutual enemies. He exhorts her to be patient, but she chides him for standing idly by and doing nothing to save her from her public disgrace. She warns him that he will not stir until his enemies have contrived his death. Secure in his sense of guiltlessness and in his belief that his loyalty will protect him, Gloucester replies that she must patiently atone for her offenses and that he would only compromise himself if he attempted to free her.

A herald summons Gloucester to a meeting of parliament at Bury. Humphrey takes leave of Eleanor and promises Sir John Stanley a reward if he treats the Duchess kindly. Discouraged and low in spirit, Eleanor says good-by to the Sheriff and prepares to accompany Sir John to the Isle of Man.

III,i. The Abbey at Bury St. Edmunds

King Henry, the Queen, and many peers have assembled for parliament. The King expresses surprise that Gloucester has not arrived. Describing Humphrey in prejudiced and unflattering terms, the Queen poisons Henry's mind against his uncle and says that the King is foolish to admit him near his person. She calls on Suffolk, Buckingham, and York to approve or refute her allegations. Winchester joins in as they unanimously agree with the Queen and attribute other crimes and offenses to the absent Duke. King Henry remonstrates that he has found Humphrey virtuous, mild, and free of treasonable intentions, but Margaret replies that the Duke's seeming innocence, like a lambskin for a wolf, merely makes him the more dangerous. At this moment Somerset enters with news that all of France is lost. The King piously accepts the disaster as God's will, but York in an aside bewails the lessening of the realms he views as his own.

Gloucester arrives, apologizing for his tardiness. Instantly Suffolk arrests him for high treason. Gloucester demands to know what his guilt is, and York charges him with accepting bribes from the French, embezzling the army's pay, and administering justice with cruel and harsh punishments. Suffolk implies that Gloucester has committed even "mightier crimes" and places him in the Cardinal's custody. When Henry invites him to speak in his own defense, Humphrey describes the envy and malice with which his many enemies have tried to discredit him and take his life. "I shall not want false witness to condemn me," he says and quotes the proverb, "A staff is quickly found to beat a dog." Winchester, Suffolk, Queen Margaret, and Buckingham heap reproaches on him until the Cardinal orders him confined under guard. As he departs, Gloucester warns Henry of the "gnarling" wolves around him.

Grief-stricken and reluctant to participate in the false indictment of Gloucester, whom he still believes innocent, Henry walks out of the parliament. Contemptuous of her husband's "foolish pity," the Queen immediately calls for Gloucester's death. Winchester agrees but says that political expediency requires a legal pretext. Suffolk wants Gloucester out of the way but fears that a formal trial will not adduce enough evidence to warrant his execution. York argues that Humphrey's ambition renders him unfit to serve the King. Suffolk maintains that his criminal actions justify killing him by any means and offers himself as executioner. The Cardinal is eager for quicker action, however, and says that he will provide the agent. The Queen, the Cardinal, York, and Suffolk agree to murder Gloucester at once.

Before they can act on their plot, a messenger arrives with news of the Irish rebellion, which requires an expedition to suppress the uprising. Ironically, York suggests that Somerset be dispatched as Regent to Ireland since he proved himself efficient in losing France. The two men start to quarrel, but the Queen silences them although she suggests that York might have done worse in France than Somerset did. The Cardinal asks York if he will lead the army to Ireland, and the Duke accepts the commission at once. Suffolk pledges to supply York with soldiers; the Cardinal promises to deal with Humphrey so that he will trouble them no more; York agrees to embark at Bristol within a fortnight. In a long soliloquy the Duke explains that the Queen and her advisers have given him the troops he lacked; on his return he will use them to seize the throne; during his absence he will hire Jack Cade "To make commotion . . . Under the title of John Mortimer," thus involving England in civil strife. Whatever happens to Cade, York stands to gain. With Humphrey gone, Henry VI alone stands between York and the crown.

III,ii. Bury St. Edmunds. A Room of State

Murderers hasten to inform Suffolk that they have killed Gloucester as he commanded. He commends them, makes certain that they have concealed traces of their crime, promises to reward them, and dismisses them as the King and others arrive. King Henry orders Suffolk to fetch Gloucester for his trial. In Suffolk's absence the King requests the peers to be fair and honest in their adduction of evidence against the Duke, and Margaret hypocritically voices the hope that Humphrey may establish his innocence.

At this point Suffolk, pale and trembling, reports that he has found Gloucester dead in his bed. Winchester comments that he dreamed "The Duke was dumb and could not speak a word." The King faints, and the Queen and Suffolk set about reviving him. Regaining consciousness, Henry orders Suffolk to remove his hands and blames him for Gloucester's death. Quickly Margaret speaks in Suffolk's defense, says that if weeping could recall Humphrey's life she would blind herself with tears, and wonders if rumor will hold her responsible for his death. Henry continues to mourn his uncle, and Margaret in a frenzy chides her husband for enticing her from France and then neglecting her.

Sounds of a commotion accompany the entrance of Salisbury, Warwick, and many commoners, who have heard that Gloucester has been murdered on the command of Suffolk and Winchester. Henry replies that he does not know the manner of Humphrey's death and directs Warwick to enter the chamber and view the body. During Warwick's absence, Henry prays that God may forgive his suspicions of foul play if they prove incorrect. Warwick returns with the corpse and calls upon the King to inspect it. While the others look on, Warwick vividly describes the symptoms on Gloucester's body that suggest his violent murder. Circumstantial evidence points to Suffolk and the Cardinal, who had custody of the unfortunate Humphrey. Suffolk protests his innocence too vigorously and challenges Warwick to call him guilty if he dares. Winchester departs without speaking. In the presence of the King and Queen, Warwick and Suffolk exchange threats until they go out to test their honor in a duel. In a moment they return, Suffolk claiming that Warwick and the citizens of Bury set upon him. Salisbury enters and tells Henry that the outraged Commons demand Suffolk's execution or banishment from England for Gloucester's murder. Otherwise they themselves will seize Suffolk and torture him in order to protect the King. While Salisbury presents their case, the Commons shout outside the hall as they await the King's decision. At last Henry directs Salisbury to inform the people that Suffolk will be banished in three days' time on pain of death. In vain the Queen pleads for Suffolk, but Henry remains firm, repeats the sentence, and takes Warwick to another room for conference.

Margaret curses Henry and Warwick. Suffolk joins in execrating their enemies. They take a long, agonizing, and passionate farewell. Vaux interrupts them to tell of the Cardinal's grievous sickness in which he blasphemes God, curses men, and appears to converse with Humphrey's ghost. Vaux goes to report to the King, and Suffolk and Margaret, professing their love for each other, say good-by.

III,iii. London. Cardinal Beaufort's Bedchamber

King Henry, Salisbury, and Warwick visit the dying Cardinal of Winchester, who is suffering physical pain and remorse. Tortured by guilt and by his memories of the murdered Gloucester, the Cardinal seeks death as a release. The King asks Winchester to lift his hand as a sign that he trusts in heavenly salvation, but the wretched churchman dies without moving. The King and his companions retire to spiritual meditation.

IV,i. The Coast of Kent

A lieutenant, other officers and seamen, and Walter Whitmore have captured the disguised Duke of Suffolk and his attending Gentlemen on a ship at sea. Two Gentlemen agree to pay their captors ransoms of a thousand crowns. Whitmore, who has lost an eye in the fight, resolves to kill Suffolk rather than accept ransom. Identifying himself as a Knight of the Garter and revealing his name and title, Suffolk offers to pay any amount placed on his head. On learning that Whitmore's given name is Walter [1] and recalling the prophecy that he should die "by Water," Suffolk shudders but decides that the name correctly pronounced is "Gaultier." Despite Suffolk's eloquent attempt to overawe them, Whitmore and the Lieutenant determine to kill the Duke for his many crimes against individuals and the state. Suffolk haughtily declares that he carries diplomatic messages from Queen Margaret. Then, too proud to plead for mercy, Suffolk dares his captors to kill him. The Lieutenant directs Whitmore to dispatch the Duke while he arranges the Gentlemen's ransoms. In a moment Whitmore returns with Suffolk's severed head and body. One of the Gentlemen prepares to carry the corpse to court.

IV,ii. Blackheath

Bevis and Holland chat while they await the arrival of Jack Cade, his lieutenants, and his band of rebels. Cade explains his claims to the throne of England while his followers indicate in a series of asides that they attach little serious significance to his pretenses of royal descent. Cade proves more successful with the rabble when he promises them cheap bread, strong beer, luxurious living, and social equality. After Dick the butcher advises that they kill all the lawyers, Cade and his henchmen hang the Clerk of Chatham because he can read and write and keep accounts. When Michael brings news of the approach of Sir Humphrey Stafford and his brother William, Cade dubs himself Sir John Mortimer so that he can meet his enemy on equal status. Cade then defies the Staffords' orders to yield, and claims to be the son of Edmund Mortimer, Earl of March. The Staffords refute his statements, but Cade's fellow rebels gullibly and naively support their leader. William Stafford charges that the Duke of York has suborned Cade. The rebel thereupon offers to leave

[1] The *l* in Walter was silent in Elizabethan pronunciation.

Henry VI on the throne on condition that he become Protector. After the rebels denounce Lord Say, the Staffords proclaim Cade and all his followers traitors and depart. Cade rallies his supporters, and they march toward battle.

IV,iii. Another Part of Blackheath

Cade and Dick the butcher congratulate themselves on their recent victory in which they slew both the Staffords. Cade awards Dick the privilege of slaughtering meat during Lent and arrays himself in Sir Humphrey's armor. Together they set out for London to open the jails and free all the prisoners.

IV,iv. London. The Palace

Queen Margaret looks at Suffolk's head and grieves for the dead Duke. She thinks on revenge, wishing that she had Suffolk's body to embrace. Buckingham inquires what answer Henry will make to the rebels' petition, and the King says that he will send a prelate to reason with the mob. In order to avert bloodshed, Henry himself will parley with Cade. Rereading the document, Henry tells Lord Say that Cade has sworn to have his head. The King chides Margaret for continuing to mourn for Suffolk, and a messenger enters with word that Cade and his rabble have reached Southwark. Buckingham urges Henry to flee to Killingworth. The Queen wishes that Suffolk were alive to suppress the rebellion. Lord Say declines to accompany the King lest his presence jeopardize the monarch's safety. Another messenger reports that Cade's forces have seized London Bridge. All hurriedly leave except Lord Say, who remains bold and confident, trusting in his innocence of any wrongdoing.

IV,v. London. The Tower

Two or three citizens request Lord Scales, who is on the wall of the Tower, to aid the Mayor of London. Scales promises to send Matthew Goffe and exhorts the citizens to fight gallantly against the rebels.

IV,vi. London. Cannon Street

Flushed with success, Cade orders the killing of a soldier who calls him Jack Cade instead of Lord Mortimer. He then directs his followers to burn London Bridge and to set fire to the Tower, and he leaves to meet the royalist troops at Smithfield.

IV,vii. London. Smithfield

Having killed Matthew Goffe and his company, Cade orders the razing of public buildings and the burning of "all the records of the realm." A messenger announces the capture of Lord Say, whom Bevis brings before Cade. Say vehemently protests that he is innocent of the preposterous charges Cade levels against him and cites his faithful service to the government and the people. Repressing a momentary feeling of remorse, Cade commands his aides to remove Lord Say and behead him. After this they are to excute Sir James Cromer, Say's son-in-law, and bring both heads "upon two poles." Cade then boasts extravagantly of the excesses he plans to practice as king until one of his rebels returns with the heads of the two knights. Cade and his followers leave to parade their gory trophies through London's streets.

IV,viii. Southwark

Cade's mob is plundering the city. Buckingham and Lord Clifford appear and proclaim a royal pardon to all rebels who desert their leader and "go home in peace." Clifford appeals to the Kentishmen to honor the memory of Henry V by demonstrating their loyalty to his son. Cade temporarily holds his forces together by flaunting the nobility and reminding the commoners of the oppression they have suffered. Clifford exposes Cade's meanness of character and points to the danger of French invasion during a time of civil turmoil. All shout that they will "follow the King and Clifford." Seeing that he has lost control of his forces, Cade flees. The crowd disperses as Buckingham declares a bounty of a thousand crowns on Cade's head.

IV,ix. Killingworth [Kenilworth] Castle

To Somerset and the Queen, King Henry observes that no subject ever longed to be a king as much as he longs to be a subject. Buckingham and Clifford come to inform the King of the dispersal of the rebels and to present a number of prisoners who, with halters about their necks, await the King's sentence. Henry pardons them all and sends them home.

A messenger brings word that the Duke of York has returned from Ireland with a powerful army and is determined to arrest Somerset as a traitor. Recognizing that York has replaced Cade as the major threat to his security, King Henry sends Buckingham to negotiate with York and commits Somerset to the Tower.

IV,x. Kent. Iden's Garden

A fugitive, famished from five days without food, Cade has climbed into Iden's garden in the hope of finding something to eat. Iden, unaware of Cade's presence, strolls into his garden, admires his modest property, and reflects on his contentment. Cade, supposing that Iden wishes to capture him, threatens the innocent man with his sword. Iden rebukes Cade for illegal entry but insists that he has no intention of betraying him. Iden chivalrously hesitates to take unfair advantage of the miserable Cade, but the rebel compels him to fight. In the struggle, Cade falls mortally wounded and tells Iden that he may boast of having killed Kent's best man. Gratified that he has slain the "monstrous traitor," Iden says that he will drag the body to a dunghill, cut off the head, and carry it to the King.

V,i. Fields between Dartford and Blackheath

At the head of his army the Duke of York declares that he has come to seize the throne. "Let them obey that know not how to rule," he says. Seeing Buckingham approaching, York hypocritically conceals his ambition and courteously explains to the King's emissary that his only purpose in keeping men under arms is to force Somerset's removal from court. On Buckingham's assurance that Somerset is a prisoner in the Tower, York dismisses his troops and directs them to assemble the following day in Saint George's Field to receive their pay. In addition, he offers his sons as hostages of his fealty and love to the King. Pleased with York's ready submission, Buckingham starts to escort him to the King's tent.

Meeting Henry and his attendants, York again states that he has brought his army for the specific purpose of removing Somerset and suppressing Cade. While the parties are conferring, Iden approaches with Cade's head, which he presents to the King. Praising God for this evidence of His justice, Henry knights Iden in token of his loyal service.

At this moment Queen Margaret and Somerset join the royal party. Furious at finding Somerset still at large, York charges Henry with breaking faith and demands that he abdicate in favor of one who can rule, namely York himself. Somerset arrests York for capital treason and orders him to kneel, but York scorns the order and sends for his sons to serve bail for him. The Queen dispatches Buckingham to fetch Clifford, and York reviles Margaret as a "blood-bespotted Neapolitan." York's sons Edward and Richard (i.e., Edward IV and

Richard, Duke of Gloucester, later Richard III) enter with their forces, followed by Clifford and his son Young Clifford and their forces. Clifford refuses to acknowledge York as ruler and kneels before Henry, asking that York be conveyed to the Tower and executed. The Queen says that York will not submit to his arrest, and his two sons rally behind him. York instructs an attendant to fetch Salisbury and Warwick, his "two brave bears." The Nevils appear, and Richard taunts Clifford, who calls the boy a "foul indigested lump" because of his physical deformity.

King Henry rebukes Salisbury and Warwick for their failure to show proper deference to him as their King. Salisbury replies that he has carefully considered the question of succession and has decided that York is rightful heir to England's throne. The King asks Salisbury how he can thus violate his sworn allegiance, and the Earl retorts that keeping a sinful oath is a greater sin than swearing to a sin. Angry words pass among the peers as the two parties threaten each other.

V,ii. Saint Albans

On the battlefield Warwick calls for Clifford to fight with him. York walks up, saying that Clifford has killed his horse. Clifford now appears; Warwick gives precedence to York in meeting Clifford and leaves. York and Clifford fight; Clifford falls; York departs. Young Clifford, wandering over the field, discovers his father's body, vows to take revenge, and carries the corpse away. Richard (York's son) fights with Somerset and kills him.

Queen Margaret chides Henry because he will neither fight nor flee. She urges him to avoid capture, and they start for London. Young Clifford laments their flight but hopes the future will hold better fortune for them.

V,iii. Fields near Saint Albans

York and his allies review their success. York inquires about Salisbury, and Richard tells of repeatedly rescuing the old man only to see him return to the battle. Salisbury approaches and thanks Richard for his assistance. York and Warwick agree to pursue the King to London.

HENRY VI (PART THREE) [1590–1591]

CHARACTERS

KING HENRY THE SIXTH.

EDWARD, Prince of Wales, his son.

LEWIS XI, King of France.

DUKE OF SOMERSET.

DUKE OF EXETER.

EARL OF OXFORD.

EARL OF NORTHUMBERLAND.

EARL OF WESTMORELAND.

LORD CLIFFORD.

RICHARD PLANTAGENET, Duke of York.

EDWARD, Earl of March, afterwards KING EDWARD IV, } his sons.
EDMUND, Earl of Rutland, } his sons.
GEORGE, afterwards DUKE OF CLARENCE, } his sons.
RICHARD, afterwards DUKE OF GLOUCESTER, } his sons.

DUKE OF NORFOLK.

MARQUESS OF MONTAGUE.

EARL OF WARWICK.

EARL OF PEMBROKE.

LORD HASTINGS.

LORD STAFFORD.

SIR JOHN MORTIMER, } uncles to *Richard*, Duke of York.
SIR HUGH MORTIMER, } uncles to *Richard*, Duke of York.

HENRY, Earl of Richmond, a youth.

LORD RIVERS, brother to *Lady Grey*.

SIR WILLIAM STANLEY.

SIR JOHN MONTGOMERY.

SIR JOHN SOMERVILLE.

Tutor to *Rutland*.

Mayor of York.

Mayor of Coventry.

Lieutenant of the Tower.

A Nobleman.

Two Keepers [SINKLO and HUMPHREY].

A Son that has killed his father.

A Father that has killed his son.

The French Admiral.

QUEEN MARGARET.

LADY GREY, a widow, afterwards Queen to *Edward IV*.

BONA, sister to the French Queen.

Soldiers, Attendants, Messengers, Aldermen, Watchmen, a Huntsman.

Scene: *England and France*

I,i. London. The Parliament House

Richard, Duke of York, and his fellow commanders recapitulate their victory at Saint Albans.[1] King Henry abandoned his men and escaped. Of the royalist leaders, Lord Clifford and Lord Stafford are dead; Edward reports that he killed or seriously wounded the Duke of Buckingham; Montague claims the blood of the Earl of Wiltshire; Richard of Gloucester produces Somerset's head. With encouragement from his sons and supporters, York seats himself on the throne as King Henry and several peers with the red roses of Lancaster in their hats arrive to convene parliament. Seeing York in the "chair of state," Henry reminds Northumberland and Clifford that they have vowed to revenge their fathers on York and his faction. All the loyal lords wish to fall upon the Yorkists at once; with some difficulty the King restrains them from turning the Parliament House into a shambles. Imperiously, King Henry demands that York vacate the throne, but the Duke refuses to yield, and both parties exchange taunts and threats.

At last King Henry and York quiet their excited followers while they argue their leaders' claims to the royal office. In an aside, Henry admits that his title is weak because of Henry IV's usurpation. Swayed by the argument, Exeter changes sides on the grounds that York's claim appears to be stronger. Northumberland and Clifford remain faithful, but Warwick summons his troops and threatens to establish York's title with bloody violence. Faced with this ultimatum, Henry offers to designate York as heir if he can continue to occupy the throne during his lifetime. Shocked at the disinheritance of Prince Edward and feeling betrayed by Henry's weak compliance and surrender, Northumberland, Clifford, and Westmoreland leave in disgust. After a sigh of regret for his son, King Henry entails the

[1] Shakespeare in this scene fuses the Battle of Saint Albans (May 22, 1455) with the Battle of Northampton (October, 1460).

crown to York and his heirs forever on condition that York cease the civil war, honor Henry as his king and sovereign, and not seek to promote himself by treason or hostility. York solemnly swears to observe these stipulations. Promptly York descends from the throne, and satisfied with the agreement, members of the Yorkist faction acknowledge Henry as king and disperse; Henry prepares to go to court "with grief and sorrow."

Before King Henry and Exeter can leave, they see Queen Margaret approaching with Edward, Prince of Wales. Noting her anger, Exeter and the King try to steal away, but she demands that they stay. Angrily, Queen Margaret wishes that she had never married or that she had never borne a son rather than see the Prince disinherited. To Prince Edward's question as to why he should not succeed, Henry lamely replies that Warwick and the Duke of York forced him to agree to these terms. Shaming Henry for his timidity and warning him that York and his confederates will grow more inexorable in their demands, the Queen forsakes the table and bed of her husband until Parliament repeals the disgraceful pact Henry has endorsed. With Prince Edward she departs to rally the Lancastrians and take the field against the Yorkists. Saddened, Henry tells Exeter that he will write Northumberland, Clifford, and Westmoreland in an effort to regain their support.

I,ii. Sandal Castle, near Wakefield, in Yorkshire

Richard (Duke of Gloucester), Edward Plantagenet, and Montague are plotting how they can persuade York to resume his campaign to depose Henry and occupy the throne. When York enters and learns the subject of their conversation, he insists that he must keep his oath permitting Henry VI to reign peacefully for life. Edward bluntly asserts that he would break a thousand oaths to reign one year. More subtly, Richard approves his father's sense of honor but offers to prove that the oath itself is invalid. First, Richard argues that an effective oath must be taken before "a true and lawful magistrate." Inasmuch as Henry is a usurper and not rightfully entitled to the throne, York's oath "is vain and frivolous." Reminding York of the desirability of the kingly office, Richard exhorts him to take the field immediately and seize the crown by violence. Richard's words fall on welcome ears, and the Duke instructs his sons and Montague to start enlisting aid. He himself will strive to keep the Lancastrians ignorant of his purposes.

A messenger [1] appears with word that Queen Margaret, with "the Northern earls and lords" and twenty thousand men, is close at hand. Rapidly countermanding his previous orders, York redirects his aides to meet this new emergency. Sir John Mortimer and Sir Hugh Mortimer arrive and offer to fight the Queen with a mere five thousand men. Contemptuous of the Queen's generalship, York and his sons confidently depart for battle.

I,iii. Battlefield between Sandal Castle and Wakefield

Rutland and his tutor try to escape, but Clifford and his soldiers overtake them. Ignoring the Tutor, whom the soldiers drag away, Clifford turns a deaf ear to Rutland's piteous appeals for mercy. Avenging his father's murder at York's hands, Clifford stabs the boy and vows not to wipe his blade until York's blood congeals on the same weapon with that of his son.

I,iv. Another Part of the Field

Alone, the Duke of York reflects on his reverses. His uncles, the two Mortimers, are dead; all of his followers are in retreat; his sons, despite their courageous efforts, have disappeared, and he does not know their fate. Faint and unable to go farther, York is surrounded by the Queen, Prince Edward, Northumberland, Clifford, and their soldiers. York defiantly struggles against his captors, who overpower him. Directing her aides to set York on a molehill, Queen Margaret sarcastically mocks her enemy, inquiring about his sons and showing him a napkin with which she wiped Rutland's blood from Clifford's rapier. At last, in a mock coronation ceremony, she places a paper crown on York's head and scoffs at his pretensions to the throne. Clifford is eager to slay his archenemy, but Margaret insists that York have a chance to speak. Reviling her unwomanly behavior and cruelty, York describes the Queen as "She-wolf of France" and a "tiger's heart wrapp'd in a woman's hide." Bewailing Rutland's assassination and cursing the Queen and Clifford for their inhumanity, York challenges his foes to kill him too. Northumberland weeps to see York's grief and passion, but Queen Margaret and Clifford stab him to death. The Queen orders that his severed head be set on the city gates, "So York may overlook the town of York."

[1] The First Folio calls the messenger "Gabriel," but many editors believe that the name designated Gabriel Spencer, the actor who played the role.

II,i. A Plain near Mortimer's Cross in Herefordshire

Edward and Richard are greatly concerned about their father, of whom they have received no news since the Battle of Wakefield. As they lead their troops, they see three suns in the morning sky. While they are discussing this portent, a messenger joins them and gives an eyewitness account of York's humiliation and violent death at the hands of the Queen and Clifford. Edward bitterly mourns for his father; Richard savagely eschews tears and vows revenge. Richard rallies his brother to action as Warwick and Montague approach with their army.

Warwick, having heard of the setback at Wakefield, had left London to intercept the Queen's forces at Saint Albans, where he and the Duke of Norfolk suffered defeat. Thereupon they set out to join the remainder of York's army under Edward and Richard. Norfolk is about six miles away, and George, Duke of Clarence, has arrived from France with reinforcements. Richard and Warwick take the initiative in planning a counterattack against the Queen; Warwick promises to place Edward on the throne; and a messenger reports the impending arrival of the Queen with a powerful force.

II,ii. In Front of York

Queen Margaret strives to cheer her companions by pointing to the Duke of York's head that is impaled on the city's gate, but Henry deplores such violence and asserts that he has kept his vow. Clifford argues that the King is far too lenient in rejecting retaliation on his enemies and is neglectful of the rights of Edward, Prince of Wales. Henry replies that he will bequeath his son his virtuous deeds and grieves over York's severed head. At the Queen's request, Henry dubs Edward knight and tells him to draw his sword in the cause of right.

A messenger brings word of Warwick's approach. Clifford and the Queen entreat Henry to leave the field because they fare better in his absence, but he resolutely remains at their side. Edward Plantagenet, his brothers Richard and Clarence, Warwick, Norfolk, Montague, and their forces appear. Edward orders "perjur'd Henry" to yield. At once, members of both parties begin to insult and threaten one another. King Henry attempts to speak, but his supporters force him to remain silent. Finally Edward Plantagenet imputes all responsibility for the rebellion to Queen Margaret, whose pride has overcome the Yorkists' willingness to prolong the rule of "the gentle King." Tired of wrangling, the Yorkists prepare for battle.

II,iii. A Battlefield between Towton and Saxton, in Yorkshire

Warwick, exhausted from combat, lies down to rest as Edward Plantagenet and Clarence come up. Both brothers are retreating and despair of success. Richard arrives with the news that Clifford has slain Montague, Warwick's brother. Aroused, Warwick vows on his knee to God that he will gain revenge or die. Encouraged by the Earl's resoluteness, Edward and Richard own their indebtedness to Warwick and rally to the cause. The three men take a fond farewell of one another and return to the fight.

II,iv. Another Part of the Field

Richard and Clifford, consumed with hatred for each other, engage in combat. Warwick approaches; Clifford flees; Richard orders Warwick to seek another foe because he is determined to hunt Clifford to death.

II,v. Another Part of the Field

Alone on the battlefield, King Henry sits on a molehill to soliloquize. Clifford and the Queen have expelled him from the battle. Committing himself to God's will, Henry wishes that the Almighty would grant him death. How much happier, the King believes, a rustic shepherd's life would be than that of a king surrounded by care, mistrust, and treason. While the King reflects, a soldier drags in the body of his father. Impressed into the King's army, the son "unawares" killed his father, whom Warwick has impressed into the Yorkist forces. While the King grieves at the spectacle, a father who has similarly slain his son bears the boy's body in front of the ruler. Both men depart with the bodies, leaving the King woeful at the tragic consequences of civil war.

Retreating before the renewed onslaughts of Warwick and the Plantagenets, the Queen, Prince Edward, and Exeter find Henry and urge him to flee the field with them.

II,vi. Another Part of the Field

Seriously wounded, Clifford laments the loss of the Lancastrian cause and bewails Henry's laxness, which has permitted the Yorkist faction to make such headway. He dies as the Yorkist commanders ride up and discover his body. Richard, Edward, and Warwick mock the dead Clifford and adjure him to speak. Finally tiring of their revengeful sport, Warwick advises that they take Clifford's head and substitute it for the Duke of York's on the gates of York. After seeing Edward crowned king, he will go to France to secure an alliance through the marriage of Edward and Lady Bona. Delegating full powers to Warwick, Edward creates George Duke of Clarence and Richard Duke of Gloucester.

III,i. A Forest in the North of England

Two Keepers [1] are posting themselves to kill deer in the forest. Seeing a man approaching, they quietly watch and listen. Disguised and carrying a prayer book, the deposed King Henry has returned from Scotland to walk on the soil that the Yorkists have taken from him. The First Keeper recognizes "the quondam King," but he delays seizing the fugitive in order to learn more. Henry has heard of Warwick's mission to arrange a diplomatic marriage, and he fears that this will undermine the efforts of Queen Margaret and Prince Edward, who have "gone to France for aid." Breaking into Henry's reveries, the two Keepers apprehend him as an enemy to King Edward, to whom they have sworn allegiance. Henry asks if they have not violated their onetime oaths to him as King, but they reply that they are true subjects of the King, whoever he happens to be at the time. Meekly submitting to the Keepers' simple philosophy of government, Henry consents to accompany them to the officers.

III,ii. London. The Palace

Lady Elizabeth Grey is petitioning King Edward to restore the lands of her husband, who died in the Battle of Saint Albans. Edward concurs with Richard that Lady Grey's suit is a reasonable one, but he pretends to put her off. She presses him for a reply while Richard and Clarence exchange comments attributing lustful motives to their brother's action. Ordering Richard and Clarence to step aside, Edward offers to restore the property to her and her three children if she will become his mistress. Indignantly, she refuses these advances, and the King denies her petition. However, her charms overwhelm the monarch, and he confesses to himself that he must possess her. To this end he proposes to marry her. With dignity she replies, "I know I am too mean to be your queen,/And yet too good to be your con-

[1] Some early editions call the keepers "Sinklo" and "Humphrey," but most editors regard these as names for the actors playing the parts.

cubine." Overriding Lady Grey's objections, Edward informs Richard and Clarence that she has agreed to wed him in order to regain her deceased husband's lands, although they scoff at the idea of their lascivious brother's marrying. A messenger comes in to announce the capture of Henry VI. Edward orders Henry's confinement in the Tower, dismisses Lady Grey, and takes Clarence to interview the man who arrested the deposed king.

Left to himself, Richard Duke of Gloucester soliloquizes on his secret ambition to ascend the throne of England. He must remove Edward, his brother Clarence, Henry VI and his son (Prince Edward), and all "the unlook'd for issue of their bodies." Supremely confident of his patience, persistence, and ability to dissemble, Richard vows to achieve his goal. Fully aware of his deformed body and repulsive appearance, he knows that he can expect little success as a lover. To compensate for his deficiencies, he will account the world but hell until he wears the crown. To gain it, he will deliberately murder while he smiles, wet his cheeks with artificial tears, "add colours to the chameleon," and "set the murderous Machiavel to school."

III,iii. France. The King's Palace

Lamenting her decline from greatness, Margaret implores Lewis XI to assist the cause of herself, King Henry, and the Crown Prince. Lewis begs her to be calm and patient while he determines the best means of helping her. At this point Warwick enters and proposes the match between King Edward and Lady Bona, sister-in-law of Lewis. Vigorously, Queen Margaret and the Earl of Oxford argue against Warwick's offer, but Lewis commands Margaret, Oxford, and Prince Edward to stand aside while he confers with Warwick. On his knightly honor, Warwick assures Lewis of Edward's just claim to the throne, of his popularity with the people, and of his true and virtuous love for Bona. After getting Bona's consent, Lewis confirms the match and calls Margaret to witness the formal agreement.

In frustration, Margaret denounces Warwick and accuses Lewis of perfidy, but Lewis insists that he remains Henry's friend and will extend Margaret his hospitality. To Warwick's insulting advice that she trouble Lewis no farther, Margaret declares that she will make the French King aware of Warwick's "sly conveyance" and Edward's "false love." A horn signals the arrival of a messenger with letters from England for Warwick, Lewis, and Margaret. The various papers inform their recipients of King Edward's marriage to Lady Grey. Lewis expresses outrage at this insult to France and to himself. Margaret says in effect, "I told you so!" Warwick protests that King Edward has dishonored him in contracting marriage with Lady Grey after sending him to arrange the match with Lady Bona. Recalling numerous offenses committed by the Yorkist monarch, Warwick angrily renounces Edward and declares that he will loyally return to the service of Henry VI and Margaret. Margaret welcomes him back to the Lancastrian ranks, and Warwick begs Lewis to supply him with troops for an invasion of England. United in purpose, Lewis, Margaret, Warwick, and Bona instruct the messenger to convey to Edward their threats of impending war. As soon as the messenger departs, Lewis asks Warwick for a pledge of his firm loyalty. To reassure the French ruler, Warwick and Margaret contract a marriage between Edward (Prince of Wales and son of Henry VI) and Warwick's daughter. Lewis issues orders to assemble the invasion force. Warwick vows to "seek revenge on Edward's mockery."

IV,i. London. The Palace

While Richard, Clarence, and Somerset are discussing the recent royal marriage, King Edward, his Queen, and their attending lords enter. Clarence is outspoken in criticizing Edward's wedding. Richard more discreetly declares that he has no wish to sever "Whom God hath join'd together." Under Edward's questioning, Clarence, Richard, and Montague point out that the King has lost the friendship of France and made an enemy of Warwick. Hastings makes light of French hostility, observing, " 'Tis better using France than trusting France." Quickly the three brothers grow angry in their discussion of Edward's policies. The Queen deplores the dissension she is causing. Edward promises to protect her and to compel his brothers' obedience to him and love for her.

At this point the messenger from France arrives and reports the reactions of the people who commissioned him. In blunt straightforwardness, Edward concedes that Lewis and Lady Bona have just cause for their indignation. His response to Warwick's defiance and alliance with Margaret is calmly to accept the threat of war. On learning of Prince Edward's engagement to Warwick's daughter, Clarence declares that he will wed her sister, and he invites those who love him and Warwick to follow. Somerset leaves with him.

Richard in an aside explains that he will remain at court "not for the love of Edward but the crown." King Edward dispatches Pembroke and Stafford to raise an army and then secures assurances of loyalty to himself from Hastings, Montague, and Richard.

IV,ii. A Plain in Warwickshire

Warwick and Oxford with a force of French troops find satisfaction in the flocking of common people to their cause. On the arrival of Clarence and Somerset, Warwick welcomes their support, agrees to marry his daughter to Clarence, and rapidly outlines his strategy of capturing Edward and restoring Henry VI to the throne.

IV,iii. Edward's Camp, near Warwick

Three watchmen are talking about King Edward's determination to stay in the field with Lord Hastings whereas he orders his chief followers to lodge in towns nearby. While they converse, Warwick, Clarence, and their companions disperse the guard and capture Edward. Hastings and Richard escape. Addressing Edward as Duke rather than King, Warwick tersely states that Edward has proved himself incompetent to govern any kingdom. Seeing that Clarence has allied himself with Warwick, Edward accepts the fact of his capture but says that he will "always bear himself as King" in spite of Fortune's malice. Removing the crown from Edward's head, Warwick declares that he will return it to the true king, Henry VI. Warwick then directs Somerset to conduct Edward to the custody of the Archbishop of York. Oxford and Warwick set out for London to restore Henry to the throne.

IV,iv. London. The Palace

Queen Elizabeth (the former Lady Grey) tells her brother (Lord Rivers) of Warwick's capture of King Edward. Determined to safeguard Edward's heir, the pregnant Queen urges Rivers to conduct her to sanctuary.

IV,v. A Park near Middleham Castle in Yorkshire

Richard, Hastings, and Sir William Stanley plan to rescue King Edward, whom the Archbishop permits to hunt under the escort of a weak guard. When Edward and a huntsman appear, the rescuers quickly inform Edward of their plan to spirit him to Flanders. The huntsman, afraid of being hanged if Edward escapes, consents to accompany them.

IV,vi. London. The Tower

Liberated by Warwick and his followers, King Henry offers to pay the Lieutenant of the Tower his "due fees." The Lieutenant declines any recompense, and craves the King's pardon. Henry expresses his gratitude to the officer for kind and courteous treatment and thanks God and Warwick for his release. Afraid that his return to the throne may incite further wars and eager to avoid bloodshed, he determines to live quietly and humbly and delegates the administration of the kingdom to Warwick. Warwick objects that Clarence would prove a more appropriate Protector, but Clarence insists that Warwick assume the office. Taking Warwick's and Clarence's hands and joining them, King Henry appoints them joint Protectors. Both men agree to rule on Henry's behalf and to pronounce Edward a traitor and confiscate all his lands and goods. Clarence approves Henry's requests for Queen Margaret's and Prince Edward's speedy return from France.

King Henry then inquires the name of a youth in the company of Somerset. On learning that the lad is Henry, Earl of Richmond, Henry VI praises his appearance and manner and prophesies that he is "Likely in time to bless a regal throne." [1] A messenger interrupts with the news of Edward's escape.

Warwick criticizes the Archbishop's carelessness in guarding his prisoner but hastens with King Henry to make preparations for any emergency. Somerset, anticipating a resumption of civil war and pinning his hopes for the future on Henry, Earl of Richmond, arranges with Oxford to send Richmond to Brittany to protect him "Till storms be past of civil enmity."

IV,vii. In Front of York

Edward, returning from the Continent with Burgundian reinforcements, greets Richard and Hastings. They find the gates of York barred to them, but Edward resolves to enter the city. Summoned to the walls, the Mayor and his colleagues at first maintain their loyalty to Henry VI and refuse to admit Edward. Edward argues, however, that he comes as Duke of York merely to claim his own dukedom. Hastings assures the Mayor that they are "King Henry's friends." Deceived by these protestations, the Mayor yields the keys of the city to Edward.

[1] Richmond defeated Richard III at Bosworth Field in 1485 to become Henry VII, or Henry Tudor.

Sir John Montgomery marches up with a column of soldiers and offers his services to King Edward. When Edward, trapped by his statement to the Mayor, replies that he presently claims the dukedom of York only, Sir John threatens to withdraw his forces unless Edward proclaims himself king. Egged on by Richard and Hastings, Edward consents to the proclamation. Hastings commands a soldier to make the formal announcement. Emboldened by this support, Edward determines to march against Henry VI, Clarence, and Warwick on the following day.

IV,viii. London. The Palace [1]

Warwick, Montague, Oxford, Clarence, King Henry, and their supporters take counsel on how best to oppose the Yorkist advance toward London. Warwick sends his commanders into their respective districts to levy troops. He will muster his own men in Warwickshire. Meanwhile, King Henry will remain in London until their return. Together in the palace, King Henry and Exeter review their chances. Exeter fears that Edward will seduce many of the King's adherents, but Henry believes that his own mildness, generosity, and kindness will hold them firm. Outside, shouts announce the arrival of Edward and Richard with their soldiers. Capturing Henry, Edward details a guard to take him incommunicado to the Tower. Edward and Richard then start for Coventry to meet Warwick.

V,i. Coventry

In Coventry, the Earl of Warwick is receiving reports on the deployment of his supporting commanders. Hearing a drumbeat, Warwick supposes that Clarence has arrived with reinforcements, but the approaching soldiers turn out to belong to Edward and Richard. Edward demands admittance to the city. Although he is vexed at being surprised, Warwick defies the taunts and threats of the two brothers. Even when Richard tells him that they have captured King Henry and left him in the Tower, Warwick refuses to yield. While the parley continues, Oxford, Montague, and Somerset lead their troops into Coventry to support Warwick.

Last to arrive is Clarence, at the head of a large detachment of men. Warwick greets him enthusiastically, but Clarence plucks the red rose of Lancaster from his hat, declares that he will not fight against his own brother, and deserts the Lancastrian cause. Denounc-

[1] Editors disagree on the exact locality of this scene.

ing Clarence as a "passing traitor, perjur'd and unjust," Warwick declines to defend Coventry but challenges Edward to meet him in battle at Barnet.

V,ii. A Battlefield near Barnet

King Edward deposits the wounded Warwick on the ground and leaves him to search for Montague. Warwick, his strength ebbing, soliloquizes on his former power over Kings and on the emptiness of worldly pomp and might when death comes. Somerset and Oxford discover the dying Warwick. Somerset wishes that Warwick could escape and help to rally the fleeing Lancastrians, but the Earl says that if he could flee he would not and asks for Montague. Somerset tells him that Montague is dead. Warwick dies. Somerset and Oxford carry off the body and go to join the army of Queen Margaret.

V,iii. Another Part of the Field

Having won the Battle of Barnet, Edward, Richard, and Clarence confidently move to meet the Queen's forces at Tewksbury.

V,iv. Plains near Tewksbury

Finding her advisers discouraged by their defeat at Barnet and by the loss of Warwick, Montague, and other supporters, Queen Margaret resolutely inspires them to continue the campaign. Praising his mother's spirit, Prince Edward invites any "fearful man" to depart before he infects others with his cowardice. Somerset and Oxford renew their pledges of loyalty as a messenger announces the approach of Edward and his brothers. Edward and Margaret exhort their followers and give signal for the fight to commence.

V,v. Another Part of the Field

Victorious, King Edward orders Oxford to imprisonment and Somerset to execution. Queen Margaret is held in custody while the Yorkists search for Prince Edward. Soldiers bring the young Prince before King Edward, who rebukes him for inciting rebellion. Haughtily, Prince Edward throws his captor's words back in his teeth and remains defiant. Richard interposes several churlish taunts and starts quarreling with Margaret and the Prince. Exasperated by Prince Edward's resoluteness, Edward, Richard, and Clarence stab the boy to death before his mother's eyes. Overcome with emotion, Margaret swoons. King Edward directs his followers to revive her, and Richard sets off hurriedly for London.

Regaining consciousness, Margaret reviles and curses the "Butchers and villains" who have slain her son and pleads with them to kill her on the spot. Clarence refuses to do her "so much ease," and Edward orders her away under guard. Learning from Clarence that Richard has gone to London, Edward suspects some rash act in the offing and sets out after him. He hopes to find that his own Queen has borne him an heir.

V,vi. London. The Tower

Richard of Gloucester is walking on the walls with King Henry and the Lieutenant of the Tower. Richard commands the Lieutenant to leave, and Henry at once anticipates villainy at Richard's hands. Toying with his victim, Richard tells King Henry that he has killed Prince Edward. Goaded to desperation, Henry prophesies that thousands will rue the hour of Richard's birth. He recalls the evil omens under which Richard was born and calls him "an indigested and deformed lump." Infuriated by this reference to his hunchback, Richard stabs Henry, who dies with a prayer on his lips. Richard gloats over his deed and stabs the dead king again. Glorying in his physical and moral deformities, Richard says that he has "neither pity, love, nor fear." He plans to poison King Edward's mind against Clarence and then kill him to remove his eldest brother's dread. After Clarence is gone, many others will die. He carries the corpse of Henry VI into another room.

V,vii. London. The Palace

Fresh from his recent victories and enjoying a sense of security, King Edward lists his former enemies by name. He instructs the Queen to let him embrace his young son and heir. In an aside, Richard vows to blast Edward's harvest. King Edward orders Clarence and Richard to kiss their princely nephew. Clarence at once complies. Richard also kisses the Prince but privately remembers that Judas Iscariot "kiss'd his master/And cried 'All hail! ' when as he meant all harm." To Clarence's inquiry, Edward directs that Margaret be deported to France and orders a series of "stately triumphs, mirthful comic shows" in celebration of what he hopes will prove the beginning of his lasting joy.

RICHARD III [1592–1593]

CHARACTERS

KING EDWARD THE FOURTH.

EDWARD, Prince of Wales, afterwards KING EDWARD V, and RICHARD, Duke of York, sons to the *King*.

GEORGE, Duke of Clarence, and RICHARD, Duke of Gloucester, afterwards KING RICHARD III, brothers to the *King*.

A Young Son of Clarence [*Edward, Earl of Warwick*].

HENRY, Earl of Richmond, afterwards KING HENRY VII.

CARDINAL BOURCHIER, Archbishop of Canterbury.

THOMAS ROTHERHAM, Archbishop of York.

JOHN MORTON, Bishop of Ely.

DUKE OF BUCKINGHAM.

DUKE OF NORFOLK.

EARL OF SURREY, his son.

EARL RIVERS, brother to *Queen Elizabeth*.

MARQUIS OF DORSET and LORD GREY, her sons.

EARL OF OXFORD.

LORD HASTINGS.

LORD STANLEY [also called EARL OF DERBY].

LORD LOVEL.

SIR THOMAS VAUGHAN.

SIR RICHARD RATCLIFF.

SIR WILLIAM CATESBY.

SIR JAMES TYRREL.

SIR JAMES BLUNT.

SIR WALTER HERBERT.

SIR ROBERT BRAKENBURY, Lieutenant of the Tower.

SIR WILLIAM BRANDON.

CHRISTOPHER URSWICK, a priest.

Lord Mayor of London.

Sheriff of Wiltshire.

TRESSEL and BERKELEY, gentlemen attending on *Lady Anne*.

ELIZABETH, Queen to *King Edward IV*.

MARGARET, widow of *King Henry VI.*

DUCHESS OF YORK, Mother to *King Edward IV.*

LADY ANNE, widow of *Edward Prince of Wales,* son to *King Henry VI;* afterwards married to *Richard, Duke of Gloucester.*

A Young Daughter of *Clarence* [Lady *Margaret Plantagenet,* Countess of Salisbury].

Ghosts of Richard's Victims.

Lords, Gentlemen, Attendants; [*Hastings*] Pursuivant, Scrivener, Page, Priest, Bishops, Aldermen, Citizens, Soldiers, Murderers, Messengers, etc.

Keeper in the Tower.

Scene: *England*

I,i. London. A Street

"Now is the winter of our discontent/Made glorious summer by this sun of York," Richard, Duke of Gloucester, exclaims as he contemplates the cessation of civil war and the pleasures of court society. Since Richard cannot be a lover because of his deformity, he resolves to be a villain. He has set his brothers against each other and has induced the King to believe that George, Duke of Clarence, will fulfill a prophecy that "G/Of Edward's heirs the murderer shall be."

Richard's scheme has proved quickly effective, for Brakenbury and an armed guard approach, conveying Clarence to the Tower. Clarence attributes his arrest to King Edward's fear of the prophecy concerning "G's" animosity. Affecting amazement, Richard insists that Queen Elizabeth has prejudiced the King against his brother. Richard and Clarence discuss the growing power of the Queen and her relatives and the influence Jane Shore, Edward's mistress, holds over her royal lover. Brakenbury protests that he is under orders to keep Clarence incommunicado. Reluctantly, Richard and Clarence part, Richard assuring George that he will free him quickly. As Brakenbury conducts his prisoner away, Richard mocks his brother, who will soon be killed, "If heaven will take the present at our hands."

Lord Hastings, recently freed from the Tower through Jane Shore's intercession with the King, joins Richard. Hastings learns of Clarence's imprisonment and informs Richard of King Edward's serious illness. Hastings departs, and Richard summarizes his plan to seize the throne. Hoping that Edward will not survive his sickness, he must first get rid of Clarence. When his two older brothers are dead, Richard, for political reasons, will marry Lady Annc ("Warwick's youngest daughter" and widow of Prince Edward of Lancaster).

I,ii. London. Another Street

Lady Anne is following the coffin of Henry VI. In mourning, she curses Richard for assassinating her father-in-law and her husband. The bearers lift the coffin, which they have rested on the ground during Anne's speech. Richard then appears and menacingly commands the bearers to put down their burden. Anne curses Richard for his misdeeds, calling him a villain and "lump of foul deformity." In a medley of falsehood, flattery, and arrogant confession, Richard tells Anne that love for her motivated him to commit his manifold crimes. In mounting fury, Anne execrates her tormentor and finally spits at him. Recounting the horrors and cruelties of the recent wars, all of which have left him unmoved by pity or remorse, Richard insists that Anne's scorn and contempt have reduced him to tears. Handing her his sword and baring his breast, he invites her to kill him in revenge for his murder of her relatives. Anne feints at him with the sword, then drops it, and says that although she wishes him dead she cannot be his executioner. Confident of his persuasiveness, Richard tells her that if she commands him to kill himself he will do so, saying,

> This hand, which for thy love did kill thy love,
> Shall for thy love kill a far truer love.

Richard's importunity dissipates Anne's hatred and revulsion until she wonders if he possibly can be sincere. Hesitatingly she permits him to place a ring on her finger. Avowing his love for her, Richard requests Anne to wait for him at Crosby House while he solemnly buries Henry VI at Chertsey monastery and wets the grave with his "repentant tears." Glad to see Richard "become so penitent," Anne calls Tressel and Berkeley, her gentlemen escorts, grants Richard's request, and leaves.

As soon as Anne has gone, Richard directs the bearers to convey Henry's corpse to Whitefriars. Alone, he derides Anne for her gullibility, gloats over having wooed her successfully in the face of overwhelming odds, and says that he will not "keep her long." In a moment of honest self-analysis, he marvels that Anne can have so quickly forgotten Prince Edward, who was superior to the deformed and malevolent Richard in every way. Ironically, Richard reflects that he must be a handsomer man than he knows himself to be. When he has time, he will hire a score or two of tailors to adorn his body and then he will strut in front of a mirror.

I,iii. London. The Palace

Lord Rivers and Lord Grey assure Queen Elizabeth that the King will regain his accustomed health. The Queen is apprehensive of the future, both for herself and for her young son, who has been placed under Richard's care. Furthermore, if King Edward dies, Richard will probably become Protector. Buckingham and Derby enter. After Derby apologizes briefly for his wife's [1] apparent discourtesy to the Queen, the two peers report that King Edward wishes to reconcile the Queen's two brothers (Lord Rivers and Lord Grey) [2] with Richard and Hastings (the Lord Chamberlain).

At this instant, Richard and Hastings enter. Richard is angrily protesting that the Queen has misrepresented him as an enemy of her and her kinsfolk. The Queen replies that Richard's hatred for her, her children, and her brothers has been readily apparent to the King. Richard continues to charge the Queen with responsibility for his own disgrace, for Clarence's confinement in the Tower, and for Hastings' late imprisonment. Infuriated by Lord Rivers' defense of the Queen and by her threat to acquaint Edward with his behavior, Richard grows more insulting in his tirade. Old Queen Margaret, who has entered quietly at the rear and has been denouncing Richard in a series of asides, can restrain herself no longer and berates him to his face. Sick of her banishment and with nothing to live for, Margaret invokes a curse on all for their past crimes. Stung by these indictments, Queen Elizabeth and her adherents unite with Richard and Hastings in attempting to silence the vindictive old woman.

From Buckingham alone, Queen Margaret has witheld her curse, since he has not soiled himself with Lancastrian blood. Turning prophetess, she warns Buckingham against Richard of Gloucester and his hypocrisy, but when he refuses to take her seriously she predicts his tragic death and leaves. Margaret's curses have unnerved all of her listeners except Richard, who observes that he repents

[1] Lady Derby, former wife of Edmund Tudor, was the mother of Henry Earl of Richmond (later Henry VII). The text calls her Countess Richmond.

[2] Shakespeare here apparently regards Lord Grey as a brother to the Queen; he was actually her son.

his part in the wrongs she has suffered. He also implies that Clarence has deserved arrest and imprisonment. Catesby summons Queen Elizabeth to the King; all except Richard accompany her.

In a brief soliloquy, Richard identifies himself as the instrument of Clarence's confinement; he gloats over his deception of Derby, Hastings, and Buckingham and the fact that they will now abet him in taking revenge on Rivers, Dorset, and Grey. Richard takes fiendish satisfaction in his ability to quote Scripture to his advantage and to seem a saint when most he plays the devil. Two Murderers come for the warrant that will admit them to Clarence's cell in the Tower. He hands them the document and warns them to dispatch Clarence quickly, before the unfortunate prisoner can stir them to pity.

I,iv. London. The Tower

After "a miserable night," Clarence tells his Keeper of a dream in which Gloucester pushed him overboard from a ship at sea. He goes on to describe his emotions when he thought he was drowning. The Keeper expresses surprise that Clarence did not waken. Depressed with his recollection of ghosts and fiends that tormented him as if he were in hell, Clarence prays the Keeper to spare his guiltless wife and children. On the guard's assurance of kindness, Clarence falls asleep.

Brakenbury enters, philosophizing. The Two Murderers follow him. They produce the warrant instructing him to deliver Clarence into their hands. He obeys, indicating the sleeping prisoner and handing them the keys. Brakenbury then departs with the Keeper. In a grimly humorous conversation the Two Murderers confer on how they should proceed with their act. For a moment they are ready to abandon the deed, but memory of their promised reward spurs them on. One gives an analysis of how conscience makes a man a coward and deters him from crime. Clarence wakens and elicits their admission that they have come to murder him. Desperately he maintains his innocence and argues that they are imperiling their chance of spiritual salvation. Seeing that they are deaf to his pleas, Clarence tells them to go to Richard, who will reward them for sparing him, but they assure him that Richard hates him. Despite Clarence's repeated pleas for mercy, they stab him. The First Murderer carries the corpse away to throw it in the malmsey butt (wine cask). The Second Murderer immediately repents his part in the crime, but his partner scornfully tells him to go as a coward. The First Murderer prepares to hide the body, collect his hire, and escape.

II,i. London. The Palace

Sick and expecting death every day, King Edward commands his contentious peers to pledge their fondness for one another. He insists that the Queen join with the others as they vow to keep "This interchange of love . . . inviolable." Richard appears and protests that he desires the love of all men and does not know any man in England with whom his soul "is any jot at odds." Queen Elizabeth, rejoicing in the apparent reconciliation of factions, begs the King to restore Clarence to favor. At this point, Richard startles everyone with the announcement that Clarence died before the King's pardon reached the prison.

Derby enters to seek Edward's mercy for one of his servants who recently killed an attendant of the Duke of Norfolk. Lamenting Clarence's death and the fact that no one petitioned on his behalf, Edward reluctantly grants the suit. Suddenly fearful lest the agents of Clarence's death murder him and his family, the King conducts the Queen to their private apartment. Richard implies that the Queen and her kindred are responsible for Clarence's assassination.

II,ii. London. The Palace

The old Duchess of York (mother of Edward, Clarence, and Richard) enters with Clarence's son and daughter. The two children ask their grandmother why she weeps and beats her breast, and bewails Clarence, but she insists that she grieves for the sickness of the King. Finally she admits that their father has been murdered. Clarence's son says that Richard told him that King Edward and the Queen "Devis'd impeachments to imprison him." Deploring Richard's character, the Duchess acknowledges his dissembling.

At this moment the Queen, accompanied by her brother Rivers and her son Dorset, appears in a disheveled condition mourning the death of King Edward. A succession of laments follows: the Queen wailing for Edward, Clarence's children for their father, the old Duchess for both of her sons. Dorset attempts to console his mother, and Rivers advises that she arrange for the immediate coronation of the young heir, Prince Edward. The arrival of Richard, Buckingham, Derby, Hastings, and Ratcliff interrupts their conversation.

Richard expresses his sympathy to the Queen and kneels to receive the Duchess's maternal blessing. She prays that God may imbue him with meekness, "Love, charity, obedience, and true duty." To all of this Richard humbly mutters, "Amen!" Buckingham advocates sending an escort to Ludlow to bring the young Prince Edward to London for his coronation. He advises that the guard be a small one in order to avoid a renewal of civil demonstrations. When everyone approves this plan, the Queen and most of her attendants leave. Buckingham and Richard agree that they will contrive to separate the Prince from "the Queen's proud kindred."

II,iii. London. A Street

Three citizens discuss King Edward's death and the dangers facing his successor and the nation. Although the young Crown Prince has both paternal and maternal uncles who might guide him through his minority, one citizen believes that bitter contention will arise between the dangerous Richard and the haughty and proud relatives of the Queen. Unable to foresee or do anything about the future, the citizens "leave it all to God" and go about their business.

II,iv. London. The Palace

Queen Elizabeth, the young Duke of York (Richard, brother of Prince Edward), the Duchess of York (grandmother of the two princes), and the Archbishop of York are awaiting the arrival of Prince Edward (Edward V) from Wales. The young Duke of York precociously talks about conversations he has had with his uncle Richard (Duke of Gloucester). He starts to discuss a rumor concerning Richard's deformed infancy when a messenger enters with news that the Crown Prince is well but that Richard and Buckingham have committed Rivers, Grey, and Vaughan as prisoners to Pomfret Castle. The messenger does not know the reasons for their confinement, but the Queen anticipates her family's ruin and destruction. The old Duchess laments this renewal of civil violence and bloodshed. Queen Elizabeth resolves to take the Duke of York with her to sanctuary, and the Archbishop gives the Queen the Great Seal of England (the symbol of sovereignty) as he prepares to accompany her.

III,i. London. A Street

Having conducted Prince Edward to London, Buckingham and Richard welcome him to the city. Denying any fatigue from the journey, the Prince says that his melancholy arises from his uncles' imprisonment. Richard quickly tells him that his uncles were dangerous, deceitful, and false. The Prince states his belief in their loyalty as the Lord Mayor and his train approach to greet him.

When this delegation has retired, Prince Edward asks for his mother and brother and inquires why the tardy Hastings has not brought word of them.

Hastings comes up and states that Queen Elizabeth and the young Duke of York have taken sanctuary. Scoffing at this precaution on the Queen's part, Buckingham requests Cardinal Bourchier to persuade the Queen to send her son to London. If this fails, Hastings is to seize the Duke of York and bring him by force. The Cardinal agrees to do what he can but warns Buckingham that no one should "infringe the holy privilege/Of blessed sanctuary." Buckingham caustically argues that conducting the Duke of York to London will not violate the principle of sanctuary because he himself did not and could not, as a minor, claim it but was led to it by his mother. Yielding to this argument, the Cardinal leaves with Hastings to fetch the Duke.

Cheered by the thought of his brother's arrival, Prince Edward asks Richard where he will stay until his coronation. Pretending to give the Prince a choice, Richard advises that he take residence in the Tower of London for a day or two. The proposal does not please the Prince, who begins a series of questions concerning the history of the Tower. While he talks with Richard and Buckingham, Hastings returns with the Cardinal and the young Duke of York.

Following a cordial greeting with his brother, York shrewdly and sagaciously banters with Richard, his uncle. At last Richard tells him that he and the Prince will wait in the Tower while Richard and Buckingham entreat the Queen to meet her sons there. With foreboding, the two young princes reluctantly depart for the Tower with Hastings, the Cardinal, and other attendants.

Buckingham and Richard agree that the Duke of York has reflected his mother's nature and instruction in his precocious chatter. Dismissing the young princes from his mind, Buckingham asks Catesby if Hastings will support the plot to set Richard of Gloucester on the throne. Catesby answers that Hastings' loyalty to Edward IV and his heirs will prevent his joining the conspiracy, and adds that Stanley (i.e., Derby) will follow Hastings. Catesby accepts the mission of sounding out Hastings, promises to make an early report, and departs. Buckingham inquires what they can do if Hastings does not enter the conspiracy. "Chop off his head," Richard retorts, and promises when he becomes King to make Buckingham Earl of Hereford and endow him with all of King Edward's treasure and personal property.

III,ii. In Front of Lord Hastings' House

A messenger from Stanley is knocking on Hastings' door at four o'clock in the morning. When Hastings appears, the messenger relates that Stanley has wakened from an ominous dream. In addition to this, Stanley has learned that Richard and Buckingham plan to hold two different council meetings, at one of which they may betray Stanley and Hastings. For these reasons Stanley is inviting Hastings to flee with him as speedily as possible. Confident of his favor in high places and of Catesby's friendship, Hastings makes light of Stanley's fears and sends the messenger back with a counterproposal that they go together to the Tower to meet Richard.

Catesby arrives, greets Hastings, and bluntly states that Richard of Gloucester is determined to seize the crown. Hastings declares that he will die before he consents to Richard's usurpation. Catesby relays Richard's invitation to Hastings to enlist on his side and tells of the imminent execution of the Queen's kinsmen at Pomfret. Hastings gloats at this purging of his enemies but steadfastly refuses to support Richard. Meanwhile he will seize the opportunity of taking vengeance on many of his unsuspecting personal rivals.

In the midst of this conversation, Stanley arrives. He is full of apprehension and misgivings, but Hastings jokingly minimizes his suspicions. Hastings sends Catesby and Stanley ahead and pauses to reward a pursuivant. The herald leaves, and Hastings speaks briefly with a priest whose recent sermon has pleased him. Buckingham comes up, and Hastings departs with him for the Tower.

III,iii. Pomfret Castle

Sir Richard Ratcliff and guards are leading Rivers, Grey, and Vaughan to their execution. Recalling the assassination of Richard II in Pomfret and the curses of Queen Margaret upon them all, Rivers and Grey view their deaths as a fulfillment of destiny. They and Vaughan embrace and prepare to die.

III,iv. London. The Tower

In council, several lords and gentlemen are discussing the coronation of the new king. Buckingham insists that he is not privy to the Lord Protector's (i.e., Richard's) mind. Hastings similarly disclaims possessing specific information, but as Lord Chamberlain he will represent Richard. At this point Richard arrives with an apology for oversleeping. Buckingham says that Hastings was on the point of speaking for the absent Duke. Richard pleasantly refers to Hastings' loyalty and asks the Bishop of Ely to procure some strawberries from his garden. Taking Buckingham aside, Richard tells him of Catesby's report that Hastings will defend Prince Edward's accession. Richard and Buckingham immediately withdraw. Derby (i.e., Stanley) advocates a delay in the coronation ceremonies; Ely returns with the strawberries; Hastings, observing that Richard is incapable of concealing his true emotions from anyone, comments on the Protector's good humor and geniality.

Reappearing with Buckingham, Richard asks his Council what punishment is appropriate for those who have conspired against his life with witchcraft and "hellish charms." Hastings at once pronounces such offenders deserving of death. Richard exposes his withered arm, which he attributes to the witchcraft of Queen Elizabeth and Jane Shore. "If they have done this deed . . . ," Hastings starts to remark; but Richard seizes upon the conditional "If," calls Hastings a traitor and protector of "this damned strumpet" (Jane Shore), and orders Lovel and Ratcliff to lead him to immediate execution.

In custody, Hastings too late perceives his folly in ignoring Stanley's dream and other omens. He, too, sees himself as a victim of Queen Margaret's curse. Lovel and Ratcliff prod him along, and Hastings starts for the block while he prophesies the coming of England's "fearfull'st time."

III,v. London. The Walls of the Tower

Having donned rotten and soiled armor, Richard and Buckingham are waiting for the arrival of Catesby and the Lord Mayor. Buckingham assures Richard that he can assume any role or counterfeit any emotion that will serve his purpose. As soon as Catesby and the Mayor come up, Lovel and Ratcliff expose Hastings' severed head. Richard pretends to mourn the execution of Hastings, whom he says he never suspected of villainy. Buckingham explains to the Mayor that Hastings headed a plot in Council to murder Richard and Buckingham. Richard adds that only extreme danger to the peace of England justified Hastings' execution without a legal trial. Agreeing that Hastings deserved his fate, the Mayor believes that the punishment will warn other traitors. Besides, the Mayor anticipated nothing good for Hastings after he began consorting with Mistress Shore. Buckingham apologizes for arranging Hastings' death before securing the Mayor's approval, but the official professes himself pleased and promises to satisfy the citizens of London that justice has been done. No sooner has the Mayor departed than Richard sends Buckingham to circulate rumors of the bastardy of King Edward's children, to stress the late King's immoral and lascivious practices, and even to suggest that King Edward himself was illegitimate. If Buckingham succeeds, he is to bring the Mayor and citizens to Baynard's Castle where Richard will be waiting with several ecclesiastical officials. Directing Lovel and Catesby to fetch Doctor Shaw and Friar Penker, Richard goes to arrange for the solitary confinement of Clarence's children.

III,vi. London. A Street

A Scrivener is looking over an indictment of Lord Hastings that he has copied for proclamation at St. Paul's. Inasmuch as Hastings died six hours after Catesby brought him the document and several hours before its publication, the Scrivener realizes that treachery and "ill dealing" are rife.

III,vii. London. Baynard's Castle

Buckingham reports to Richard that the citizens of London have not responded to the rumors he has attempted to instigate. Even after Buckingham exhorted the people to cheer for "Richard, England's royal King," they remained silent. When some ten of Buckingham's own followers repeated the cheer, he thanked the crowd for their general applause. Inasmuch as the Lord Mayor and his party will come soon to the Castle, Buckingham rapidly coaches Richard on how he is to receive the delegation. Richard departs as the Mayor arrives.

Catesby publicly advises Buckingham that Richard is presently engrossed in religious meditation with two "reverend fathers" and does not wish to be disturbed. Buckingham sends Catesby back to tell Richard that he, the Mayor, aldermen, and citizens desire to confer with him on matters of great moment and public concern. In Catesby's absence, Buckingham contrasts Richard's piety and prayerful devotion with the late King Edward's worldly and lustful indulgences. Catesby returns to report that Richard hesitates to appear because he fears some harm to his person. At Buckingham's insistence, Catesby goes back once more to persuade Richard to face the crowd.

In the carefully prearranged scene, Richard comes into view between two Bishops. Affecting deep humility, Richard inquires what offense he has committed that has inspired the parley. Offering himself as spokesman, Buckingham says that Richard has offended his countrymen by declining to ascend the throne. Richard pretends to be angry at this suggestion and rebukes Buckingham for proposing it. After a long plea by Buckingham, the Lord Mayor adds his voice to those of Buckingham and Catesby. Once again Richard protests that he is "unfit for state and majesty" and declines. In assumed anger Buckingham swears that he will entreat no more, and Richard piously rebukes him for profanity. Buckingham leads the Mayor and citizens away, but Catesby pleads with Richard to recall them. Professing the greatest reluctance to accept regal responsibilities, Richard calls the delegation back, and, inviting the Almighty to witness his unwillingness, says that he will assume the throne. All unite in cheers for "King Richard," and Richard retires with the Bishops to resume his "holy work."

IV,i. London. In Front of the Tower

Queen Elizabeth, the Duchess of York, and the Marquis of Dorset meet Lady Anne (wife of Richard) and Lady Margaret Plantagenet (Clarence's daughter). All have come to visit the two young princes in the Tower. Brakenbury appears and says that "The King" has forbidden anyone to visit the prisoners. Instantly he changes the title to that of Lord Protector, but he obstinately refuses to violate his orders and departs.

Stanley arrives and dismays the ladies by summoning Anne to Westminster for Richard's coronation. Frantically, Queen Elizabeth advises Dorset to flee and join Richmond on the Continent, and Stanley endorses her counsel, promising to send letters to Richmond by Dorset's hand. Fearfully, Anne recalls how she yielded to Richard's impetuous wooing and married him. Since her marriage she has not enjoyed one hour's sound sleep because of his fitful dreams. She knows that Richard hates her because of her father, Warwick, and she suspects that he will shortly get rid of her. The Duchess of York invokes a blessing on Dorset as he goes to Richmond; she hopes that good angels will watch over Anne; she urges Queen Elizabeth to find sanctuary, and with a heavy heart she prepares herself for death. Queen Elizabeth looks back apprehensively on the Tower, the "Rude ragged nurse" of her two young sons.

IV,ii. London. The Palace

Richard ascends the throne in pomp but at once reminds Buckingham that young Edward and his brother still live. Bluntly, Richard asks Buckingham to kill the two princes. When Buckingham demurs and asks for time, Richard becomes annoyed. Deciding that Buckingham has suddenly grown prudent, Richard sends a page for Tyrrel and resolves that Buckingham will no longer be his confidant.

In rapid succession, Stanley reports that Dorset has fled abroad to join Richmond, and Richard directs Catesby to start a rumor that Anne is "very grievous sick" and to arrange a marriage between Clarence's daughter and "some mean poor gentleman." In an aside, Richard reveals his plans to marry his own niece (daughter of Edward IV and Queen Elizabeth) and to assassinate his two nephews. The scheme is risky, but he has gone too far to turn back. The page returns with Sir James Tyrrel, who readily agrees to commit the murders Richard demands.

When Tyrrel has gone, Buckingham enters and says that he has been thinking about Richard's recent request. Ignoring his former favorite, Richard warns Stanley, Richmond's stepfather, to take note of Dorset's flight. Buckingham tries to remind Richard of his promises of the earldom of Hereford and other rewards, but Richard pays him no attention and continues to talk about Richmond and the prophecies relating to him. Exasperated by Buckingham's repeated interruptions, Richard says that he is "not in the giving vein" and stalks off. Suddenly realizing that he has fallen from favor, Buckingham remembers the fate of Hastings and decides to flee for Brecknock at once.

IV,iii. London. The Palace

Tyrrel is soliloquizing on the "piteous massacre" he has carried out for Richard. Even Dighton and Forrest, two "flesh'd villains, bloody dogs" whom he paid to do the actual butchery, wept when they described smothering their innocent victims. Richard comes in and asks for a report, and Tyrrel replies that he saw the princes dead and that the chaplain of the Tower has buried them in some secret place. After Richard commends Tyrrel and promises him a reward, Tyrrel leaves. Briefly, Richard reflects on his disposal of Clarence's children, the deaths of the two princes and Anne, and his scheme of marrying his niece, Princess Elizabeth. Ratcliff arrives to report that Morton, Bishop of Ely, has fled to join Richmond and that

Buckingham is raising an army in Wales. Fearing Morton more than Buckingham, Richard goes to muster his own forces.

IV,iv. London. In Front of the Palace

Old Queen Margaret reveals that she has come to London to watch the decline of her enemies. She retires from view when the Duchess of York and Queen Elizabeth approach. Uniting in grief for the death of the princes, the two women sit to mourn their fate. Coming forward, Queen Margaret joins them and augments the list of Richard's crimes. Together the three widows recall the atrocities, violent deaths, and recurring sorrows of their lives. At last Queen Margaret leaves, and the Duchess suggests to Queen Elizabeth that they "in the breath of bitter words" smother Richard, who smothered the two princes.

A trumpet announces the royal procession. The Duchess and Queen Elizabeth heap curses on Richard, who commands his drums and trumpets to drown out their imprecations. Persistently, the Duchess recounts the burdens and vexations Richard has imposed on her throughout his life. Impatiently, Richard starts to march on, but the Duchess deters him while she invokes a fatal curse upon him and leaves.

Queen Elizabeth starts to add her curse, but Richard interrupts to say that he must have a word with her about her daughter Elizabeth. Supposing that Richard intends to slay the Princess, the Queen pleads desperately for her life and boldly denounces Richard for his crimes. Intoxicated with success, Richard audaciously insists that he loves the Princess Elizabeth and wishes to make her his queen. Arguing that the match would restore the Queen and Dorset to favor and insure the peace of England, Richard persists in his suit. At long last Queen Elizabeth says that she will go and shortly inform Richard of her decision. Confident that he has persuaded the Queen to approve the marriage, Richard contemptuously describes her as a "Relenting fool, and shallow, changing woman."

Learning from Ratcliff of the appearance of Richmond's fleet off the English coast, Richard in his excitement issues conflicting orders to Catesby and Ratcliff and with some embarrassment has to clarify them. Stanley arrives with confirmation of Richmond's invasion and asks for instructions. Beginning to distrust everyone, Richard hesitates to permit Stanley to levy troops but finally does so on condition that he leave his son, George Stanley, as a hostage. In swift succession, Richard learns of rebellion in Devonshire, Kent, and Yorkshire. He is so frustrated that he strikes a messenger who brings word of the dispersal of Buckingham's army by floods. Catesby reports the capture of Buckingham but tempers it with news that Richmond has landed with a large force at Milford. Richard starts for Salisbury, where he hopes to confront Buckingham.

IV,v. Lord Derby's House

Sir Christopher Urswick informs Derby of several important persons who have joined Richmond, and Derby sends word to Richmond of George Stanley's detention as a hostage and of Queen Elizabeth's hearty approval of the espousal of Richmond and Princess Elizabeth.[1]

V,i. Salisbury. An Open Place

Leading Buckingham to execution on All Souls' Day, the Sheriff adamantly refuses to permit him to speak with King Richard. Moodily, Buckingham remembers the numerous people whose deaths he arranged and thinks that their ghosts must be mocking him. He also recalls many false oaths he swore by All Souls' Day. Queen Margaret's prophecy (see I,iii above) has proved true, and he directs the officers to conduct him to "the block of shame."

V,ii. Camp near Tamworth

Having received Derby's encouraging letter, Richmond inspires his followers to hasten into action against "The wretched, bloody, and usurping boar," who lies within one day's march. Oxford, Blunt, and Herbert voice their enthusiastic support.

V,iii. Bosworth Field

Commanding soldiers to pitch his tent, Richard takes Norfolk, Surrey, and Ratcliff to reconnoiter the field for the impending battle. Richmond, heading a much smaller army than Richard's, pitches his tent nearby and issues orders to his commanders for the next day's engagement. After sending Blunt with a message to Lord Stanley, Richmond leads his companions into his tent for further consultation.

On the other side, Richard reviews his equipment and arrangements with Ratcliff, Norfolk, and Catesby. Giving detailed orders to each one, Richard retires inside his tent and falls asleep. Meanwhile Derby (Stanley) has come to Richmond with encouragement from

[1] Evidence that the Queen was not as stupid and shallow as Richard assumed. (See IV,iv above.)

Lady Derby (Countess of Richmond) to her son. Derby will render whatever help he can without imperiling the life of "tender George," who remains a hostage in Richard's possession. Richmond commands his attending Lords to conduct Derby safely back to his regiment. Praying for victory and commending his soul to God, Richmond sleeps.

Immediately the Ghosts of Richard's victims [1] visit his tent and pass on to Richmond's. To Richard, they recall the violence they have suffered and end their speeches with the words, "Despair and die!" To Richmond, they promise success and prosperity, many of them repeating the refrain, "Live and flourish!"

Rousing in a cold sweat, Richard analyzes the fear that the specters have instilled in him. At last he realizes that no creature loves him and that he can no longer love himself or pity himself. Ratcliff comes to waken him, and Richard confesses that his nightmare has badly frightened him. Ratcliff tries to reassure the King, but Richard takes Ratcliff to eavesdrop on his own followers to learn if any intend to desert him.

In contrast, Richmond tells his comrades that he has enjoyed "The sweetest sleep, and fairest-boding dreams/That ever ent'red in a drowsy head." Learning that it is already four o'clock in the morning, Richmond arms himself and delivers a short oration to his soldiers: in following him and suppressing Richard, they are fighting a holy war on God's side against God's enemy. Confident in the righteousness of their cause, they march toward the battlefield.

Although Richard dislikes the bad omen of a sunless day, he comforts himself that the same heaven that frowns on him "looks sadly" on Richmond too. He has also cheered himself with the knowledge that Richmond is without military training or experience. Norfolk arrives with word that the enemy has already taken the field. Swiftly, Richard calls for his horse, sends an order for Stanley to bring support, and issues other directions for the battle. Norfolk approves Richard's tactics; then he shows the King a paper he found on his tent. In doggerel, the writer implies that bribery has undermined Richard's cause. Viewing this as enemy propaganda, Richard calls to his aides to ignore their "babbling dreams" and consciences and to trust in their strong arms and swords. Addressing his army, Richard sneeringly refers to Richmond as a "paltry fellow" and

[1] The sequence of Ghosts is as follows: (1) Prince Edward, son of Henry VI; (2) Henry VI; (3) Clarence; (4) Rivers, Grey, and Vaughan; (5) Hastings; (6) the two Princes; (7) Lady Anne; (8) Buckingham.

"milksop" and to his forces as "A sort of vagabonds, rascals, and runaways,/A scum of Britons and base lackey peasants." With this denigration of the enemy, Richard orders his knights, yeomen, and archers into action.

At this moment, a messenger reports that Lord Stanley has refused to support Richard. Immediately, the King orders the execution of George Stanley, whom he still holds as hostage, but Norfolk advises postponing this act of vengeance because Richmond's army is already on the attack.

V,iv. Another Part of the Field

Catesby shouts for Norfolk to lend assistance. He reports that Richard has lost his charger but continues on foot to search for Richmond. Suddenly Richard appears shouting, "A horse! a horse! my kingdom for a horse!" Catesby offers to assist him from the field to a horse, but Richard, who has already slain five men disguised as Richmond, fiercely resolves to risk his life in a final desperate effort.

V,v. Another Part of the Field

In hand-to-hand combat, Richmond kills Richard. Derby acknowledges Richmond as rightful successor to the throne and assures him of the safety of young George Stanley. At Richmond's request, Derby names the prominent casualties. Directing suitable burial for these men, Richmond proclaims a general pardon to all surviving Yorkists who return, submit, and pledge their loyalty to him. Declaring an end to the Wars of the Roses, Richmond announces his forthcoming marriage with Elizabeth of York to seal the division between York and Lancaster and thus insure a lasting peace.

HENRY VIII [1612–1613]

CHARACTERS

KING HENRY THE EIGHTH.

CARDINAL WOLSEY.

CARDINAL CAMPEIUS.

CAPUCIUS, Ambassador from the Emperor Charles V.

CRANMER, Archbishop of Canterbury.

DUKE OF NORFOLK.

DUKE OF BUCKINGHAM.

DUKE OF SUFFOLK.

EARL OF SURREY.

LORD CHAMBERLAIN.

LORD CHANCELLOR.

GARDINER, Bishop of Winchester.

BISHOP OF LINCOLN.

LORD ABERGAVENNY.

LORD SANDYS.[1]

SIR HENRY GUILDFORD.

SIR THOMAS LOVELL.

SIR ANTHONY DENNY.

SIR NICHOLAS VAUX.

Secretaries to *Wolsey*.

CROMWELL, servant to *Wolsey*.

GRIFFITH, Gentleman-Usher to *Queen Katherine*.

Three Gentlemen.

DOCTOR BUTTS, Physician to the *King*.

Garter King-at-Arms.

Surveyor to the *Duke of Buckingham*.

BRANDON, and a Sergeant-at-Arms.

Doorkeeper of the Council Chamber.

Porter, and his Man.

Page to *Gardiner*.

A Crier.

QUEEN KATHERINE,[2] wife to *King Henry*, afterwards divorced.

ANNE BULLEN, her Maid of Honour, afterwards Queen.

[1] Some editors prefer to spell the name Sands. Although the Folio in II,i refers to him as Sir Walter, his correct name was William.

[2] Katherine in the First Folio; some editors change to Katharine.

An Old Lady, friend to *Anne Bullen.*

PATIENCE, woman to *Queen Katherine.*

Lords, Ladies, Bishops, Judges, Priests and Gentlemen; Lord Mayor of London and Aldermen; Scribes, Officers, Guards, Women attending upon the Queen, Attendants, and Others.

Spirits.

Scene: *London; Westminster; Kimbolton*

The Prologue

Warning the audience not to expect a "merry bawdy play" or the antics of a clown, the Prologue advises that he and his fellow actors will excite pity with "noble scenes." Those who can "see/The very persons of our noble story/As they were living" will "in a moment, see/How soon this mightiness meets misery."

I,i. London. A Room in the Palace

Buckingham and Norfolk greet each other for the first time since returning from France. Because Buckingham's ague prevented his viewing the pageantry of the Field of the Cloth of Gold,[1] Norfolk vividly describes the pomp and splendor of that meeting. On learning that Wolsey, "the right reverend Cardinal of York," planned and directed the spectacle, Buckingham curses him as a lump of fat that gets his ambitious finger in every man's pie. Norfolk replies that Wolsey, although of humble ancestry, possesses innate qualities that enable him to weave his spiderlike political web and gain the King's favor. Abergavenny can find no heavenly derived virtues in Wolsey, but rather a pride that must come from hell. Buckingham and Abergavenny know several important people whom Wolsey's exorbitant levies have bankrupted, and Norfolk fears that the results of the recent alliance will not justify its expense. Buckingham grows so caustic in his denunciation of the Cardinal that Norfolk warns him of the danger in flaunting this powerful and malicious man.

Wolsey, accompanied by two Secretaries and guards bearing his seal of office, makes a pretentious entry. Exchanging disdainful glares with Buckingham, Wolsey tells his Secretary that he is ready to interview Buckingham's Surveyor (i.e., Overseer) and strides out. Sensi-

[1] Name designating a place between Guines and Ardres where Henry VIII and Francis I of France staged a series of tournaments and lavish entertainments in June, 1520.

tive to Wolsey's animosity, Buckingham begins another tirade against the Cardinal and threatens to appeal to the King for justice. Norfolk urges Buckingham to control his anger and to let reason govern him. Buckingham admits the soundness of this advice, says that he will follow it, but adds that he knows the Cardinal to be "corrupt and treasonous." To support this charge, Buckingham declares that Wolsey not only has betrayed England in the recent agreement with France, but that he has also entered into secret negotiations with Emperor Charles V.

In the thick of this conversation, Brandon, a Sergeant-at-Arms, and guardsmen enter, arrest Buckingham for high treason, and start to convey him to the Tower. When Buckingham turns to bid farewell to his son-in-law, Brandon says that Abergavenny must accompany Buckingham to the Tower to await the King's pleasure. Brandon reveals that he holds warrants for the arrest of several of Buckingham's associates, and the Duke realizes that Wolsey has suborned his Surveyor into betraying him.

I,ii. London. The Council Chamber

Entering with the Cardinal and other followers, King Henry thanks Wolsey for exposing Buckingham's treason and sends for the Surveyor to testify. Meanwhile Queen Katherine, escorted by Norfolk and Suffolk, comes into the chamber. Humbly and courteously, she petitions the King to relieve the people who are suffering grievously from the taxes Wolsey has imposed. Wolsey admits only limited knowledge of what the Queen is talking about, but she persists in criticizing the severity of the burden that has changed the people's allegiance and prayers to curses. Wolsey defends himself vigorously, but King Henry is displeased and commands the Cardinal to reduce the assessments. Wolsey privately instructs his Secretary to implement the order but to make it appear that the Cardinal himself has influenced the King to lessen the tribute.

As the Surveyor enters, Queen Katherine expresses sorrow that Buckingham has incurred displeasure. King Henry praises Buckingham's eloquence and natural endowments but says that he has misdirected his talents and invites the Queen to listen to the Surveyor's testimony. Under the interrogation of the King and the Cardinal, the Surveyor describes Buckingham's ambitions to succeed to the throne and his dislike for Wolsey. The Queen cautions the discharged man to bear faithful witness, but the Surveyor proceeds to tell of Buckingham's threats against Wolsey, Lovell, and the

King's own life. Persuaded of Buckingham's treachery, King Henry orders the Duke brought to trial immediately.

I,iii. London. A Room in the Palace

Lord Sandys and the Lord Chamberlain are chatting about the artificial fashions and manners recently borrowed from France. Sir Thomas joins them and tells of the proclamation banning such imported affectations and daring deportment. After a number of bawdy quibbles, the three men turn their conversation to Wolsey's forthcoming banquet.

I,iv. A Hall in St. James's [York] Palace

Sir Henry Guildford welcomes Anne Bullen and other ladies and gentlemen to the banquet hall. Close on their heels arrive the Lord Chamberlain, Lord Sandys, and Sir Thomas Lovell. Amid much gaiety and jesting the guests seat themselves. Sandys kisses Anne Bullen.

To the accompaniment of hautboys, Cardinal Wolsey enters with his attendants. Drinking the health of all, the Cardinal chides the gentlemen for failing to amuse the ladies sufficiently. A drum and trumpet are heard, and small cannon fire salutes.[1] A servant investigates and returns with word that a number of strangers have left their barge and are approaching the palace in the manner of foreign ambassadors. Wolsey directs the Lord Chamberlain, who can speak French, to welcome the visitors.

In a moment, to the accompaniment of music, the Lord Chamberlain ushers in King Henry and his companions masqued as shepherds. They pass in front of Wolsey and salute him. The Lord Chamberlain explains that they have come to help celebrate the occasion by viewing the ladies and reveling with them. With the Cardinal's permission the masquers choose partners for dancing, the King selecting Anne Bullen, whose beauty he praises. In a whispered conversation the Lord Chamberlain identifies King Henry to Wolsey, who at once yields the chair of state to his monarch. The King amiably congratulates Wolsey on the success of his feast. Learning the name of his fair partner from the Lord Chamberlain, Henry again extols her beauty and calls for a toast. At Wolsey's suggestion the entire company stops dancing and seeks fresher air in the next chamber.

[1] Most scholars believe that the discharge of this salute in the Globe Theater started the fire in the thatched roof that destroyed the building on June 29, 1613.

II,i. Westminster. A Street

One Gentleman tells another how, at his trial, Buckingham pleaded innocent, but his peers, after hearing "divers witnesses," found him guilty of high treason. The two Gentlemen believe Cardinal Wolsey to be behind Buckingham's indictment. At this moment Buckingham passes on his way to execution under the escort of Lovell, Vaux, Sandys, and officers. A crowd of common people has assembled, and Buckingham addresses the populace, with whom he is extremely popular. With dignity, Buckingham declares his innocence in spite of the judgment passed upon him. Although he wishes that those testifying against him had been more Christian, he forgives them and bears no malice toward the law for his death sentence. He commends the mercies of King Henry and requests his own friends to pray for him. Lovell implores Buckingham's forgiveness and turns the prisoner over to Sir Nicholas Vaux, who commands that the barge be fitted in a style appropriate to Buckingham's rank and position. Buckingham remonstrates, saying that whereas he came to trial as Lord High Constable and Duke, he now leaves as "poor Edward Bohun." He recalls his father's execution by Richard III and his own restoration to honor and title by Henry VII, and he says that he is thankful for his noble trial. Warning his hearers to beware of false friends, and asking them to remember his sad fall, he departs with his guards.

Together again, the two Gentlemen deplore Buckingham's fate. They then discuss the revival of a rumor concerning the pending separation of King Henry and Katherine. In addition to the belief that Wolsey has inspired Henry's mistrust of Katherine, popular opinion holds that Cardinal Campeius has arrived in England to aid Wolsey in his intrigues. People also believe that Wolsey, having failed to obtain the archbishopric of Toledo from Emperor Charles V, is taking this method of getting revenge.[1] Apprehensive of conversing in a public place, the two Gentlemen seek more private quarters.

II,ii. London. A Room in the Palace

Having learned of Wolsey's forcible and highhanded seizure of certain fine horses, the Lord Chamberlain shares Norfolk's and Suffolk's distrust of the prelate. The three men believe that Wolsey has been encouraging Henry to divorce Katherine and to arrange a marriage with the French King's sister. The Lord Chamberlain trusts

[1] Charles V was Queen Katherine's nephew.

that Heaven will open the King's eyes to the machinations of the Cardinal; Norfolk suggests that they pray for deliverance from Wolsey's power; Suffolk proposes to ignore the Cardinal and to leave him to the Pope, who promoted him. The Lord Chamberlain excuses himself to attend to other business; Norfolk and Suffolk remain until Henry draws back the curtain behind which he is reading.

Becoming aware of the Dukes' presence, the King rebukes them for intruding on his privacy. Wolsey and Campeius enter. After the King dismisses Norfolk and Suffolk, Wolsey introduces Campeius as Rome's representative to serve with him in judging Henry's petition for a divorce. Wolsey admonishes the King to provide Katherine with competent counsel and summons Stephen Gardiner, Henry's new Secretary. Before stepping aside to confer with the King, Gardiner assures Wolsey of his lasting loyalty to him as his sponsor. Campeius takes this opportunity to advise Wolsey of popular suspicions that the Cardinal drove Doctor Pace, Gardiner's predecessor, to madness because of envy. Wolsey explains that Pace was virtuous, whereas Gardiner will obey him (Wolsey) as his true master. Henry directs Gardiner to summon Queen Katherine to Blackfriars.

II,iii. London. A Room in the Queen's Apartments

Anne Bullen describes Queen Katherine as an upright and honorable lady whom no one can reproach. Her attendant, an Old Lady, adds that people with the hardest hearts sympathize with the Queen. Filled with pity for Katherine, Anne says that she would not be a queen on any condition. In jesting and bawdy words, the Old Lady accuses her of hypocrisy. In the middle of their conversation the Lord Chamberlain enters to inform Anne that King Henry has created her Marchioness of Pembroke with an annual income of a thousand pounds. Observing Anne's beauty and honor, the Lord Chamberlain speculates that she may well bear an heir to the throne. He then retires to convey her thanks and obedience to the King. Lamenting her sixteen years of unrewarded service in court, the Old Lady intimates that Henry's gifts will demand more return from Anne than mere respect. Protesting that she finds no joy in Queen Katherine's distress, Anne cautions the Old Lady to conceal what she has heard.

II,iv. London. A Hall in Blackfriars

Numerous bishops, gentlemen, attendants, scribes, the two Cardinals, King Henry, Queen Katherine, and others enter the hall and take their respective positions for the review of Henry's petition for divorce. When the crier calls her name, Queen Katherine rises and kneels at the King's feet. Briefly the Queen reviews her foreign background, her long marriage during which she has borne several children, her fidelity, obedience, and faithfulness to Henry. Furthermore, the best legal experts of Europe have declared her marriage to Henry lawful.[1] She wants time to call additional counsel in her defense but is submissive to the King's pleasure.

Wolsey denies her request for a postponement on the grounds that adequate and qualified counsel [2] is present and available to her. Cardinal Campeius supports Wolsey's opinion and directs that the arguments in the trial proceed.

Proudly scorning tears, Queen Katherine turns on Wolsey, charges him with being her enemy, and demands that he disqualify himself from serving as her judge. Wolsey stoutly denies her accusations and asks King Henry to corroborate his complete innocence in the matter. Upbraiding Wolsey for his obsequiousness and false humility, Katherine again declines to accept him as a judge, says that she appeals to the Pope, curtsies to the King, and departs. On the suggestion of Campeius, King Henry calls Katherine back, but she steadfastly declares that she will not again appear in "any of their courts."

Watching Katherine depart, King Henry testifies to her many virtues and noble birth and conduct. Wolsey requests Henry to absolve him of complicity in the divorce, and the King declares that Wolsey has often tried to halt the proceedings. King Henry goes on to explain that the French Ambassador raised questions concerning the legitimacy of Mary because of the dubious validity of the marriage between Henry and Katherine. Inasmuch as no male heir to the throne survived, Henry has become apprehensive lest heaven is punishing him for his irregular relationship with the Queen. Greatly concerned by the absence of a male successor and determined to effect a remedy, Henry has consulted the Bishop of Lincoln. Lincoln admits that he has advised Henry to undertake the divorce action. With Lincoln's advice King Henry secured the sanction of the Archbishop of Canterbury to proceed with the trial. Emphatically, the King insists that he entertains no dislike for Katherine and that he will preserve the marriage if the Bishops declare it lawful.

[1] Katherine's first husband was Arthur, Henry's older brother, who died in 1502. In the face of strong ecclesiastical objection, the marriage between Henry and Katherine had been arranged under papal dispensation.

[2] The Bishops of Ely, Rochester, and Saint Asaph.

Campeius reserves judgment for a later date and says that meanwhile the Queen must be induced to recall her appeal to the Pope. Henry perceives that the Roman legate is trifling with him, calls the Archbishop of Canterbury to a private conference, and adjourns the court.

III,i. London. A Room in the Queen's Apartments

Sad and depressed, the Queen commands one of her women to sing to the accompaniment of a lute. A gentleman announces that Cardinals Wolsey and Campeius seek audience with her. She consents to see them. When Wolsey suggests that they retire into a private chamber, the Queen commands him to speak openly, for she has nothing to conceal from her attendants. He begins his statement in Latin, but changes to English when Katherine again objects and says that her sins may be absolved in English.

Wolsey and Campeius maintain that they come in no sense of condemnation or accusation but rather to learn her reaction to the divorce and to offer helpful service and counsel. Protesting that she is a friendless woman of "weak wit," Katherine again pleads for time and adds that the only advice she can trust will come from her Spanish countrymen. The Cardinals assure Katherine that her best course is to throw herself on the King's mercy and not risk the exposure and disgrace of a legal trial. Angrily, Katherine denounces the two churchmen and says that she cannot hope for justice from them or from the King. Once more the Cardinals insist that she misjudges them and that they come as "peacemakers, friends, and servants." Frustrated and on the defensive, Katherine apologizes for her unmannerly words and tells them to bestow their advice upon her.

III,ii. London. A Room in the Palace

Several peers are talking about the political and domestic problems of the court. Norfolk, strongly seconded by Surrey, believes that the time has come to present a united complaint against the Cardinal. Although the Lord Chamberlain is sympathetic to the proposal, he fears that no one can discredit Wolsey so long as the wily churchman has access to the King's ear. Norfolk replies that Henry has learned that Wolsey, although he has given the impression of favoring the royal divorce, is secretly exhorting the Pope to deny the petition. Suffolk explains that interception of a letter to Rome has revealed the Cardinal's duplicity. In addition, Wolsey has written about

Henry's infatuation for Anne Bullen. The Lord Chamberlain reports the King has already married Anne. Suffolk adds that orders have been issued for Anne's coronation, and he hopes that a blessing may result to England from the marriage.[1] Cardinal Campeius has returned to Rome without taking formal leave, presumably to further Wolsey's intrigues.

Meanwhile Cranmer has reported that almost all the famous colleges in Christendom approve the King's divorce. The peers believe that Henry will shortly announce Anne's marriage and coronation and will proclaim Katherine the dowager princess of Prince Arthur. They agree that Henry will appoint Cranmer Archbishop of Canterbury for his services. During their discussion, Wolsey and Cromwell enter. The Cardinal quizzes Cromwell about the King's reaction to certain documents, and Cromwell relays Henry's command for Wolsey to attend on him. Wolsey dismisses his servant. In an aside, he reveals his scheme for Henry to marry the Duchess of Alençon. He will not tolerate the King's marriage to Anne, who may be virtuous and well-deserving but is also a "spleeny Lutheran." Besides, the heretic Cranmer "Hath crawl'd into the favour of the King."

At this moment King Henry, scanning a document, enters with Lovell. By accident, King Henry has found an inventory of Wolsey's tremendous wealth, so great as to convince the King of the Cardinal's worldly ambition. Wolsey addresses the King, who cryptically comments on the difficulties the Cardinal must have in finding enough time for both his spiritual and earthly duties. Henry recalls the many favors and rewards he has heaped upon Wolsey. All these the Cardinal acknowledges; he voices his gratitude and insists that he has rendered loyal and diligent service to his King and to the state. Pretending to accept Wolsey's statements, Henry hands him some papers, tells him to read them, and stalks out.

Sensing the King's displeasure, Wolsey glances at one of the papers and sees that the itemizing of his fortune has undone him. The second paper is Wolsey's secret letter to the Pope (see III,ii). Quickly he realizes that he has passed the height of his power and influence and must henceforth decline. Norfolk, with several other Lords, appears and orders Wolsey to resign the Great Seal of England and to go into confinement at Asher House. Defiantly, Wolsey refuses to yield the seal to anyone but King Henry himself. Furiously, Surrey charges Wolsey with Buckingham's execution. The two men

[1] Elizabeth I was daughter of Henry VIII and Anne Bullen.

quarrel until Surrey, Norwolk and Suffolk repeat six of the nine articles in Wolsey's official indictment,[1] which has been presented to the King. The Lord Chamberlain pities the Cardinal; Surrey forgives him; Suffolk tells him that he has forfeited all of his "goods, lands, tenements,/Chattels, and whatsoever" because of his assertion of papal authority in England. With his fellow peers Norfolk goes to report Wolsey's refusal to surrender the Great Seal.

Alone, Wolsey soliloquizes on his splendid rise to power and his subsequent fall from greatness. His "high-blown pride" has broken under him and left him "Weary and old with service" to the mercy of forces that will hide him forever. Suddenly, Wolsey detests the vain pomp and glory of the world and feels his "heart new open'd." Cromwell enters in amazement and inquires about his master's welfare. Wolsey replies that he has found a new peace of spirit since the King has removed the burdens of his conscience. At Wolsey's request for news Cromwell reports: (1) Henry's displeasure with Wolsey; (2) Sir Thomas More's appointment as Lord Chancellor; (3) Cranmer's return and consecration as Archbishop of Canterbury; (4) the public appearance of Anne as Henry's queen and rumors of her forthcoming coronation. Recognizing the King's affection for Anne as the primary cause of his downfall, Wolsey describes himself as "a poor fall'n man" unworthy to be Cromwell's master and urges his servant to offer his duty and services to Henry. Reluctantly Cromwell prepares to obey. Apologizing for his unmanly tears, Wolsey takes a fond farewell of Cromwell and adjures him to eschew ambition, love himself last, and strive honestly and justly for the good of the country and the King. Summarizing his life, Wolsey says,

> Had I but serv'd my God with half the zeal
> I serv'd my king, he would not in mine age
> Have left me naked to mine enemies.

Placing his hopes in heaven, the Cardinal goes out with his servant.

IV,i. A Street in Westminster

Meeting again, the two Gentlemen post themselves to watch Anne's coronation procession. They talk about the conferring of titles and honors and other celebrations. They also discuss Queen Katherine's divorce in a trial at Dunstable, where a convocation of bishops

[1] A list of charges specifying instances of Wolsey's intriguing diplomacy, dishonesty, and abuse of his position.

finalized the decree. Trumpets and hautboys signal the approach of the procession consisting of the Queen and numerous peers, judges, bishops, and other attendants, in splendid and magnificent array. As the parade leaves, a third Gentleman comes up and describes the ceremony in Westminster Abbey. Most notable were the modesty and graciousness of Anne, the impressive ritual and music, and the acclaim of the people. The King has also promoted several persons, among them Cromwell, who has become Master of the Jewel House. The three Gentlemen leave together.

IV,ii. Kimbolton

Griffith repeats to Katherine, now Princess Dowager and sick unto death, that Wolsey has died penitently at Leicester. Although she wishes peace to his soul, Katherine cannot refrain from recalling the Cardinal's many weaknesses and defects of character. To balance this criticism, Griffith mentions Wolsey's successful rise from humble stock, his scholarship, his encouragement of learning, and his true repentance at the time of his fall from favor. Katherine tolerantly admits the truth of Griffith's eulogy, asks her maid Patience to minister to her comfort, and falls asleep. In a vision, six personages in white robes with garlands on their heads, golden vizards on their faces, bay or palm branches in their hands, dance before Katherine. She stirs in her sleep, makes signs of rejoicing, and holds up her hands to heaven. The personages vanish, but the music continues. Waking, Katherine asks Griffith and Patience if they have also seen the spirits, but when Griffith insists that they have not, she orders the music to cease. Patience and Griffith think that Katherine is dying when a messenger announces a gentleman to see her.

A visitor whom Katherine recognizes as Capucius brings greetings from her nephew, Emperor Charles V. Katherine gives Capucius a letter in which she petitions Charles to assume the guardianship of the Princess Mary and to support her faithful ladies and gentlemen in waiting. Capucius promises to convey her requests to the Emperor; Katherine thanks him and says farewell to him and to Griffith. She commands Patience to put her to bed and to arrange her embalmment and royal burial.

V,i. London. A Gallery in the Palace

At one o'clock in the morning a page with a torch is lighting the gallery for Gardiner, now Bishop of Winchester, who has left King Henry playing cards with the Duke of Suffolk. They meet Sir Thomas

Lovell hastening to the King with news that Queen Anne is in labor. Gardiner wishes the infant well but adds that England will not prosper until Cranmer, Cromwell, and Anne are in their graves. Lovell protests that Anne and Archbishop Cranmer are among the most prominent people in the kingdom and that Cromwell has rapidly advanced in the King's favor. Furthermore, Cranmer is "the King's hand and tongue," and who dares speak against him? Gardiner retorts that he has turned members of the Council against Cranmer by representing the Archbishop as "A most arch-heretic, a pestilence/ That does infect the land." At the Council's insistence, Henry has summoned Cranmer for examination. With the comment that Cranmer is a rank weed that must be "rooted out," Gardiner leaves.

King Henry and Suffolk join Lovell in the gallery. Concerned about Anne's painful travail, the King requests Suffolk's prayers for the Queen and bids the Duke good night. Sir Anthony Denny enters to announce the arrival of Cranmer, whom he immediately ushers in. Dismissing Denny and Lovell, King Henry tells Cranmer of the complaints against him and of the forthcoming investigation. The King advises him to stay in the Tower of London until he can face his accusers in open trial. Sure of his virtue and honesty, Cranmer replies that he fears nothing that can be said against him. Henry reminds him of his many powerful enemies and of the likelihood of perjured testimony. Cranmer answers that he trusts God and the King to protect him. Warning Cranmer to keep his appointment with the Council, the King promises to back him and gives him a ring which will signify the King's special protection.

As Cranmer weeps from gratitude and departs, the Old Lady enters to announce that Queen Anne has borne a daughter as like the King "As cherry is to cherry." Rewarding the Old Lady with a hundred marks, Henry hastens to see the Queen.

V,ii. Lobby in Front of the Council Chamber

Archbishop Cranmer starts to enter the chamber, but the Keeper tells him that he must wait until he is called for. Doctor Butts appears, suspects that "a piece of malice" is in the making, and hastens to inform the King. Chagrined by his detention, Cranmer reflects that the Council is trying to shame him. Meanwhile, Butts and the King come to a window from which they look down on the lobby. Displeased with the discourtesy Cranmer has endured, Henry tells Butts not to interfere but to let him listen to the proceedings about to commence.

V,iii. The Council Chamber[1]

The Lord Chancellor and other members of the Council take their seats at the table. Cromwell serves as secretary. When Cranmer appears, the Lord Chancellor asserts that the Archbishop has been teaching and sponsoring heresies and new opinions throughout the kingdom. Gardiner interposes the opinion that his correction must be sudden lest commotions and uproars similar to recent civil and religious disturbances in Germany result. Maintaining the uprightness and propriety of his public and private life, Cranmer asks that his accusers meet him face to face. Suffolk says that since Cranmer is a Councillor, no man dares accuse him. Gardiner says that to save time the King and Council will commit Cranmer to the Tower where, reduced to the status of private citizenship, he will learn of more accusers than he will be able to refute. Cranmer ironically thanks Gardiner for this demonstration of friendship and asserts that he is confident of clearing himself. Gardiner states that Cranmer is a member of a heretical sect, and when Cromwell objects that Gardiner is "too sharp" and disrespectful with the Archbishop, he starts quarreling with the Secretary. After rebuking Gardiner and Cromwell for their wrangling, the Lord Chancellor commits Cranmer to the Tower to await the King's pleasure. When Gardiner commands a guard to lead Cranmer away, the Archbishop shows the ring he has received and appeals to the King. Recognizing the ring as genuine and a mark of the King's favor, most of the members of the Council wish that they were clear of the attempt to impugn Cranmer. Cromwell particularly regrets his industry in collecting "tales and informations" against the enviably honest Archbishop.

Frowning, King Henry enters and takes his seat. Gardiner welcomes the King, praising the wisdom, piety, and concern for the Church that induce him to sit in judgment on a great offender. Brushing aside this fulsome flattery, Henry tells Gardiner that he has a cruel and bloody nature. Inviting Cranmer to sit, the King dares any member of the Council to wag his finger at the Archbishop. Suffolk tries to speak, but Henry interrupts him to rebuke the Council for its unmannerly and malicious behavior. Finally the Lord Chancellor explains that the Council committed Cranmer to the Tower to insure his fair trial at a later date. Charging the Council to treat the Archbishop with respect and reaffirming his indebtedness

[1] The New Arden edition continues scene ii at this point.

to the man, King Henry requests Cranmer to stand as godfather to the infant princess. Humbly, Cranmer accepts the invitation. Gardiner promises the King to "embrace and love" Cranmer, and Henry hastens to the baptism of his daughter.

V,iv. The Palace Yard [1]

The Porter's Man is protesting to the Porter that he has been physically unable to keep out the crowd of people who have pushed their way in to see the christening of the princess. The Lord Chamberlain appears and rebukes the two servants for permitting the multitude to enter. Trumpets signal the approach of the baptismal procession, and the Chamberlain orders the Porter and his Man to clear the way.

V,v. The Palace

With trumpets sounding, officials, members of the peerage, godparents, marshals, and the infant princess enter. The Garter King-at-Arms (Chief Herald) calls upon heaven to send prosperous and long life to "the high and mighty Princess of England, Elizabeth." There is another flourish of trumpets, and the King and his guard appear. Cranmer kneels before the King, who kisses Elizabeth and blesses her.

Receiving permission, Cramer delivers a long prophecy envisioning the virtues and blessings of the future Queen, now in her cradle. After her a ruler equally blessed will inherit Elizabeth's "peace, plenty, love, truth, . . . honour." Cranmer also foretells Elizabeth's long reign as a virgin and "most unspotted lily." Thanking Cranmer for his prophetic eulogy and others for their attendance at the ceremony, King Henry declares a holiday and leads the assembly forth to visit the Queen.

The Epilogue

Conceding that the play cannot have pleased every member of the audience, the Epilogue apologizes for having kept some spectators awake and for boring others. The play's chief value has been in "The merciful construction of good women," and therefore all who have seen the work will applaud it.

[1] The New Arden edition designates this scene as iii and the concluding scene as iv.

BIOGRAPHICAL INDEX TO CHARACTERS IN SHAKESPEARE'S HISTORY PLAYS

For the subject matter of his ten history plays, Shakespeare selected incidents spanning a period of more than three hundred years. The reign of King John began in 1199; the death of Katherine of Aragon in *Henry VIII* occurred in 1536. Shakespeare filled his history plays with persons whose names, titles, and actions he found in chronicle sources. Many characters bearing identical titles are actually different people; sometimes a man using a particular title in one play appears with another title in a succeeding play. For example, in *Henry V* the Archbishop of Canterbury is Henry Chichele; in *Richard III* he is Thomas Bourchier; in Act II, scene iv of *Henry VIII* the Archbishop is William Warham, whereas in later scenes of the same play the Archbishop of Canterbury is Thomas Cranmer, who took office in 1533. The careful reader will identify four different Dukes of Norfolk, five different Earls of Northumberland. The Duke of Aumerle in *Richard II* is the same person as the Duke of York in *Henry V*.

The following biographical notes will assist the reader in identifying the majority of these people and events in their proper chronological setting. In addition to those persons actually appearing on the stage, the list includes many figures who are merely mentioned but about whom some information is helpful. Readers seeking fuller details should consult the works cited below, since they are the principal sources from which these notes derive.

The Dictionary of National Biography
The Encyclopædia Britannica
Shakespeareana Genealogica, compiled by George Russell French (London and Cambridge: Macmillan and Co., 1869). Cited as French.
W. H. Thomson, *Shakepeare's Characters: A Historical Dictionary* (Altrincham: John Sherratt and Son, 1951). Cited as Thomson.
Webster's Biographical Dictionary.

Key to abbreviations of titles of the plays:

		PAGE IN THIS BOOK
1H.IV	*Henry IV* (Part One)	29
2H.IV	*Henry IV* (Part Two)	41

		PAGE IN THIS BOOK
H.V	*Henry V*	55
1H.VI	*Henry VI* (Part One)	71
2H.VI	*Henry VI* (Part Two)	86
3H.VI	*Henry VI* (Part Three)	102
H.VIII	*Henry VIII*	133
John	*King John*	2
R.II	*Richard II*	15
R.III	*Richard III*	116

Abbot of Westminster. *See* Westminster, Abbot of.

Abergavenny, Lord (*H.VIII*). George Nevil (*c.*1471–1535); favorite of Henry VII; chief larderer of England; married Mary Stafford, daughter of Duke of Buckingham; officiated at coronation of Anne Bullen.

Admiral. *See* French Admiral.

Alençon, Duchess of. *See* French King's Sister.

Alençon, Duke of (*H.V*). John, 1st Duke of Alençon (d.1415); killed the Duke of York at Agincourt and was himself slain in the battle.

Alençon, Duke of (*1,2 H.VI*). John, 2nd Duke of Alençon (d.1476); son of 1st Duke, who died at Agincourt; intrigued against Charles VII; arrested for rebellion and died in prison.

Ambassadors, French (*H.V*). Louis, Earl of Vendome; William Bouratin, Archbishop of Bourges; Bishop of Lisieux; Lords of Ivry and Braquemont; Jean Andree and Gualtier Cole, Secretaries. (French)

Amurath (*2H.IV*, V,ii, 47–48). Amurath (Murad) III succeeded his father, Selim II, as Ottoman sultan in 1574; began his reign by assassinating five younger brothers; his reign saw beginning of diplomatic relations between England and Turkey; his son and successor (1595) murdered nineteen of his brothers.

Angus (*1H.IV*). George Douglas (1380?–1403); 1st Earl of Angus; illegitimate son of William, 1st Earl of Douglas, and Margaret Stewart, Countess of Angus; captured at Homildon; died of plague.

Anne Mortimer (*2H.VI*, II,ii, 38,43). Anne Mortimer (b.1388); daughter of Roger Mortimer, 4th Earl of March, and Eleanor Holland; wife of Richard, Earl of Cambridge; mother of Richard Plantagenet, Duke of York; grandmother of Edward IV and Richard III.

Anne, Lady (*R.III*). Anne Nevil (1452–1485), daughter of Richard Nevil, Earl of Warwick; married: (1) Edward, Princes of Wales (son of Henry VI) and (2) Richard III; crowned in 1483; died at Middleham Castle. Many historians doubt that Richard poisoned her.

Anne Bullen. *See* Bullen, Anne.

Another Lord (*R.II*, IV,i). Thomson suggests the name of Thomas 4th Lord Morley, for this role.

Archbishop of Canterbury. *See* Canterbury, Archbishop of.

Archbishop of York. *See* York, Archbishop of.

Archdeacon of Bangor. *See* Bangor, Archdeacon of.

Archibald, Earl of Douglas. *See* Douglas, Earl of.

Armagnac, Earl of (*1H.VI*). John IV (d.1451), son of Barnard VII; formed alliance with English against Charles VII. His daughter mentioned as a possible bride for Henry VI.

Arthur, Duke (Count) of Brittany (*John*). (1187–1203); posthumous son of Geoffrey of Brittany and Constance; on death of Richard Coeur-de-Lion in 1199, Arthur claimed throne of England and declared himself vassal of Philip II of France; captured at Mirabeau; subsequently disappeared at Rouen.

Arthur, Prince. *See* Arthur, Duke of Brittany.

Arthur, Prince of Wales (*H.VIII*). (1486–1502); 1st son of Henry VII and Elizabeth of York; married Katherine of Aragon (1501); died in Ludlow Castle less than five months after marriage.

Athol, Earl of (*1H.IV*). Walter Stewart (d.1437); 2nd son of Robert II, King of Scotland; active in return of James I to Scotland in 1424; executed for his part in James's assassination.

Attorney, King's. *See* King's Attorney.

Aumerle, Duke of (*R.II*). *See* York, Duke of.

Austria, Duke of (*John*). Following earlier writers, Shakespeare confused:
(1) Leopold (d.1195), Archduke of Austria; captured Richard Coeur-de-Lion and held him for ransom in 1192.
(2) Widomar, Viscount of Limoges; opposed Richard at time of Richard's death in 1199.

Auvergne, Countess of (*1H.VI*). French suggests Mary, wife of Bertrand III, Lord de la Tour, Count of Auvergne.

Bagot (*R.II*). Sir William Bagot (d.1407); Sheriff of Leicester; M.P. in 1397; committed to the Tower in 1400 (Thomson); released, returned to parliament (French). Holinshed calls him Sir John Bagot.

Bangor, Archdeacon of (*1H.IV*). Dean Daron; supported Owen Glendower. (Thomson)

Banister (*H.VIII*). Ralph Banister; servant of Henry Stafford, Duke of Buckingham; betrayed his master for the £1,000 reward offered by Richard III. (Thomson)

Barbary (*R.II*). Name Shakespeare gives to Richard II's favorite horse, on which Henry IV rode to his coronation. Many scholars think Shakespeare created the name and story on the basis of Froissart's account of Mathe, a greyhound of Richard's that deserted his master and fawned on Bolingbroke in Flint Castle.

Bardolph, Lord (*2H.IV*). Thomas (1368–1408); 5th Baron Bardolph (or Bardolf); supported Percy rebellion in 1403; died of wounds received at Bramham Moor.

Basset (*1H.VI*). Possibly Robert Basset or Philip Basset; Lancastrian.

Bastard. *See:* Faulconbridge, Philip; Orleans, Bastard of.

Bayonne, Bishop of (*H.VIII*). Jean du Bellay. In history the envoy was Grammont, Bishop of Tarbes. (Thomson)

Beaufort. *See:* Exeter, Duke of; Somerset, Duke of; Winchester, Bishop of.

Beaumond, Lord of (*R.II*). Henry (d.1413); 5th Baron Beaumond; Constable of Dover Castle.

Beaumont (*H.V*). French noble; killed at Agincourt in 1415.

Bedford, Duke of. *See* John of Lancaster.

Berkeley, Lord (*R.II*). Thomas (d.1417); 5th Baron Berkeley; commissioner of parliament for deposing Richard II; Warden of Welsh marches; harassed Owen Glendower; father-in-law of Richard Beauchamp, Earl of Warwick.

Berkeley (*R.III*). Possibly a son of James, 6th Lord Berkeley. (French)

Berri, Duke of (*H.V*). Jean (John) (1340–1416); 1st Duke of Berri (or Berry); 3rd son of John II, King of France; brother of Philip the Bold, Duke of Burgundy; patron of arts and literature.

Bigot (*John*). Roger Bigot (or Bigod) (d.1221); 2nd Earl of Norfolk; opposed King John and promoted Magna Carta.

Bishop. *See:* Carlisle, Bishop of; Lincoln, Bishop of; etc.

Black Prince, The. *See* Edward the Black Prince.

Blanch(e) of Spain (Castile) (*John*). (1187?–1252); daughter of Alfonso IX of Castile and of Elinor (1162–1214), who was daughter of Henry II and Elinor of Aquitaine and sister of King John; married the Dauphin Louis (Lewis) in 1200; Queen of France and mother of Louis IX.

Blount. *See* Blunt.

Blunt (*R.II*). Sir Thomas Blunt (or Blount) (d.1400); remained loyal to Richard II and refused to recognize Henry IV; helped Abbot of Westminster and others plan conspiracy against Henry IV; betrayed by Aumerle and executed at Oxford.

Blunt, Sir James (*R.III*). (d.1493); son of Sir Walter Blunt, 1st Baron Mountjoy; loyal supporter of Henry Richmond, for whom he fought at Bosworth Field.

Blunt, Sir John (*2H.IV*). (d.1418); son of Sir Walter Blunt; one-time Governor of Calais; served at Harfleur under Henry V; died in siege of Rouen.

Blunt, Sir Walter (*1,2H.IV*). (d.1403); served with Edward the Black Prince in Spain; died at Shrewsbury when Douglas mistook him for Henry IV.

Blunts, Both the (*2H.IV*). Probably Sir Walter Blunt and Sir John Blunt.

Bohun, Edward. *See* Buckingham, Duke of (*H.VIII*).

Boleyn, Anne. *See* Bullen, Anne.

Bolingbroke, Henry. *See* Henry IV.

Bolingbroke, Roger (*2H.VI*). (d.1441); "a cunning necromancer" who burned a wax image representing King Henry VI; testified that Eleanor, Duchess of Gloucester, sponsored him; hanged, drawn, and quartered at Tyburn; mentioned by contemporaries as one of most learned men of his period.

Bona (*3H.VI*). Princess Bona (Bonne) (d.1485); 3rd daughter of Louis, 1st Duke of Savoy; sister of Charlotte, queen of Louis XI of France; married Duke of Milan in 1468; mother-in-law of Maximilian I.

Bonville, Lord (*3H.VI*). William Lord Harrington (d.1461); Yorkist; executed after second Battle of St. Albans; his widow, Catherine Nevil, subsequently married Lord Hastings.

Bourbon, Duke of (*H.V*). John (d.1433); succeeded his father, Louis the Good in 1410; died while a prisoner in England.

Bourchier, Cardinal. *See* Canterbury, Archbishop of.

Brackenbury. *See* Brakenbury.

Bracy, Sir John (*1H.IV*). J. Dover Wilson says, "No trace . . . in the histories of the period." Thomson cites a Bracy family in Worcestershire.

Brakenbury, Sir Robert (*R.III*). (d.1485); Constable of Tower of London; refused Richard III's order to murder Edward IV's two sons; gave keys of Tower to Tyrrel; fought for Richard III at Bosworth Field.

Brandon (*H.VIII*). R.A. Foakes suggests that Shakespeare had Charles Brandon, Duke of Suffolk, in mind; J. Dover Wilson believes that Shakespeare intended to identify no specific person.

Brandon, Sir William (*R.III*). (d.1485); accompanied Henry Richmond from Brittany to England; father of Charles Brandon, Duke of Suffolk (see above); slain by Richard III at Bosworth Field.

Bretagne, Duke of (*John*). *See* Arthur, Duke of Brittany.

Bretagne, Duke of (*R.II*). John IV de Montfort (d.1399); Duke of Brittany; befriended Henry Bolingbroke during his exile; his widow, Joan of Navarre, became 2nd wife of Henry IV.

Bretagne, Duke of (*H.V*, II,iv). John V of Montfort (d.1442); fought at Agincourt.

Bretagne, Duke of (*2H.VI*, I,1,7). Francis I (1414–1450); Duke of Brittany; fought against the English in Normandy.

Britaine, Duke of. *See* Bretagne, Duke of.

Briton, Duke of (*R.II*). *See* Bretagne, Duke of.

Brittany. *See* Bretagnc.

Brocas (*R.II*). Sir Bernard Brocas (d.1400); son of a favorite of Edward the Black Prince; chamberlain to Anne of Bohemia (1st queen of Richard II); executed by Henry IV.

Buckingham, Duke of (2,3*H.VI*). Humphey Stafford (1402–1460); 1st Duke of Buckingham; grandson of Thomas of Woodstock, youngest son of Edward III; served under Henry V in France; Constable of France; tried to make terms with Cade; Warden of the Cinque Ports; supported Queen Margaret against Yorkists; killed beside tent of Henry VI on eve of Battle of Northampton.

Buckingham, Duke of (*R.III*). Henry Stafford (1454?–1483); 2nd Duke of Buckingham; grandson of Humphrey, 1st Duke (see *2H.VI*); as Lord High Steward of England pronounced sentence on George, Duke of Clarence, in 1478; married Katherine Woodville (sister of Elizabeth, consort of Edward IV); aided Richard III in his usurpation of the throne; deserted Richard and with encouragement from Morton, Bishop of Ely, supported Henry Richmond; betrayed, captured, and beheaded at Salisbury on All Souls' Day, 1483; father of Edward Stafford, 3rd Duke (see *H.VIII*).

Buckingham, Duke of (*H.VIII*) Edward Stafford (1478–1521); 3rd Duke of Buckingham; son of Henry Stafford, 2nd Duke; Lord High Constable of England and K.G.; married Alianore, daughter of Henry Percy, 4th Earl of Northumberland; rival and enemy of Wolsey; father-in-law of Earl of Surrey and of Lord Abergavenny; executed; his betrayer was probably Robert Gilbert rather than Charles Knevet (or Knyvet), his Surveyor.

Bullen, Anne (*H.VIII*). (1507–1536); daughter of Sir Thomas Bullen; 2nd wife of Henry VIII; secretly married 1533; mother of Elizabeth I; charged with infidelity and beheaded on Tower Hill. (Thomson and some others argue that she was born in 1501.)

Bullen, Sir Thomas (*H.VIII*). (1477–1539); Viscount Rochford and Earl of Wiltshire and Ormonde; ambassador to Charles V and the pope; father of Anne Bullen; retired from public life after Anne's execution.

Bulmer, Sir William (*H.VIII*). Holinshed mentions Bulmer as having incurred Henry VIII's displeasure for leaving the King's service and entering that of Buckingham. Thomson lists him as Sir William Blomer. The Folio reads "Blumer."

Burgh, Hubert de. *See* Hubert de Burgh.

Burgundy, Duchess of (*3H.VI*). Isabella (1397–1471); daughter of John I of Portugal; granddaughter of John of Gaunt and hence distant cousin to Edward IV; married Philip the Good, Duke of Burgundy; mother of Charles the Bold.

Burgundy, Duke of (*H.V*). John the Fearless (1371–1419); son of Philip the Bold; formed alliances with the English in 1414 and 1416; assassinated at instigation of the Dauphin (later Charles VII).

Burgundy, Duke of (*H.V, V,ii; and 1H.VI*). Philip the Good (1396–1467); son of John the Fearless (see *H.V.*); formed alliance with Henry V and made peace with Charles VII; married Isabella of Portugal; founded Order of the Golden Fleece; patron of arts and letters.

Burgundy, Duke of (*3H.VI*). Charles the Bold (1433–1477); son of Philip the Good; lifelong struggle against Louis XI of France; in 1468 married Margaret Plantagenet, sister of Edward IV; last Duke of Burgundy.

Bushy (*R.II*). Sir John Bushy (or Bussy) (d.1399); three times Speaker of House of Commons; flattered Richard II to gain favor; captured at Bristol and executed without trial.

Butts, Doctor (*H.VIII*). Sir William Butts (d.1545); principal physician to Henry VIII; helped to found College of Physicians; friend to Cranmer and Reformation.

Cade, Jack (*2H.VI*). (d.1450); claimed descent from Edmund Mortimer, 3rd Earl of March; rebel; fled Sussex for murder; returned to England from France; headed Kentish rebellion in 1450; won temporary victory at Sevenoaks; entered London; later denied readmission to the city and defeated at London Bridge; a fugitive, with a price on his head, captured by Alexander Iden, Sheriff of Kent; died of wounds on way to London.

Cambridge, Earl of (*H.V; 1,2H.VI*). Richard (d.1415); son of Edmund Langley, Duke of York, and Isabel of Castile; brother of Aumerle (see *R.II*); married Anne Mortimer; father of Richard Plantagenet, Duke of York (see *1,2,3 H.VI*); father-in-law of Henry Bourchier, Earl of Essex; married (1) Anne Mortimer; married (2) Maud Clifford, daughter of Thomas Lord Clifford; conspired with Lord Scroop and Sir Thomas Grey against Henry V; executed at Southampton.

Campeius, Cardinal (*H.VIII*). Lorenzo Campeggio (1474?–1539); cardinal; papal legate; appointed Archbishop of Salisbury by Henry VIII; colegate with Wolsey to hear Henry VIII's divorce suit against Katherine of Aragon; deprived of bishopric; died in Rome.

Canterbury, Archbishop of (*John*). Stephen Langton (d.1228); Biblical scholar; made cardinal priest in 1206; consecrated archbishop in 1207, but King John opposed his occupation of the see; first subscribing witness to Magna Carta.

Canterbury, Archbishop of (*R.II*). Thomas Arundel (1353–1414); Archbishop of Canterbury and Lord Chancellor of England; 3rd son of Richard Fitzalan, Earl of Arundel and Warenne; consecrated archbishop in 1396; landed with Bolingbroke at Ravenspurgh; witnessed Richard II's abdication; crowned Henry IV on Oct. 13, 1399; bitter opponent of Lollardy; buried at Canterbury.

Canterbury, Archbishop of (*H.V.*). Henry Chichele (or Chicheley) (1364–1443); Carthusian monk; envoy to Rome; consecrated in 1414; founded St. Bernard's and All Souls' Colleges at Oxford.

Canterbury, Archbishop of (*R.III*). Thomas Bourchier (1404?–1486); descendant of Edward III and Thomas of Woodstock; Archbishop of

Canterbury and Lord Chancellor; crowned Edward IV and Elizabeth Woodville; installed as cardinal in 1473; crowned Richard III (1483) and Henry VII (1485); married Henry VII and Elizabeth of York (1486); buried in Canterbury.

Canterbury, Archbishop of (*H.VIII*, II,iv). William Warham (1450?–1532); Bishop of London and Lord Chancellor; Archbishop of Canterbury (1504–1532); crowned Henry VIII and Katherine of Aragon; agreed to Katherine's divorce; friend of Erasmus and John Colet; noted for charity and generosity.

Canterbury, Archbishop of (*H.VIII*). Thomas Cranmer (1489–1556); succeeded Warham as archbishop in 1533; voided marriage of Henry VIII and Katherine of Aragon; pronounced marriage of Henry and Anne Bullen; crowned Anne queen; stood godfather to Elizabeth; promoted translation of Bible into vernacular; encouraged union among Reformed churches; chief composer of the Articles of Religion; condemned for treason; excommunicated; condemned for heresy; burned at the stake.

Capucius (*H.VIII*). Eustachius Campucius (or Chapuyso); Spanish legate in service of Emperor Charles V.

Car, John de la (*H.VIII*). John de la Court; chaplain to Duke of Buckingham; testified against Buckingham in 1521. (Thomson)

Cardinal Beaufort. *See* Winchester, Bishop of.

Carlisle, Bishop of (*R.II*). Thomas Merke (d.1409); Benedictine monk; member of commission to arrange dowry of Queen Isabella in 1389; arrested for loyalty to Richard II but later pardoned by Henry IV.

Cassado, Gregory de (*H.VIII*). English ambassador to Rome; Wolsey's agent to negotiate secret treaty between Henry VIII and Duke of Ferrara without Henry's knowledge. (Thomson)

Catesby, Sir William (*R.III*). (d.1485); Sheriff of Northamptonshire under Edward IV; succeeded Hastings as Chancellor of Exchequer (1483); Speaker of House of Commons; beheaded three days after Battle of Bosworth Field.

Catherine. *See* Katherine.

Charles V, Emperor (*H.VIII*). (1500–1558); Holy Roman Emperor and King of Spain as Charles I; son of Philip of Burgundy; grandson of Ferdinand and Isabella; married Isabella of Portugal (1503–1539); active in suppressing Protestantism; retired to monastery in Spain.

Charles VI (*H.V*). Charles the Well-Beloved (1368–1422); son of Charles V of France; married Isabel of Bavaria in 1385; suffered recurring attacks of insanity; defeated by Henry V at Agincourt; father of two queens of England (Isabel, 2nd wife of Richard II; and Katherine, consort of Henry V).

Charles VII (*1H.VI*). (1403–1461); 5th son of Charles VI and Isabel of Bavaria; raised siege of Orleans with aid of Joan of Arc; recovered all French territory except Calais from the English; instituted many reforms; initiated standing army; strengthened power of the throne.

Chatillon (*John*). Thomson cites Hugh de Chatillon, who is listed among the Grand Peers of France in 1223. J. Dover Wilson says, "not a historical character."

Clarence, Duke of (*1,2H.IV*). Thomas (1388?–1421); 2nd son of Henry IV and Mary de Bohun; campaigned in France; accompanied Henry V at Harfleur but not at Agincourt; remained in France and was killed fighting against French and Scottish forces at Beauge.

Clarence, Duke of (*1,2H.VI*). Lionel of Antwerp (1338–1368); 1st Duke of Clarence; 3rd son of Edward III; brother of John of Gaunt, Edmund of Langley, and Thomas of Woodstock; his only daughter Philippa married Edmund Mortimer, 3rd Earl of March; Lionel was great-great-grandfather of Richard Plantagenet, Duke of York.

Clarence, Duke of (*3H.VI; R.III*). George (1449–1478); 3rd surviving son of Richard Plantagenet, Duke of York; born in Dublin; brother of Edward IV, Richard III, and Rutland; married Isabella, elder daughter of Richard Nevil, Earl of Warwick; joined father-in-law against Edward IV (1469–1470); rejoined Edward on his return from France in 1471; charged with plotting Edward's death through necromancy; committed to Tower; executed.

Clarence, Young Daughter of. *See* Margaret Plantagenet.

Clarence, Young Son of. *See* Edward, Earl of Warwick.

Clifford (*2H.VI*). Thomas Clifford (1414–1455); 8th Baron Clifford; grandson of Hotspur; supported Henry VI in Wars of the Roses; died in first Battle of St. Albans.

Clifford, Lord. *See* Clifford, Young.

Clifford, Young (*2,3H.VI; R.III*). John Clifford (1435–1461); 9th Baron Clifford; son of Thomas Clifford; reported to have participated in murder of Edmund, Earl of Rutland, at Battle of Wakefield (1460), for which deed he earned title of "The Butcher"; also reported to have decapitated corpse of Richard Plantagenet, Duke of York, and presented his head to Queen Margaret; killed at Ferrybridge.

Clifton (*1H.IV*). Sir John Clifton (d.1403); knight from Nottinghamshire; died at Shrewsbury. (Thomson)

Cobham, Eleanor (*2H.VI*). (d.1454); Duchess of Gloucester; daughter of Sir Reginald Cobham and granddaughter of Reginald Lord Cobham (see *R.II*); married Humphrey, Duke of Gloucester, in 1428; tried for witchcraft, heresy, and treason in 1441; committed to custody of Sir John Stanley and imprisoned at Chester and Kenilworth; transferred to Isle of Man, where she died.

Cobham, Lord (*R.II*). Rainold (Reginald); 1st Baron Cobham of Sternborough; companion of Henry Bolingbroke. (Thomson)

Cobham, Lord (*3H.VI*). Sir Edward Brooke; Lord Cobham of Kent; M.P. 1445–1460; fought with Yorkists in first Battle of St. Albans and at Northampton. (Thomson)

Colevile, Sir John (*2H.IV*). Possibly the governor of Wisbeach Castle in 1416; some sources state that he survived the action at Gaultree and accompanied Henry V to France in 1415.

Constable of France (*H.V*). Charles de la Bret (Delabreth) (d.1415); natural son to Charles the Bad, King of Navarre; half brother to Joan of Navarre, who married Henry IV of England in 1402; mortally wounded at Agincourt.

Constance, Lady (*John*). (d.1201); wife of Geoffrey of Brittany, 3rd surviving son of Henry II of England; mother of Arthur, Duke of Brittany; remarried in 1187 and again in 1199.

Courtney, Sir Edward (*R.III*). (or Courtenay) (d.1509); joined his cousin, Bishop of Exeter, in opposing Richard III; joined Henry Richmond in Brittany; created Earl of Devonshire in 1485; resisted Perkin Warbeck's attack on Exeter.

Coventry, Mayor of. *See* Mayor of Coventry.

Cranmer, Thomas. *See* Canterbury, Archbishop of.

Cromer, Sir James (*2H.VI*). Shakespeare identifies him as Lord Say's son-in-law and a fellow victim in Cade Rebellion; history mentions a Sir William Cromer, Sheriff of Kent in 1450, father-in-law of Lord Say.

Cromwell (*H.VIII*). Thomas Cromwell (1485?–1540); Earl of Essex; son of an artisan and tradesman; legal adviser to Wolsey; gained favor of Henry VIII; Chancellor of Exchequer; effected Act of Supremacy; directed suppression and confiscation of monasteries; accused of treason; attainted, condemned without trial, and beheaded on Tower Hill.

Darc, Jacques (*1H.VI*). Devout peasant of Domremy; father of Joan of Arc; designated as Old Shepherd in the play.

Dauphin (*John*). See Lewis, Dauphin of France.

Dauphin of France (*H.V*). Under the name of Lewis the Dauphin, Shakespeare combines three sons of Charles VI:

(1) Lewis, who died at age of 19 shortly after Agincourt;
(2) Jean (or John), who succeeded to his brother's title in 1415 and died in 1416;
(3) Charles, who ultimately succeeded his father in 1422 as Charles VII.

Dauphin (*1H.VI*). *See* Charles VII.

Denny, Sir Anthony (*H.VIII*). (1500–1549); favorite of Henry VIII; member of Council of Regency for Edward VI; supporter of Reformation.

Derby, Earl of (*R.III*). *See* Stanley, Lord.

Dighton (*R.III*). John Dighton; one of the murderers of Edward IV's two sons; bailiff of Aiton, Staffordshire; subsequently hanged.

Dorset, Lady Marquess (*H.VIII*). Margaret Wotton; mother of Marquis of Dorset; godmother of Elizabeth. (Thomson)

Dorset, Marquis of (*R.III*). Thomas Grey (1451–1501); 1st Marquis of Dorset; son of Sir John Grey (see *3H.VI*) and Elizabeth Woodville; fought with Edward IV at Tewkesbury and participated in assassination of Edward, Prince of Wales (son of Henry VI); took sanctuary in Brittany on accession of Richard III; returned to England after Battle of Bosworth Field; early patron of Wolsey.

Dorset, Marquis of (*H.VIII*). Henry Grey (d.1554); 3rd Marquis of Dorset and Duke of Suffolk; grandson of 1st Marquis; carried scepter at coronation of Anne Bullen; attended christening of Elizabeth; supported Reformation; father of Lady Jane Grey; executed for part in rebellion opposing marriage of Mary Tudor to Philip II of Spain.

Douglas, Earl of (*1,2H.IV*). Archibald (1372–1424); 4th Earl of Douglas and 1st Duke of Touraine; captured by Hotspur at Homildon Hill in 1402; prisoner of English (1403–1408); aided Charles VII of France; killed at Verneuil.

Douglas, Earl of (*1H.IV*, I,iii,261). Archibald (1391?–1439); 5th Earl of Douglas and 2nd Duke of Touraine; fought with Charles VI against English at Beauge; escorted James I from England to Scotland; died of fever.

Edmund, Earl of Rutland (*3H.VI; R.III*). (?–1460); son of Richard Plantagenet, Duke of York; cruelly killed by Young Clifford at Wakefield. French gives date of his birth as 1443; Thomson implies that he was born in 1448.

Edmund of Langley. *See* York, Duke of.

Edward the Confessor (*H.VIII*, **IV,i,88**). (1002?–1066); son of Ethelred the Unready; favored Norman advisers; enfranchised the Cinque Ports; founded Westminster Abbey; first English king to employ the royal touch as a cure for scrofula (see *Macbeth*, IV,iii, 140–156); last of Anglo-Saxon line.

Edward III (*R.II; 2H.IV; H.V; 1,2H.VI*). (1312–1377); known as Edward of Windsor; eldest son of Edward II; married Philippa of Hainaut; won brilliant military and naval victories over French; had seven sons and five daughters.

Edward IV (*2,3H.VI; R.III*). (1442–1483); Earl of March, Duke of York, and King of England (1461–1470; 1471–1483); born in Rouen; son of Richard Plantagenet, Duke of York, and Cicely Nevil, daughter of 1st Earl of Westmoreland; major figure in Wars of the Roses; married Elizabeth Woodville (Lady Grey) in 1464, thereby offending the Earl of Warwick; defeated Warwick at Barnet in 1471 and Queen Margaret at Tewkesbury, the last engagement leading to the murder of Prince Edward and Henry VI.

Edward V (*3H.VI; R.III*). (1470–1483); son of Edward IV and Elizabeth Woodville; created Prince of Wales in 1471; confined to Tower with his brother Richard in 1483; deposed on charge of illegitimacy; murdered, presumably by smothering, on order of Richard III.

Edward the Black Prince (*R.II; H.V; 1,2H.VI*). Edward of Woodstock (1330–1376); eldest son of Edward III and Philippa of Hainaut; one of original Knights of the Garter; campaigned widely in Europe; married Joan, "The Fair Maid of Kent"; father of Richard II.

Edward, Earl of Warwick (*R.III*). (1475–1499); son of George, Duke of Clarence, and Isabel Nevil, daughter of Earl of Warwick; confined by Richard III in Sheriff Hutton Castle in 1484; in 1485 transferred by Henry VII to the Tower, where he remained for life; suffered mental lapses because of rigorous confinement; beheaded on pretext of conspiracy against Henry VII.

Edward Plantagenet. *See* Edward IV; Edward, Earl of Warwick; York, Duke of (*R.II; H.V*).

Edward Plantagenet, Prince of Wales (*3H.VI; R.III*). (1453–1471); son of Henry VI and Margaret of Anjou; taken by mother to Harlech Castle after Lancastrian defeat in 1460; fled to France with Queen Margaret in 1462; returned to Scotland; married Anne Nevil, younger daughter of Earl of Warwick "the Kingmaker"; slain by Yorkists after Battle of Tewkesbury; last legitimate Lancastrian male heir to English throne.

Eleanor Cobham, Duchess of Gloucester. *See* Cobham, Eleanor.

Eleanor Mortimer (*2H.VI*; **II,ii,38**). (d.1418); younger daughter of Roger Mortimer; married 11th Earl of Devonshire. (Thomson)

Eleanor. *See* Elinor.

Elinor, Queen (*John*). Elinor (1122?–1204) of Aquitaine; daughter of William X, Duke of Aquitaine; known as "Damsel of Brittany"; married Louis VII of France in 1137 and divorced on pretext of consanguinity in 1152; married Henry II of England (1152); supported her sons' rebellion against their father; mother of Richard Coeur-de-Lion, John, and Geoffrey of Brittany.

Elizabeth I (*H.VIII*). (1533–1603); Queen of England; daughter of Henry VIII and Anne Bullen; reigned 1558–1603; appears as infant in V,v of the play.

Elizabeth of York (*R.III*). (1465–1503); daughter of Edward IV and Elizabeth Woodville; queen of Henry VII; mother of Henry VIII.

Elizabeth Woodville, Queen of Edward IV (*3H.VI; R.III*). (1437?–1492); daughter of Sir Richard Woodville, 1st Earl Rivers; married Sir John Grey (killed 1461); married Edward IV in 1464; took sanctuary in 1470; her two sons, Edward V and Richard, Duke of York, were murdered in Tower in 1483; her daughter Elizabeth married Henry VII.

Ely, Bishop of (*H.V*). John Fordham (d.1425); one-time secretary to Richard II; Bishop of Durham; demoted to bishopric of Ely in 1390.

Ely, Bishop of (*R.III*). John Morton (1420?–1500); Bishop of Ely; Archbishop of Canterbury (1486–1500); Cardinal of St. Anastasia (1493); Chancellor of Oxford; Lancastrian in sympathy but submitted to Edward IV; encouraged Buckingham to rebel against Richard III; sent Urswick to warn Henry Richmond of danger from Richard; advocated marriage of Henry VII and Elizabeth of York; known as author of "Morton's fork."

Ely, Bishop of (*H.VIII*). Nicholas West (1461–1533); elevated to bishopric of Ely in 1515; diplomat; chaplain to Katherine of Aragon; opposed her divorce.

Emperor (*John*). Henry VI (1165–1197); King of Germany and Sicily; Holy Roman Emperor (1190–1197); son of Frederick I; captured Richard Coeur-de-Lion and held him prisoner (1193–1194).

Emperor (*H.V; 1H.VI*). Sigismund (1368–1437); King of Hungary and Bohemia; Holy Roman Emperor (1411–1437); inaugurated Council of Constance (1414); implicated in death of John Huss.

Emperor (*H.VIII*). *See* Charles V, Emperor.

Erpingham, Sir Thomas (*R.II;* H.V). (1357–1428); member of Norfolk family; landed with Bolingbroke at Ravenspurgh; Warden of the Cinque Ports; field commander at Agincourt; K.G.; suspected of Lollardy.

Essex, Earl of (*John*). Geoffrey Fitzpeter (d.1213); Lord Chief Justice and Vice-Regent of England; opposed William Longchamp; supported John in extortions.

Exeter, Bishop of (*R.III*). Peter Courtenay (d.1492); appointed Bishop of Exeter in 1478; Yorkist, but opposed Richard III after his succession; restored to bishopric by Henry VII. (Thomson)

Exeter, Duke of (*R.II*, II,i,281; and V,iii,137). John Holland (1352?–1400); Duke of Exeter and Earl of Huntingdon; 3rd son of Thomas Holland, 1st Earl of Kent; half brother of Richard II; married Elizabeth, daughter of John of Gaunt and sister of Henry IV; served in Spain with John of Gaunt; Chamberlain of England; aided Richard II; executed for conspiracy against Henry IV.

Exeter, Duke of (*H.V; 1H.VI*). Thomas Beaufort (d.1427); 3rd son of John of Gaunt and Katherine Swynford; half brother of Henry IV; legitimized in 1397; campaigned in France but historically present neither at Agincourt nor at Henry VI's coronation.

Exeter, Duke of (*3H.VI*). Henry Holland (d.1473); 2nd Duke of Exeter; grandson of John Holland, Duke of Exeter; son of Earl of Huntingdon; brother-in-law to Edward IV; remained faithful to Henry VI; attainted by Edward IV; died in poverty.

Exton. *See* Pierce of Exton.

Falconbridge (*3H.VI*). William Nevil (d.1463); Baron Faulconberg; 2nd son of Ralph, 1st Earl of Westmoreland; grandson of John of

Gaunt; commander of English fleet in 1458; elevated to earldom of Kent for valor at Ferrybridge.

Falstaff, Sir John (*1,2H.IV; H.V*). Non-historical; Shakespeare's great comic character in the plays indicated; in creating him, Shakespeare may have incorporated features of Sir John Fastolfe and Sir John Oldcastle.

Fastolfe, Sir John (*1H.VI*). (1378?–1459); distinguished service at Agincourt; governor of Anjou and Maine; captured John II, Duke of Alençon; accused of cowardice against Joan of Arc at Pataye; took refuge in Tower of London during Cade Rebellion; retired to Norfolk, where he died.

Faulconbridge, Philip (*John*). Holinshed mentions Philip, the bastard son of Richard I, to whom his father assigned the castle and honor of Coinacke. According to this source, Philip killed the Viscount of Limoges in revenge for Richard's death. Philip Faulconbridge may also be partially identified with Falkes de Breauté (d.1226), likewise a bastard, to whom John gave several honors and favors. J. Dover Wilson states that Philip "appears to be compounded of most of the valiant bastards of English history."

Ferdinand, King of Spain (*H.VIII*, II,iv. 47). (1452–1516); King of Castile and Aragon; married Isabella of Castile; organized the Spanish Inquisition; conquest of Granada (1492); aided Columbus; father of Katherine of Aragon, consort of Henry VIII; grandfather of Emperor Charles V.

Ferrers, Walter Lord. *See* Walter Lord Ferrers.

Fife, Earl of. *See* Mordake.

Fisher, John. *See* Rochester, Bishop of.

Fitzwalter. *See* Fitzwater.

Fitzwater, Lord (*R.II*). Walter (d.1407); 5th Baron Fitzwater; summoned to parliament in 1390; Holinshed says that he was first to defy Aumerle in the "gage scene."

Forrest (*R.III*). Miles Forrest; one of murderers of two sons of Edward IV; appointed Keeper of the Wardrobe in Barnard Castle; died soon after his crime.

French Admiral (*3H.VI*). Louis; Count of Rousillon; natural son of Charles, Duke of Bourbon. (French)

French Ambassadors. *See* Ambassadors, French.

French King's Sister (*H.VIII*). Margaret; sister to Francis I of France; widow of Charles II, Duke of Alençon, who was grandson of John II (see *1H.IV*); in history she married Henry II of Navarre in 1527. (French)

Froissart (*1H.VI*). Jean Froissart (1333?–1400?); French historian; his famous work, known as *Froissart's Chronicles,* treats the history of France, England, Scotland, and Spain between 1325 and 1400.

Gam, Davy (*H.V*). Dafydd ab Llewelyn (d.1415); Welsh soldier who remained loyal to Henry IV during Glendower Rebellion; died at Agincourt. (Thomson)

Gardiner, Stephen. *See* Winchester, Bishop of.

Gargrave, Sir Thomas (*1H.VI*). Member of Yorkshire family; killed in siege of Orleans in 1428.

Garter King-at-Arms (*H.VIII*). Thomas Wriothesley (1505–1550); 1st Baron Wriothesley of Titchfield and 1st Earl of Southhampton; Lord

Chancellor of England (1544–1547); enemy of Cranmer; grandfather of Henry Wriothesley, 3rd Earl of Southampton, Shakespeare's patron.

Gascoigne, Sir William. *See* Lord Chief Justice.

Gaunt. *See* John of Gaunt.

Gawsey, Sir Nicholas (*1H.IV*). Several scholars identify this knight as Sir Nicholas Goushill of Hoveringham, Nottinghamshire.

General of the French Forces (*1H.VI*). French identifies two commanders of the French forces at Castillon:
(1) Andreas de Valle, Lord of Leheauc;
(2) Sieur de Jalognes.

Gentleman Usher to Wolsey (*H.VIII*). George Cavendish (1500?–1562); remained loyal to Wolsey; retired to his home in Suffolk; famous for his biography, *Life of Wolsey.*

Geoffrey (*John*). Geoffrey (1158–1186); Count of Brittany; 4th son of Henry II; joined his brothers in rebellion against their father; later opposed Richard I; father of Arthur, Duke of Brittany.

George, Duke of Clarence. *See* Clarence, Duke of.

Glansdale, Sir William (*1H.VI*). English knight who died during siege of Orleans in 1428.

Glendower, Owen (*R.II; 1,2H.IV; 2H.VI*). Owain ab Gruffydd (1359?–1416?); last independent prince of Wales; headed Welsh Rebellion against Henry IV; joined Northumberland uprising; captured Harlech and Aberystwith in 1404; failed to establish independent and united Wales.

Gloucester, Duchess of (*R.II*). Eleanor de Bohun (d.1399); daughter of Humphrey X and co-heiress of earldoms of Hereford, Essex, and Northampton; married Thomas of Woodstock, Duke of Gloucester in 1374; sister of Mary de Bohun, Queen to Henry IV.

Gloucester, Duchess of. *See* Cobham, Eleanor.

Gloucester, Duke of. *See* Humphrey, Duke of Gloucester; Richard III; Thomas of Woodstock.

Goffe, Matthew (*2H.VI*). Matthew Goffe (or Gough) (d.1450); English soldier; served in France under Talbot, Fastolfe, and Scales; killed on London Bridge during Cade Rebellion.

Governor of Harfleur. *See* Harfleur, Governor of.

Governor of Paris. *See* Paris, Governor of.

Gower (*2H.IV*) (*H.V, ?*). Probably Thomas Gower, member of a Yorkshire family. Thomson believes that he is also the Gower in *Henry V*; French holds that these characters are not the same.

Grandpré (*H.V*). (d.1415); French noble killed at Agincourt.

Green (*R.II*). Sir Henry Green (d.1399); favorite of Richard II; captured at Bristol by Henry IV and executed without trial.

Grey, Lady. *See* Elizabeth Woodville, Queen of Edward IV.

Grey, Lord (*R.III*). Sir Richard Grey (d.1483); younger son of Sir John Grey and Elizabeth Woodville; brother of Thomas Grey, Marquis of Dorset; coguardian with Earl Rivers of Edward V; executed at Pomfret (Pontefract).

Grey, Sir John (*3H.VI; R.III*). (d.1461); 8th Lord Ferrers; married Elizabeth Woodville (later the consort of Edward IV) in 1450; Lancastrian adherent; died at second Battle of St. Albans. Shakespeare erroneously refers to him as Sir Richard.

Grey, Sir Richard (*3H.VI,* III,ii,2). Shakespeare erroneously ascribes this name to Sir John Grey in this line.

Grey, Sir Thomas (*H.V*). (d.1415; 2nd son of Sir Thomas Grey of Berwick; married Alice Nevil, daughter of Ralph Nevil, Earl of Westmoreland; conspired with Richard Earl of Cambridge and Lord Scroop against Henry V; executed at Southhampton.

Griffith (*H.VIII*). French and Thomson fail to identify this character, although Cavendish calls him "Master Griffith."

Guildford, Sir Henry (*H.VIII*). (d.1533); Master of the Horse to Henry VIII; Standard-Bearer for England for life; served against Moors in Spain.

Guildfords (*R.III*). Prominent Kentish family, including Sir John Guildford and his son, Sir Richard; the latter was father of Sir Henry Guildford (see *Henry VIII*).

Gurney, James (*John*). Probably non-historical, but French cites Hugh de Gurney, whose name appears in treaties of 1196 and 1204 between France and England.

Hal, Prince. *See* Henry V.

Harcourt (*2H.IV*). (d.1417) properly identified as Sir Thomas Harcourt of Oxfordshire and Sheriff of Berkshire.

Harfleur, Governor of (*H.V.*). Jean Lord D'Estouteville; captured and transported as a prisoner to England.

Hastings, Lord (*2H.IV*). Sir Ralph Hastings; not actually a "Lord"; historians disagree on the date and manner of his death.

Hastings, Lord (*3H.VI; R.III*). William Hastings (1430?–1483); Baron; Yorkist; Master of the Mint; Chamberlain of Royal Household; Captain of Calais; ambassador; loyal to Edward IV and his children; rebuffed Richard III in his attempt to seize throne; charged with treason and beheaded without trial.

Henry III (*John*). (1207–1272); King of England; son of John and Isabella; strongly assisted by Earl of Pembroke, Hubert de Burgh, and Stephen Langton; married Eleanor of Provence; warred against Simon de Montfort; rebuilt Westminster Abbey.

Henry IV (*R.II; 1,2H.IV; 1,2,3H.VI*). (1367–1413); also known as Bolingbroke, Hereford, and Henry of Lancaster; King of England; son of John of Gaunt and Blanche, Duchess of Lancaster; campaigned in Europe and the Holy Land; banished by Richard II in 1398; returned to depose Richard; proclaimed King in 1399; plagued with series of insurrections; persecuted Lollards; married (1) Mary de Bohun and (2) Joan of Navarre; four sons and two daughters by first marriage.

Henry V (*1,2H.IV; H.V; 1,2,3H.VI*). (1387–1422; ruled 1413–1422); also known as Prince Hal and Harry of Monmouth; eldest son of Henry IV and Mary de Bohun; distinguished himself in actual command against the Percies at Battle of Shrewsbury shortly before his 16th birthday; invaded France and won notable victory at Agincourt (Oct. 25, 1415); married Katherine of Valois (daughter of Charles VI and sister of Isabella, consort of Richard II) in 1420; recognized as regent and heir to throne of France; died in France; buried in England.

Henry VI (*H.V, Epilogue; 1,2,3 H.VI; R.III*). (1421–1471); son of Henry V and Katherine of Valois; succeeded to throne in infancy; married Margaret of Anjou in 1445; his reign saw loss of French possessions, Jack Cade's Rebellion (1450), and beginning of Wars of the Roses; subject to periods of mental derangement; imprisoned in Tower after Margaret's defeat at Tewkesbury; probably murdered; pious, scholarly; patron of arts and letters; founded Eton (1440) and King's College, Cambridge (1441).

Henry VII (*3H.VI; R.III; H.VIII*). (1457–1509); also known as Henry, Earl of Richmond, and Henry Tudor; son of Edmund Tudor, Earl of Richmond, and Margaret Beaufort (descendant of John of Gaunt); lived as exile in Brittany throughout most of Wars of the Roses; defeated and killed Richard III at Bosworth Field (1485); acknowledged as King Henry VII; married Elizabeth of York (daughter of Edward IV); instituted Star Chamber.

Henry VIII (*H.VIII*). (1491–1547); also known as Bluff King Hal; son of Henry VII and Elizabeth of York; met Francis I of France on Field of the Cloth of Gold (1520); obtained Act of Supremacy establishing the Church of England; married six times; father of Edward VI, Mary Tudor, and Elizabeth I.

Henry, Earl of Richmond. *See* Henry VII.

Henry, Prince (*John*). *See* Henry III.

Henry, Prince (*1,2H.IV*). *See* Henry V.

Henton, Nicholas. *See* Hopkins, Nicholas.

Herald (*H.V*). French identifies three heralds serving Henry V at Agincourt: (1) John Ashwell; (2) John Wrexworth; (3) John Kitteby.

Herbert, Sir Walter (*R.III*). Son of William Herbert, Earl of Pembroke (see *3 Henry VI*).

Hereford, Duke of. *See* Henry IV.

Holland, Thomas. *See* Surrey, Duke of.

Hopkins, Nicholas (*H.VIII*). Holinshed refers to "one Nicholas Hopkins, a Monke of an house of the Chartreux order, beside Bristow." The Folio text reads "Nicholas Henton."

Horner, Thomas (*2H.VI*). Shakespeare's name for William Catur (d.1446), an armorer accused of high treason by his own servant, John David; ordered to defend his innocence in personal combat, Catur entered the lists while he was intoxicated and was killed at Smithfield.

Hotspur. *See* Percy, Henry.

Howard, John. *See* Norfolk, Duke of.

Hubert de Burgh (*John*). (d.1243); Chief Justiciar of England; Chamberlain to King John; created Earl of Kent (1227); outlawed for treason, pardoned, restored to title and estates; last of justiciars to hold political powers; J. Dover Wilson thinks Shakespeare may have confused this character and a dramatic figure of lower rank.

Hume, John (*2H.VI*). Priest; adviser to Eleanor Cobham, Duchess of Gloucester; arrested in 1441; pardoned.

Humphrey, Duke of Gloucester (*2H.IV; H.V; 1,2H.VI*). Humphrey (1391–1447); Duke of Gloucester and Earl of Pembroke; 4th and youngest son of Henry IV; wounded at Agincourt; Regent of England (1420–1421); Protector during Henry VI's minority; Married (1) Jacoba of Holland; (2) Eleanor Cobham, his mistress; patron of literature; 1st donor of books to library at Oxford; known as "The Good Duke Humphrey"; died in custody.

Hungerford, Lord (*1H.VI*). Sir Walter Hungerford (d.1449); loyal Lancastrian; M.P. from Wiltshire; served with Henry V in France.

Hungerford, Lord (*3H.VI*). Sir Thomas Hungerford; deserted Edward IV to join Warwick in restoration of Henry VI; executed at Salisbury. Shakespeare errs in ascribing marriage of Lord Hungerford's daughter to Lord William Hastings rather than to his son, Sir Edward Hastings.

Huntingdon, (*H.V.*, V,ii,85). John Holland (1395–1447); Earl of Huntingdon and Duke of Exeter; son of Duke of Exeter (see *Richard II*); fought with distinction at Agincourt; campaigned successfully in France.

Iden, Alexander (*2H.VI*). Sheriff of Kent, succeeding Cromer, who was executed by Cade's rebels; captured Cade in Sussex and collected reward posted for apprehension of the rebel leader.

Innocent III. *See* Pope.

Isabel (*H.V*). Isabel (or Elizabeth) (1370–1435); daughter of Stephen II, Duke of Bavaria; consort of Charles VI of France; after Charles succumbed to attacks of insanity, Isabel took active part in politics and gained notoriety for scandalous personal behavior; mother of Charles VII, of Isabella (consort of Richard II), and of Katherine of Valois.

Isabella (*R.II*). (1389–1409); 2nd daughter of Charles VI of France; 2nd wife of Richard II; married at Calais in 1396; returned to France after death of Richard; in 1406 married Charles, Duke of Orleans.

Jack Cade. *See* Cade, Jack.

Jamy (*H.V*). French and Thomson note that James I (1394–1437), campaigned with Henry V in France. That Shakespeare intended to identify James I with Jamy seems unlikely.

Joan la Pucelle. *See* Joan of Arc.

Joan of Arc (*1H.VI*). (1412–1431); the Maid of Orleans; born at Domremy; at age of 13 claimed to have received divine messages; raised siege of Orleans and relieved Dunois in 1428–1429; encouraged Charles VII's coronation at Rheims in 1429; captured by Burgundians in 1430 and sold to English, who permitted her trial by Inquisition at Rouen; found guilty of witchcraft and heresy; burned at the stake; her trial revised and her innocence proclaimed in 1455; beatified in 1909; canonized in 1920.

John, Duke of Lancaster. *See* John of Lancaster.

John, King (*John*). (1167?–1216); also known as John Lackland; son of Henry II; married Isabella of Angoulême; succeeded his brother, Richard I, in 1199; lost duchies of Normandy, Anjou, Maine, and Touraine; difficulties with Pope Innocent III; signed Magna Carta at Runnymede on June 15, 1215.

John Morton. *See* Ely, Bishop of.

John of Gaunt (*R.II; 1,2H.IV; 1,2H.VI*). (1340–1399); Duke of Lancaster; 4th son of Edward III and Philippa of Hainaut; born in Ghent; married: (1) Blanche of Lancaster, (2) Constance of Castile, by whom he claimed title to Castile and Leon, (3) Katherine Swynford, his mistress; campaigned in Spain, in Aquitaine, and at Limoges; failed to establish rule over Duchy of Aquitaine; father of Henry IV, by his first wife; father of the Beauforts, legitimized issue of Katherine Swynford, who was sister-in-law of Geoffrey Chaucer; died following Henry Bolingbroke's banishment.

John of Lancaster (*1,2H.IV; H.V; 1,2H.VI*). (1389–1435); also known as Prince of Lancaster and Duke of Bedford; 3rd son of Henry IV; Regent during Henry V's French invasions; campaigned successfully in France during early reign of Henry VI; Regent of England and France; permitted execution of Joan of Arc; effected Henry VI's coronation as King of France; married: (1) Anne of Burgundy, (2) Jacqueline of St. Pol, Luxembourg; died and buried at Rouen.

John, Prince. *See* John of Lancaster.
Jourdain, Margery (*2H.VI*). The "Witch of Eye"; charged with sorcery in 1433 but released to her husband's custody; subsequently executed.

Kate. *See* Percy, Lady.
Katherine (*H.V*). Katherine of Valois (1401–1437); daughter of Charles VI of France; wife of Henry V; sister of Isabella, consort of Richard II; mother of Henry VI; after death of Henry V, married Owen Tudor by whom she was mother of Edmund Tudor, whose son Henry Richmond became Henry VII (see *Richard III*); died in obscurity in Bermondsey Abbey.
Katherine (*H.VIII*). Katherine of Aragon (1485–1536); daughter of Ferdinand and Isabella of Spain; married Arthur, Prince of Wales (d.1502); became 1st Queen of Henry VIII; mother of Mary Tudor; gave birth to four other children, all of whom died in infancy; marriage to Henry declared void in 1533; died at Kimbolton.
Kent (*R.II*). *See* Surrey, Duke of.
Kent, Earl of (*2H.IV*). Edmund Holland (1384–1408); 4th Earl of Kent; succeeded his brother Thomas (see Surrey, Duke of, in *Richard II*); died in Brittany.
Ketly, Sir Richard (*H.V*, IV,viii,109). French identifies this officer as Sir Richard Kighley; Thomson calls him Sir Richard Kelly. Little is known about him except that his retinue at Agincourt consisted of "6 lances and 18 archers."
Kildare (*H.VIII*). Gerald Fitzgerald (d.*c.*1534); 9th Earl of Kildare; Deputy of Ireland; replaced by Earl of Surrey (later Duke of Norfolk) in 1520; died in Tower of London.
King's Attorney (*H.VIII*, II,i,15). Sir John Fitzjames (*c.*1470?–1542); as attorney-general conducted Buckingham's trial in 1521; Chief Justice of King's Bench; signed articles impeaching Wolsey in 1526; assisted at trials of More and Fisher. (Thomson)

Lancaster, Duke of. *See* Henry IV; John of Gaunt; John of Lancaster.
Lancaster, Prince John of. *See* John of Lancaster.
Langley, Edmund of. *See* York, Duke of.
Langton, Stephen. *See* Canterbury, Archbishop of.
Leicester, Abbot of (*H.VIII*). Not identified.
Leopold. *See* Austria, Duke of.
Lewis XI (*3H.VI*). Louis XI (1423–1483); King of France; son of Charles VII; prolonged struggle with Burgundy; assisted Warwick and Queen Margaret in support of Henry VI against Edward IV; sometimes called the "bourgeois king."
Lewis, Dauphin of France (*John*). Louis VIII (1187–1226); also called le Lion or Coeur de Lion; son of Philip II; married Blanche of Castile; offered crown of England by rebel barons; invaded England (1216–1217); fought against Albigenses (1215–1219); 12 children.
Lewis, the Dauphin (*H.V*). *See* Dauphin of France (*Henry V*).
Lieutenant of the Tower (*3H.VI*). French and Thomson suggest that Shakespeare combined two historical figures:
  (1) John Tiptoft (or Tibetoft) (1427–1470); 1st Earl of Worcester; Yorkist; English humanist; called "the butcher of England"; appears in IV,vi of the play.
  (2) John Sutton (1401–1487), 6th Baron Dudley; appears in V,vi.

Limoges. *See* Austria, Duke of.

Lincoln, Bishop of (*H.VIII*). John Longland (1476–1547); Bishop of Lincoln; confessor to Henry VIII; Chancellor of Oxford; said to have been first to suggest Henry's divorce from Katherine; lover of architecture.

Lionel, Duke of Antwerp. *See* Clarence, Duke of.

London, Bishop of (*3H.VI*, V,i,45). Thomas Kemp (d.1489); adherent of Somerset but adapted himself to the Yorkist dynasty. (Thomson)

London, Bishop of (*H.VIII*). John Stokesley (1475–1539); created Bishop of London in 1530; tried to enlist foreign support for Henry's divorce of Katherine; christened Elizabeth; opposed translation of Bible into vernacular.

London, Lord Mayor. *See* Lord Mayor of London.

Lord Chamberlain (*H.VIII*). Two men held this office during period covered in *Henry VIII:*

(1) Charles Somerset (1460?–1526), Earl of Worcester; illegitimate son of Henry Beaufort, 3rd Duke of Somerset; responsible for arrangements for Field of the Cloth of Gold; took part in trial of Duke of Buckingham. (Some sources date his death in 1520.)

(2) Sir William Sandys (or Sands); see Sandys, Lord.

(Thomson believes that Shakespeare intended his character to represent Somerset throughout the play.)

Lord Chancellor (*H.VIII*). Three men occupied this office during the period covered in *Henry VIII*:

(1) Sir Thomas More (1478–1535); statesman, author, humanist; friend of Erasmus and Colet; successful lawyer; succeeded Wolsey as Lord Chancellor; 1st layman to hold chancellorship; resigned in 1532; wrote *Utopia;* beheaded; beatified in 1886; canonized in 1935.

(2) Sir Thomas Audley (1488–1544); appointed Chancellor in 1533; presided at trial of Sir Thomas More; tried Anne Bullen (1536); founded Magdalene College, Cambridge.

(3) Thomas Wriothesley; see Garter King-at-Arms.

(It is likely that Shakespeare had More in mind throughout the play.)

Lord Chief Justice (*2H.IV*). Sir William Gascoigne (1350?–1419); one of attorneys representing Bolingbroke during period of his banishment; created Lord Chief Justice in 1400; reputation for fairness and uprightness.

Lord Marshall (*R.II*). *See* Surrey, Duke of (in *Richard II*).

Lord Marshal (*1H.IV*). *See* Mowbray, Thomas (in *1 Henry IV*).

Lord Mayor of London (*1H.VI*). John Coventry, a mercer, held this office in 1425.

Lord Mayor of London (*R.III*). Sir Edmund Shaw (or Shaa) (d.*c.*1487); goldsmith; ardent Yorkist; brother of Doctor Shaw.

(Lord) Mayor of London (*H.VIII*). Thomson identifies this official as Sir Thomas Peacock.

Louis. *See* Lewis.

Lovel, Lord (*R.III*). Francis (1454– ?); Viscount Lovel; staunch adherent of Richard III; delegated to oppose Buckingham and invasion of Richmond in 1485; fought at Bosworth Field; ultimately fled to Yorkshire; possibly died at Stoke in 1487, but another version says that he died in a secret room in his manor in Oxfordshire.

Lovell (*R.III*, IV,iv,518; *H.VIII*). Sir Thomas Lovell (d.1542); Esquire of the Body to Henry VII, whom he supported at Bosworth Field; Treasurer of the Household; Constable of the Tower under Henry VIII; loyal Roman Catholic; his funeral was famous for its splendor.

Lucy, Lady (*R.III,* III,vii,5). Elizabeth Lucy; mistress of Edward IV and mother of his illegitimate son, Arthur Plantagenet.

Lucy, Sir William (*1H.VI*). (d.1466); Sheriff of Warwickshire; Yorkist sympathizer; buried in church at Stratford-on-Avon; his descendant, Sir Thomas Lucy, has sometimes been equated with Justice Shallow in *2 Henry IV* and *The Merry Wives of Windsor* (French). Thomson lists another William Lucy, killed in Battle of Northampton in 1460.

Lymoges. *See* Austria, Duke of.

March, Earl of. *See* Edward IV; Mortimer.

Margaret (*1,2,3H.VI; R.III*). Margaret of Anjou (1430–1482); daughter of René of Anjou; married Henry VI by proxy in 1445; supported Duke of Somerset and opposed Richard Plantagenet, Duke of York; defeated Richard Nevil, Earl of Warwick at St. Albans in 1461; allied herself with Warwick and temporarily restored Henry VI to throne; defeated at Tewkesbury in 1471; after five years in prison, was ransomed by Louis XI. There is no historical basis for her illicit relationship with Suffolk in the plays.

Margaret Plantagenet (*R.III*). (1473–1541); Countess of Salisbury; daughter of George, Duke of Clarence, and Isabel Nevil; last of the Plantagenets; governess to Mary Tudor; executed by order of Henry VIII.

Margery Jourdain. *See* Jourdain, Margery.

Mary Tudor (*H.VIII*). (1516–1558); also known as Mary I and Bloody Mary; Queen of England; daughter of Henry VIII and Katherine of Aragon; succeeded Edward VI in 1553; married Philip II of Spain in 1554; permitted vigorous persecution of Protestants; lost Calais to French in 1558.

Mayor of Coventry (*3H.VI*). John Brett; Mayor of Coventry; deprived of sword of office because of loyalty to Henry VI; subsequently restored to favor.

Mayor of London. *See* Lord Mayor of London.

Mayor of York (*3H.VI*). Thomas Beverley; Mayor of York in 1460 and again in 1471, when Edward IV visited the city.

Melun (*John*). A Count de Melun is mentioned in a treaty of 1194 between France and England. (French)

Mentieth (*1H.IV*). Another title for Mordake (*q.v.*).

Michael, Sir (*1H.IV,* IV,iv). Historians fail to identify this character.

Monmouth, Harry of. *See* Henry V.

Montacute, Lord (*H.VIII,* I,i,217). Sir Henry Pole (1492?–1538); Baron Montacute (or Montague); brother of Reginald Pole (Cardinal and Archbishop of Canterbury); married Joan, daughter of Lord Abergavenny; beheaded for treason.

Montague, Marquess of (*3H.VI*). Sir John Nevil (d.1471); Marquess of Montague and Earl of Northumberland; brother of Richard Nevil, Earl of Warwick, "the Kingmaker"; allied himself with Warwick throughout Wars of the Roses; killed at Battle of Barnet.

Montgomery, Sir John (*3H.VI*). Actually Sir Thomas Montgomery (d.1495); supported Edward IV in Wars of the Roses; one of "knights of the body" to Richard III.

Mordake (*1H.IV*). Murdach (or Murdock) Stewart (d.1425); 2nd Duke of Albany and Earl of Fife; Regent of Scotland during imprisonment of James I in England; executed for treason.

More, Sir Thomas. *See* Lord Chancellor.

Mortimer, Anne. *See* Anne Mortimer.

Mortimer, Edmund (*2H.VI*, II,ii,36ff., IV,ii,144). (1351–1381); 3rd Earl of March; married Philippa, daughter of Lionel of Antwerp, Duke of Clarence; Lieutenant of Ireland; father-in-law of Hotspur.

Mortimer, Edmund (*1H.IV*). Sir Edmund de Mortimer (1376–1409); 2nd son of Edmund (1351–1381) and Philippa; brother of Roger de Mortimer, 4th Earl of March; married daughter of Owen Glendower. Shakespeare and early historians frequently confused him with Edmund de Mortimer (1391–1425), 5th Earl of March (*q.v.*). Occasionally Shakespeare confused Edmund, 5th Earl of March, with his father, Roger the 4th Earl.

Mortimer, Edmund de (*1,2H.VI*). (1391–1425); 5th Earl of March, succeeding to title at age of seven; placed under guard on accession of Henry IV; restored to estates by Henry V in 1413; in 1415 he revealed the conspiracy of Richard Earl of Cambridge, Lord Scroop, and Sir Thomas Grey; Lieutenant of Ireland; died of plague.

Mortimer, Elizabeth. *See* Percy, Lady.

Mortimer, Sir Hugh (*3H.VI*). (d.1460); uncle to Richard Plantagenet, Duke of York; possibly illegitimate; died in Battle of Wakefield.

Mortimer, Sir John (*3H.VI*). (d.1460); uncle to Richard Plantagenet, Duke of York; possibly illegitimate; died in Battle of Wakefield.

Mortimer, Roger de (*2H.VI*, II,ii,37ff., IV,ii,144). (1374–1398); 4th Earl of March; son of Edmund, 3rd Earl; Lieutenant of Ireland; grandfather of Richard Plantagenet, Duke of York; killed fighting in Ireland.

Mortimer of Scotland (*1H.IV*, III,ii,164). George Dunbar (1338–1420); 11th Earl of Dunbar and March; participated in Scottish victory at Chevy Chase (1388); fought with Hotspur at Homildon Hill; warned Henry IV of Percy conspiracy and rescued him from Douglas at Shrewsbury; returned to Scotland in 1409. Because of similarity of his Scottish title (Earl of March) with hereditary title of the Mortimers, Shakespeare calls him "Lord Mortimer of Scotland."

Morton, John. *See* Ely, Bishop of (*R.III*).

Mowbray, Thomas (*R.II*). *See* Norfolk, Duke of.

Mowbray, Thomas (*2H.IV*). (1386–1405); Earl Marshal and 3rd Earl of Nottingham; son of Thomas Mowbray, 1st Duke of Norfolk (see *Richard II*); resenting father's banishment and his own exclusion from title, joined Scroop, the Archbishop of York, in Northumberland Rebellion against Henry IV; captured at Shipton Moor and beheaded.

Murray (*1H.IV*). Thomas Dunbar; 4th Earl of Murray; captured by Hotspur at Homildon Hill.

Nevil, Anne. *See* Anne, Lady.

Nevil, Cicely. *See* York, Duchess of.

Nevil, George. *See* Abergavenny, Lord; York, Archbishop of (*3H.VI*).

Nevil, Isabella. *See* Clarence, Duke of (*3H.VI; R.III*).

Nevil, John. *See* Montague, Marquess of (*3H.VI*).

Nevil, Ralph (*1,2H.IV; H.V*). (1364–1425); 1st Earl of Westmoreland; Warden of Scottish Marches; married (2nd wife) Joan Beaufort, daughter of John of Gaunt and half sister of Henry IV; joined Henry

Bolingbroke against Richard II; rival of the Percies; captured (possibly through betrayal) Archbishop Scroop and Thomas Mowbray at Shipton Moor; historically did not accompany Henry V to France; had 23 children; grandfather of Edward IV and Richard III.

Nevil, Ralph (*3H.VI*). (d.1484); 2nd Earl of Westmoreland; grandson of 1st Earl (above); married Elizabeth Percy, widow of John Clifford and daughter of Hotspur. (Thomson)

Nevil, Richard (*2H.VI*). (1400–1460); 1st Earl of Salisbury; son of Ralph Nevil, 1st Earl of Westmoreland, by Joan Beaufort; married Alice Montacute, daughter of Thomas de Montacute, 4th Earl of Salisbury; brother-in-law of Richard Plantagenet, Duke of York; assisted in arrest of Humphrey, Duke of Gloucester; supported York's claim to throne; Lord Chamberlain; father of Richard Nevil "the Kingmaker"; captured at Wakefield and beheaded at Pomfret (Pontefract).

Nevil, Richard (*2,3H.VI; R.III*). (1428–1471); Earl of Warwick and Salisbury, "the Kingmaker"; son of Richard, 1st Earl of Salisbury; married Anne, daughter of Richard Beauchamp, Earl of Warwick; aided Yorkists at First Battle of St. Albans (1455); captured Henry VI at Northampton (1460); defeated Queen Margaret at Second Battle of St. Albans (1461); proclaimed Edward IV as King; took offense while on mission to France and instigated revolt against Edward IV in Yorkshire; joined Queen Margaret and Lancastrians in restoring Henry VI in 1470; father-in-law of George, Duke of Clarence, and of Richard III; defeated and killed at Barnet.

Nobleman, A (*3H.VI*, III,ii). Sir James Harrington, who captured Henry VI at Waddington Hall. (French)

Noblemen, Two (*H.VIII*, V,v). Stage direction calls for "two Noblemen bearing great standing bowls for the christening gifts." Thomson identifies them as:

(1) Sir Robert Radcliffe (or Ratcliffe) (1482–1542); 1st Earl of Sussex, 1st Viscount Fitzwalter; and

(2) Henry Somerset (1499–1548); 2nd Earl of Worcester.

Noblemen, Four (*H.VIII*, V,v). Stage direction calls for "four Noblemen bearing a canopy." Thomson lists them as:

(1) George Lord Rochford (d.1536); son of Thomas Bullen and brother of Anne Bullen; Warden of the Cinque Ports; executed for high treason and incest.

(2) Sir John Hussey (d.1537); Comptroller of household of Henry VII; Chief Butler of England; Chamberlain to Princess Mary Tudor; executed in Northern uprising of 1536 ("the Pilgrimage of Grace").

(3) William Howard (1510–1573); 1st Baron Howard of Effingham; convicted of treason for protecting his niece, Katherine Howard (consort of Henry VIII), but pardoned; defended London against Sir Thomas Wyatt; Lord Chamberlain; Privy Seal.

(4) Thomas Howard (1473–1554); see Surrey, Earl of.

Norbery, Sir John (*R.II*). Companion of Henry Bolingbroke; Governor of Guisnes; Treasurer of the Exchequer. (Thomson)

Norfolk, Duchess of (*H.VIII*). Agnes; 2nd wife and widow of Thomas Howard, Earl of Surrey and 2nd Duke of Norfolk (Howard line).

Norfolk, Duke of (*R.II; 2H.IV*). Thomas Mowbray (1366–1399); 12th Baron Mowbray and 1st Duke of Norfolk; son of John III de Mowbray; summoned to parliament as Earl to Nottingham; Marshal of England;

Captain of Calais (1391); emissary to arrange Richard II's marriage with Isabella of France; possibly responsible for death of Thomas of Woodstock, Duke of Gloucester; betrayed by Henry Bolingbroke; banished by Richard II; died at Venice.

Norfolk, Duke of (*3H.VI*). John Mowbray (1415–1461); 3rd Duke of Norfolk, and Earl Marshal of England; delayed joining Yorkist cause but fought gallantly at Towton. (Thomson)
French argues that this character was John Mowbray (1444–1476); 4th Duke of Norfolk and son of the 3rd Duke; last of the Mowbray line.

Norfolk, Duke of (*R.III*). John Howard (1430?–1485); 1st Duke of Norfolk (Howard line), also known as "Jack of Norfolk"; supported Yorkists; created Earl Marshal of England; legate to France and Flanders; Lord Admiral; led vanguard of archers at Bosworth Field, where he was killed; attainted by Henry VII.

Norfolk, Duke of (*H.VIII*). Thomas Howard (1443–1524); Earl of Surrey (see *Richard III*) and 2nd Duke of Norfolk (Howard line); supported Edward IV and fought for Richard III at Bosworth Field, where he was wounded and captured; after three years in the Tower, fought for Henry VII against the Scots; negotiated marriage between Princess Margaret (daughter of Henry VII) and James IV of Scotland; Privy Councilor; rival of Wolsey; as Lord High Steward passed judgment on Buckingham in 1521; common ancestor of all Howards of main stock. (Appears as Earl of Surrey in *Richard III*.)

Northampton, Sheriff of. *See* Sheriff of Northampton.

Northumberland, Earl of (*R.II*; 1,2H.IV). Henry Percy (1342–1408); 1st Earl of Northumberland; Earl Marshal of England; supported Richard II in 1397 but joined Bolingbroke in 1399; revolted with his eldest son (Hotspur) in 1403; submitted to Henry IV in 1404; joined conspiracy of Glendower and Sir Edmund de Mortimer; killed at Bramham Moor.

Northumberland, Earl of (*3H.VI*, I,i,4 and V,vii,8). Henry Percy (1394–1455); 2nd Earl of Northumberland; son of Hotspur; restored to title and estates by Henry V; campaigned against the Scots; married Eleanor Nevil, daughter of Ralph Nevil, 1st Earl of Westmoreland; joined Lancastrians; killed in first Battle of St. Albans.

Northumberland, Earl of (the active character in *3H.VI*; *R.III*, I,iii, 187). Henry Percy (1421–1461); 3rd Earl of Northumberland; son of 2nd Earl and grandson of Hotspur; invaded Scotland in 1448; defeated Richard Plantagenet, Duke of York, at Wakefield in 1460; led van of Lancastrian army at Towton, where he died.

Northumberland, Earl of (R.III, V,iii,68). Henry Percy (1446–1489); 4th Earl of Northumberland; great-grandson of Hotspur; professed loyalty to Richard III but failed to bring troops into Battle at Bosworth Field; gained favor of Henry VII; killed in a riot when he attempted to enforce the subsidy of the King.

Northumberland, Earl of (*H.VIII*, IV,ii,12). Henry Algernon Percy (*c.*1502–1537); 6th Earl of Northumberland; page to Wolsey; commissioned to arrest Wolsey in 1530; sat on trial of Anne Bullen, with whom he had fallen in love as a boy, but became ill and had to retire; died without issue.

Northumberland, Lady (*2H.IV*). Maud, 2nd wife of Northumberland (1342–1408); not the mother of Hotspur.

Nottingham, Earl of. *See* Mowbray, Thomas (1386–1405).

Old Shepherd (*1H.VI*). *See* Darc, Jacques.
Oldcastle, Sir John (*1H.IV*). (1377–1417); Baron Cobham; friend of Henry V; commanded troops in France; arrested and convicted of heresy in 1413; escaped; participated in Lollard movement; captured, hanged, and burned for heresy and treachery. Shakespeare adapted him as a character and used his name until his widow's descendants forced the playwright to substitute the name of Sir John Falstaff.
Orleans, Bastard of (*1H.VI*). John (1403?–1468); Count of Dunois and Bastard of Orleans; illegitimate son of Louis, Duke of Orleans; defended city of Orleans until Joan of Arc lifted the siege; conquered Normandy and Guienne from English; legitimized in 1439.
Orleans, Duke of (*H.V*). Charles D'Angoulême (1391–1465); Duke of Orleans; nephew of Charles VI of France; joint commander at Agincourt; captured and held prisoner in England for some 25 years; married Isabella, widow of Richard II, in 1406; author of rondels and ballads; father of Louis XII of France, by 3rd wife, Mary of Cleves.
Orleans, Duke of (*H.VIII*, **II,iv,174**). Charles (1522–1545); Duke of Orleans; 3rd son of Francis I of France; grandson of Louis XII of France; commanded armies in Low Countries; at one time suggested as husband for Princess Mary Tudor.
Oxford, Earl of (*R.II*, **V,vi,8**). Aubrey de Vere (1340–1400); 10th Earl of Oxford; secured favor under Richard II; failed to gain favor under Henry IV. Historically had no part in the rebellion. First Folio reads Spencer in place of Oxford in this line (see Spencer).
Oxford, Earl of (*3H.VI; R.III*). John de Vere (1443–1513); 13th Earl of Oxford; suspected of conspiring with Lancastrians, he fled to France in 1469; returned with Warwick to restore Henry VI in 1470; routed Hastings at Barnet; fled to France, returned; captured in Cornwall in 1473; escaped, joined Henry Richmond, and commanded one wing of Richmond's army at Bosworth Field; enjoyed favor of Henry VII.

Pace, Doctor (*H.VIII*). Richard Pace (1482–1536); private secretary to Henry VIII; succeeded John Colet as Dean of St. Paul's; followed in secretaryship by Stephen Gardiner (see Winchester, Bishop of).
Page, A (*R.III*). Probably John Green, an esquire of the body to Richard III; procured Tyrrel to direct assassination of two sons of Edward IV; reported to have been "walled up alive" by order of Henry VII. (French)
Pandulf. *See* Pandulph.
Pandulph, Cardinal (*John*). (d.1226); papal legate to England by commission of Pope Innocent III; excommunicated King John in 1211; received John's submission (1213); Bishop of Norwich; arrogantly powerful during reign of Henry III; recalled in 1221 at insistence of Hubert de Burgh and Stephen Langton; died in Rome; buried in Norwich; historically not a cardinal, although Thomson notes that he was appointed "Cardinal of the Twelve Apostles" in 1182.
Paris, Governor of (*1H.VI*). French and Thomson suggest that this official was John of Luxembourg.
Patience (*H.VIII*). French and Thomson suggest that Shakespeare was characterizing Mary de Salucci, member of an illustrious Spanish family, in whose arms Katherine of Aragon died. R. A. Foakes says, "Katherine's maid Patience is wholly an invention."
Peck, Gilbert (*H.VIII*). Sir Gilbert Peck, chancellor to the Duke of

Buckingham and arrested with him; Shakespeare's sources gave his name as "Perke"; records of the trial read "Robert Gilbert, Clerk." J. Dover Wilson accepts "Parke."

Pembroke, Earl of (*John*). William Marshal (d.1219); 1st Earl of Pembroke and Strigul; crusader; one of regents during absence of Richard I; commanded Henry III's army against Louis at Battle of Lincoln (1217).

Pembroke, Earl of (*3H.VI*). William Herbert (d.1469); 1st Earl of Pembroke (Herbert line); grandson of Davy Gam (see *Henry V*); ardent Yorkist; appointed guardian of young Henry Richmond; quarreled with Earl of Warwick; captured and beheaded by Lancastrians at Northampton.

Pembroke, Earl of (*R.III*, IV,v,14; V,iii,29). Jasper Tudor (1431?–1495); Earl of Pembroke and Duke of Bedford; 2nd son of Owen Tudor and Katherine (widow of Henry V); half brother of Henry VI; fought with Lancastrians at St. Albans (1455); Henry Richmond born in his residence; helped Warwick restore Henry VI in 1470; companion and guardian of Henry Richmond in Brittany; married Katherine Woodville, widow of Henry Stafford, 2nd Duke of Buckingham, and sister of Elizabeth Woodville (consort of Edward IV).

Penker, Friar (*R.III*). A provincial of the Augustinian Friars; popular preacher during period of Richard III.

Percy, Henry (*R.II; 1,2H.IV*). (1364–1403); Hotspur; son of Henry Percy, 1st Earl of Northumberland; engaged in active military service at age of 14; border warfare; campaigned in France; in folk ballads a hero at Otterburn and Chevy Chase; fought against Scots; defeated Douglas; captured by Sir John Montgomery and ransomed (Richard II contributing £3000); Warden of Carlisle and the West March; supported Bolingbroke in 1399; received numerous appointments from Henry IV; campaigned aggressively for Henry IV but could not collect arrears in pay; during quarrel over Scottish prisoners and ransom of Hotspur's brother-in-law, Henry IV denounced him as traitor and struck him; formed plot to proclaim Edmund Mortimer as king; killed at Shrewsbury; disinterred; his head fixed on one of the gates of York.

Percy, Henry. *See* Northumberland, Earl of.

Percy, Lady (*1,2H.IV*). Elizabeth Mortimer (d.1444); daughter of Edmund Mortimer (1351–1381), 3rd Earl of March; sister of Sir Edmund Mortimer (1376–1409); married Henry Percy (Hotspur); mother of Henry Percy (1394–1455), 2nd Earl of Northumberland; subsequently married Thomas Lord Camoys. Some historians refer to her as Eleanor; Shakespeare calls her Kate.

Percy, Thomas. *See* Worcester, Earl of.

Perke. *See* Peck, Gilbert.

Perkes, Clement (*2H.IV*). Possibly Clement Purchase (or Perkis). A family by this name lived at Stinchcombe Hill, near Dursley in Gloucestershire.

Peter (*2H.VI*). In history Peter was John David, servant or apprentice of William Catur, armorer (see Horner, Thomas); having accused his master of treason, David killed Catur in personal combat at Smithfield in 1446; later confessed that his charge against Catur was false.

Peter of Pomfret (*John*). Historically, a hermit who enjoyed great popularity with the common people; located at Pomfret or Wakefield; either inspired with spirit of prophecy or notably skilled in "art Magike"; more a deluder of the people than an instrument of Satan; hanged, together with his son, by the King's order; people interpreted John's yielding of crown to Pandulph as fulfillment of Peter's prophecy.

Philip, King of France (*John*). Philip II (1165–1223); or Philip Augustus; King of France; son of Louis VII and Adele of Champagne; accompanied Richard Coeur-de-Lion on 3rd Crusade but quarreled with him; seized French provinces from John; famous as a builder; granted first charter to University of Paris (1200).

Philip the Bastard. *See* Faulconbridge, Philip.

Pierce of Exton (*R.II*). Mentioned in Holinshed as "sir Piers of Exton"; probably a near relation of Sir Nicholas Exton, Sheriff of London in 1385.

Plantagenet, Richard. *See* first name for entry.

Ponton de Santrailles (*1H.VI*). French commander who captured Talbot as Pataye in 1429; was captured and exchanged for Talbot in 1431.

Pope (*John*). Innocent III (1161–1216); real name: Giovanni Lotario de' Con'ti; brought papal power to its highest point; urged 4th Crusade; warred against the Albigenses; opposed King John and placed England under interdict (1208); crowned Frederick II of Sicily; presided over Fourth Lateran Council (1215).

Pope (*1H.VI*). Eugenius IV (1383–1447; Pope 1431–1447); real name: Gabriele Condolmieri (or Condulmer); resided for ten years in Florence; deposed by Council of Basel (1439), which established Felix V, last of antipopes.

Pope (time of *H.VIII*). Clement VII (1478–1534; Pope 1523–1534); real name: Giulio de' Medici; natural son of Giuliano de' Medici; entered league against Emperor Charles V; quarreled with England and refused to sanction Henry VIII's divorce from Katherine of Aragon.

Prince Hal. *See* Henry V.

Prince Henry. *See* Henry III; also Henry V.

Prince John. *See* John of Lancaster.

Queen to Richard II (*R.II*). *See* Isabella.

Quoint, Francis (*R.II*). Possibly confused with Francis Point; a descendant of the Point family in Gloucestershire was Sheriff of the County during reign of Richard II. (Thomson)

Rambures (*H.V*). (d.1415); David, Seigneur de Ramouxes, Master of the Crossbows; killed at Agincourt. (French)

Ramston (*R.II*). Historically, Sir John Ramston; Warden of the Tower during Richard II's confinement; Admiral of the Fleet; drowned in the Thames. (Thomson)

Ratcliff, Sir Richard (*R.III*). (d.1485); son of Sir Thomas Ratcliff (or Ratcliffe); knighted at Tewkesbury by Edward IV; one of Richard III's chief advisers; executed Hastings, Rivers, Grey, and Vaughan; died at Bosworth Field.

Recorder, A (*R.III*, III,vii,30). Thomas Fitzwilliam, "a sad man and an honest, which had newly come to the office" in June, 1483.

Reignier (*1H.VI*). René I (1409–1480); called René the Good; Duke of Anjou and Lorraine, titular King of Naples; retired to Provence in 1442; his court became center of poets and artists; author of poems and romances; father of Margaret of Anjou, Queen of Henry VI.

Rice ap Thomas (*R.III*, IV,v,15). Rice or (Rhys) ap Thomas (1449–

1525); owned property in Carmethen, Wales; aided Henry Richmond at Bosworth Field and was knighted there.

Richard I (*John*). Richard Coeur-de-Lion (or Lion-Hearted) (1157–1199); King of England; 3rd son of Henry II; rebelled against his father; joined Philip II of France on 3rd Crusade; recaptured Jaffa from Saladin (1192); captured in Austria and held for ransom; married Berengaria of Navarre; wounded by arrow at Limoges and died.

Richard II (*R.II; 1,2H.IV; 1,3H.VI; R.III*). Richard of Bordeaux (1367–1400); son of Edward the Black Prince and Joan "the Fair Maid of Kent"; married (1) Anne of Bohemia (1366–1394) and (2) Isabella of France (1389–1409); no legitimate issue; suppressed Wat Tyler's Rebellion in 1381; banished Bolingbroke and Mowbray in 1398; deposed 1399; imprisoned and possibly murdered.

Richard III (*2,3H.VI; R.III; H.VIII*). Richard Crouchback (1452–1485); Duke of Gloucester, King of England; son of Richard Plantagenet, Duke of York; brother of Edward IV; married Anne Nevil, daughter of Earl of Warwick; assumed crown in 1483; blamed for death of his brother George, Duke of Clarence; announced deaths of Edward V and Richard, Duke of York; defeated and killed at Bosworth Field; despite his cruelty, violence, and ruthlessness, Richard was intelligent, active, and courageous; many historians believe descriptions of his physical deformity to be exaggerated.

Richard, Duke of Gloucester. *See Richard III.*

Richard, Duke of York. *See* York, Duke of.

Richard, Earl of Cambridge. *See* Cambridge, Earl of.

Richard Plantagenet. *See* Faulconbridge, Philip; Richard III; York, Duke of.

Richmond, Countess of (*R.III*). Margaret Beaufort (1443–1509); Countess of Richmond and Derby; daughter of John Beaufort, 1st Duke of Somerset, and heiress of John of Gaunt; in 1455 married Edmund Tudor, Earl of Richmond; mother of Henry Richmond (Henry VII); married (2) Henry Stafford, son of Duke of Buckingham; married (3) Thomas Stanley, 1st Earl of Derby, in 1482; patron of education; endowed professorships at Oxford and Cambridge; helped Caxton and Wynkyn de Worde.

Richmond, Earl of. *See* Henry VII.

Richmond, Henry. *See* Henry VII.

Rivers, Lord (*3H.VI; R.III*). Anthony Woodville (1442?–1483); 2nd Earl Rivers; brother of Elizabeth, consort of Edward IV; married Elizabeth, daughter of Lord Scales; grandson of John of Lancaster; enjoyed favor of Edward IV; fought for Edward at Barnet; incurred hatred of Richard III; beheaded at Pomfret (Pontefract).

Rochester, Bishop of (*H.VIII*). John Fisher (1459–1535); Roman Catholic churchman and martyr; confessor to Countess of Richmond; professor of divinity at Cambridge; Bishop of Rochester (1504); opponent of Luther and church reform; refused to acknowledge Henry VIII as head of church under Act of Supremacy; beheaded; canonized (1935).

Rochford, Viscount. *See* Bullen, Sir Thomas.

Ross, Lord (*R.II*). William de Ross (d.1414); 7th Baron Ross; M.P. 1394–1413; Lord Treasurer under Henry IV.

Rotherham, Thomas (*R.III*). (1423–1500); also known as Thomas Scott; Bishop of Rochester (1468); Bishop of Lincoln (1471); Chancellor of England; favorite of Elizabeth Woodville (Queen of Edward IV); Archbishop of York (1480); cardinal; removed from chancellorship by Richard III; withdrew to Oxford after accession of Henry VII.

Rutland, Earl of. *See* York, Duke of. (*R.II*)

Rutland, Earl of (*3H.VI; R.III*). *See* Edmund, Earl of Rutland.

Rutland, Tutor to. *See* Tutor to Rutland.

Saint Asaph, Bishop of (*H.VIII*). Henry Standish (d.1535); Franciscan friar; court preacher to Henry VIII; opposed Colet and Erasmus; consecrated Bishop of St. Asaph by Warham in 1518; one of Queen Katherine's counsel in divorce trial; renounced Roman jurisdiction after Cranmer's consecration as archbishop.

Salisbury, Earl of (*John*). William Longsword (d.1226); also called William de Longespee; 3rd Earl of Salisbury; illegitimate son of Henry II; Warden of Cinque Ports and of Welsh Marches; faithfully supported King Henry III; Holinshed calls him Nicholas.

Salisbury, Earl of (*R.II*). John de Montacute (1350?–1400); 3rd Earl of Salisbury (Montacute line); Lollard; deputy marshal of England; joined conspiracy against Henry IV; beheaded.

Salisbury, Earl of (*H.V; 1H.VI*). Thomas de Montacute (1388–1428); 4th Earl of Salisbury; son of John, 3rd Earl, who was beheaded in 1400 (see *Richard II*); married Eleanor Holland, daughter of 2nd Earl of Kent; distinguished military record in France and at Agincourt; killed during siege of Orleans.

Salisbury, Earl of (*2H.VI*). *See* Nevil, Richard (1400–1460).

Sands. *See* Sandys.

Sandys, Lord (*H.VIII*). Sir William Sandys (d.1540); distinguished military service in France under Henry VII and Henry VIII; present at Field of the Cloth of Gold; succeeded Charles Somerset, Earl of Worcester, as Lord Chamberlain; took part in trial of Anne Bullen; died at Calais.

Saunder Simpcox. *See* Simpcox, Saunder.

Say, Lord (*2H.VI*). James Fiennes (d.1450); Lord Say; campaigned in France with Henry V; Sheriff of Kent; Constable of Dover and Warden of the Cinque Ports; supported Suffolk; Lord Treasurer in 1449, dismissed by Parliament; Lord Scales surrendered him to Cade's rebels, who executed him.

Scales, Lord (*1,2,3H.VI*). Thomas (*c.*1399–1460); 7th Baron Scales; campaigned with Henry V in France; served under Talbot and Fastolfe; captured at Pataye; ransomed and continued to serve with John of Lancaster and Duke of Somerset; resisted Cade Rebellion; defended Tower against Yorkists until Salisbury compelled him to surrender; killed by London boatmen as he was trying to escape.

Scroop, Cousin (*1H.IV*, IV,iv,3). Thomson identifies this character as William Scroop, Earl of Wiltshire, (*q.v.*) who was executed at Bristol in 1399. Why or how the Archbishop is sending him a communication at this date is not clear.

Scroop, Lord (*H.V*). Henry (1376?–1415); 3rd Baron Scroop of Masham; envoy to France; Treasurer of England (1410–1411); joined Richard Earl of Cambridge and Sir Thomas Grey in conspiracy against Henry V; executed at Southampton.

Scroop, Richard. *See* York, Archbishop of.

Scroop, Sir Stephen (*R.II*). (d.1408); brother of William Scroop, Earl of Wiltshire; loyal to Richard II until his surrender at Flint Castle; Deputy-Lieutenant of Ireland under Henry IV; died of plague; his widow married Sir John Fastolfe.

Scrope. *See* Scroop.

Secretaries to Wolsey (*H.VIII*). (1) Richard Pace, *q.v.* (2) William Burbank, Archdeacon of Carlisle. (Thomson)

Seely, Sir Bennet (*R.II*, V,vi,14). Historians fail to agree on identification of this character.

Seymour, Lord (*R.II*, II,iii,55). Richard de St. Maur; 5th Baron Seymour; M.P. 1380–1400.

Shaw, Doctor (*R.III*). John (or sometimes, Ralph) Shaw (d.1484); brother of Sir Edmund Shaw, Lord Mayor of London; one-time chaplain to Edward IV; preached sermon in 1483 questioning validity of Edward's marriage to Elizabeth Woodville and implying bastardy of Edward IV and George, Duke of Clarence.

Shepherd, Old. *See* Darc, Jacques.

Sheriff of London (*2H.VI*, II,iv). John Sutton and William Wetynghale were Sheriffs of London at this time. One of them would have escorted the Duchess of Gloucester. (Thomson)

Sheriff of Northampton (*John*). Sir Simon de Pateshall (d.1217?); Sheriff during part of reigns of Richard I and King John.

Sheriff of Wiltshire (*R.III*). Henry Long (d.1490); three times sheriff of the county. (Thomson)

Sheriff of Yorkshire (*2H.IV*, IV,iv,99). Sir Thomas de Rokeby (d.1418); M.P. for Yorkshire; two times sheriff of county; loyal to Henry IV in opposing the Percies. (Thomson)

Shirley (*1H.IV*, V,iv,41). Various editors identify this character as Sir Hugh Shirley, Master of the Hawks to Henry IV.

Shore, Jane (*R.III*). (1445?–1527); daughter of Thomas Wainstead (or Warnstead), a London mercer; married William Shore, goldsmith; became mistress of Edward IV (1470–1483); subsequently mistress of Marquis of Dorset; persecuted by Richard III. Sir Thomas More praised her influence on Edward.

Shrieve of Yorkshire. *See* Sheriff of Yorkshire.

Simpcox, Saunder (*2H.VI*). The names of this character and his wife are fictitious, but the incident in which they figure is based on a similar one that historians describe as taking place at St. Albans during reign of Henry VI.

Shrewsbury, Earl of. *See* Talbot.

Skogan (*2H.IV*, III,ii,33). No certain identification; Hardin Craig and J. Dover Wilson mention John Skogan (or Scoggan), who flourished *c.*1480 and was court jester for Edward IV. Professor Wilson also notes that Henry Scogan (d.1407), friend of Chaucer and tutor to sons of Henry IV, once addressed a ballad to Prince Hal and his brother.

Somerset, Duke of (*1H.VI*). John Beaufort (1403–1444); 3rd Earl and 1st Duke of Somerset; grandson of John of Gaunt and Katherine Swynford; served with distinction in France during reign of Henry VI; his only child was Margaret Beaufort, Countess of Richmond and Derby, mother of Henry VII.

Somerset, Duke of (*2H.VI*; *3H.VI*, I,i,18, V,i,73, and V,vii,5). Edmund Beaufort (? –1455); 2nd Duke of Somerset and Earl of Dorset; brother of John, 1st Duke; campaigned successfully in France; captured Harfleur in 1440; married Alianor, daughter of Richard Beauchamp, Earl of Warwick; bitter enemy of Richard Plantagenet, Duke of York; killed at first Battle of St. Albans; first nobleman to die in Wars of the Roses.

Somerset, Duke of (active character in *3H.VI*). History offers two possibilities:

(1) Henry Beaufort (1436–1464); 3rd Duke of Somerset; son of Edmund, 2nd Duke; supported Lancastrians in France, at Wakefield, and at second Battle of St. Albans (1461); submitted to Edward IV but subsequently deserted to Queen Margaret; executed on field after Battle of Hexham.

(2) Edmund Beaufort (1438–1471); called the 4th Duke of Somerset; commanded Lancastrian archers at Barnet (1471); commanded part of Margaret's army at Tewkesbury; captured and beheaded by order of Edward IV.

Of these two figures French favors Edmund; Thomson favors Henry.

Somerville, Sir John (*3H.VI*). In history Sir Thomas Somervile (d. 1500); member of a Gloucestershire family. (French)

Southwell, John (*2H.VI*). Thomas Southwell, priest and Canon of St. Stephen's in Westminster; arrested but died in Tower before his appointed execution. (French, who cites Hall)

Spain, King of (*John*, II,i,423). Alfonso VIII (sometimes IX) of Castile (d.1214); married Eleanor, daughter of Henry II and sister of King John; defeated Moors at Navas de Tolosa (1212); father of Blanche, consort of Louis VIII of France.

Spencer (*R.II*, V,vi,8). Thomas Despenser (1373–1400); supported Richard II; involved in death of Thomas of Woodstock, Duke of Gloucester; conspired against Henry IV; beheaded.
(Quarto edition of the play lists Oxford, *q.v.* The Folio reads "Spencer.")

Stafford, Humphrey (*2,3H.VI*). *See* Buckingham, Duke of.

Stafford, Sir Humphrey (*2H.VI*). (d. 1450); Sheriff of Gloucestershire; Governor of Calais; killed by Cade's rebels. (Do not confuse with Humphrey Stafford, 1st Duke of Buckingham.)

Stafford, Lord of (*1H.IV*, V,iii,7; *2H.IV*, I,i,18). Edmund (d.1403); 5th Earl of Stafford; married Anne, daughter of Thomas of Woodstock, Duke of Gloucester; killed at Shrewsbury.

Stafford, Lord (*3H.VI*, I,i,7ff.). Humphrey Stafford (d.1455); eldest surviving son of Humphrey, 1st Duke of Buckingham; married Margaret Beaufort, daughter of Edmund, 2nd Duke of Somerset; fatally wounded in first Battle of St. Albans.

Stafford, Lord (appears in *3H.VI*, IV,i). Sir Humphrey Stafford (1439–1469); Lord Stafford and Earl of Devon; commissioned to oppose Robin of Redesdale; quarreled with Earl of Pembroke and withdrew his forces; executed.

Stafford, William (*2H.VI*). Brother of Sir Humphrey Stafford who died in 1450; slain by Cade's rebels (1450).

Stanley, George (*R.III*). (d.1497); eldest son of Thomas Stanley, 1st Earl of Derby; left as hostage with Richard III prior to Battle of Bosworth Field; fought gallantly at Stoke.

Stanley, Sir John (*2H.VI*). In history, Sir Thomas Stanley (d.1458–1459); Governor of Isle of Man; Lieutenant Governor of Ireland; Lord Chamberlain (1455). The misidentification occurs in two of Shakespeare's sources.

Stanley, Lord (*R.III*). Thomas Stanley (1435–1504); 2nd Baron Stanley and 1st Earl of Derby; married: (1) Eleanor Nevil, sister of Earl of Warwick "the Kingmaker," and (2) Margaret Beaufort, Countess of Richmond; fought with Lancastrians at Northampton but succeeded in winning favor of Edward IV; stepfather of Henry Richmond (Henry VII); maintained neutrality at Bosworth Field; placed crown on Henry Richmond's head; Lord High Steward of England.

Stanley, Sir William (*3H.VI; R.III*, IV,v,13). (1435–1495); brother of Thomas, 1st Earl of Derby; joined Yorkists and received appointments from Edward IV; deserted Richard III to support Henry Richmond; his timely reinforcement of Richmond at Battle of Bosworth Field turned tide of battle; joined Perkin Warbeck conspiracy; beheaded for high treason on Tower Hill.

Stokesley, John. *See* London, Bishop of.

Suffolk (*H.V*, IV,vi,10ff.). Michael de la Pole (1394–1415); 3rd Earl of Suffolk; served at siege of Harfleur; fought bravely at Agincourt, where he died.

Suffolk (*1,2H.VI*). William de la Pole (1396–1450); 4th Earl and 1st Duke of Suffolk and Earl of Pembroke; brother of 3rd Earl; served under Henry V and John of Lancaster in France; captured by Joan of Arc in 1429; opposed Humphrey, Duke of Gloucester; negotiated marriage of Henry VI and Margaret of Anjou, serving as Henry's proxy; supported Duke of Somerset against Richard Plantagenet, Duke of York; banished by Henry VI; seized aboard ship off Dover and beheaded.

Suffolk, Duke of (*H.VIII*). Charles Brandon (d.1545); 1st Duke of Suffolk; son of Sir William Brandon (see *Richard III*); favorite of Henry VIII; present at Field of Cloth of Gold; supported Henry's divorce from Katherine of Aragon; defied Wolsey; attended christening of Elizabeth.

Surrey (*R.II*). Thomas Holland (1374–1400); 3rd Earl of Kent and Duke of Surrey; half brother of Richard II; degraded from dukedom in 1399; beheaded for conspiring against Henry IV.

Surrey (*2H.IV*). Thomas Fitzalan (1381–1415); 11th Earl of Arundel and 5th Earl of Surrey; campaigned in France; Lord Treasurer under Henry V; Warden of the Cinque Ports; died of dysentery.

Surrey (*R.III*). Thomas Howard (1443–1524); see Norfolk, Duke of.

Surrey, Earl of (*H.VIII*). Thomas Howard (1473–1554); Earl of Surrey and 3rd Duke of Norfolk; son of Thomas Howard (1443–1524); in 1495 married Anne, daughter of Edward IV and sister of Elizabeth of York (consort to Henry VII); after Anne's death married Elizabeth Stafford, daughter of Duke of Buckingham; enemy of Wolsey; opposed Cromwell; Lord High Admiral; uncle of Anne Bullen and of Katherine Howard; father of the poet, Henry Howard, Earl of Surrey.

Surveyor to Duke of Buckingham (*H.VIII*). Charles Knyvet (or Knevet); onetime steward to Duke of Buckingham; possibly a relation of the Duke. (Thomson)

Talbot, Gilbert (*H.V*, IV,iii,54). (1383–1419); elder brother of John Talbot, 1st Earl of Shrewsbury; fought against Owen Glendower; died at Rouen.

Talbot, Sir Gilbert (*R.III*, IV,v,13). (d.1517); joined Henry Richmond at Newport; fought gallantly at Bosworth Field; K.G.; Governor of Calais.

Talbot, John (*1H.VI*). (1388?–1453); 1st Earl of Shrewsbury; English soldier; with Sir John Oldcastle imprisoned on suspicion of Lollardy; released and appointed Lord Lieutenant of Ireland; fought with distinction in France; defeated and captured by Joan of Arc in 1429; subsequently exchanged and campaigned successfully until slain in Battle of Castillon.

Talbot, John (*1H.VI*). (d.1453); son of John, 1st Earl of Shrewsbury; grandson of Richard Beauchamp, Earl of Warwick; died at Castillon.

Thomas, Duke of Clarence. *See* Clarence, Duke of.

Thomas of Woodstock (*R.II, passim; 2H.VI,* **II,ii,16**). (1355–1397); Duke of Gloucester; youngest surviving son of Edward III and Philippa of Hainaut; married Eleanor de Bohun; Constable of England; campaigned in France; helped suppress Essex uprising in 1381; involved in political intrigues; opposed Richard II's marriage to Isabella; arrested at Pleshy (Plashy) and deported to Calais, where he was probably murdered; his death inspired quarrel between Bolingbroke and Mowbray and damaged reputation of Richard II.

Tressel (*R.III*). Possibly a misprint for Trussel; Sir William Trussel was onetime Sheriff of Warwickshire; he or his brother Edmund may be the character in the play. (French)

Tutor to Rutland (*3H.VI*). Robert Aspall; priest, chaplain, and schoolmaster; presumably from a Norfolk family.

Tyrrel, Sir James (*R.III*). (d.1502); son of Sir William Tyrrel of Suffolk; Yorkist; knighted after Battle of Tewkesbury; M.P. in 1477; acted as agent for murder of the two sons of Edward IV; received general pardon in 1486; beheaded for high treason sixteen years later.

Umfrevile, Sir John (*2H.IV,* **I,i,34**). J. Dover Wilson and Thomson are unable to identify a historical character by this name; French mentions a Sir Robert Umfrevile.

Urswick, Christopher (*R.III*). (1448–1522); ecclesiastic; confessor to Countess of Richmond; chaplain to Henry Richmond; promoted marriage of Henry and Elizabeth of York; friend of Erasmus.

Vaughan, Sir Thomas (*R.III*). (d.1483); Yorkist; closely allied with Edward IV; appointed chamberlain and counselor to Prince of Wales (Edward V); arrested by Richard III while escorting the Prince to London; summarily executed with Grey and Rivers.

Vaux, Sir Nicholas (*H.VIII*). (d. 1523); son of Sir William Vaux (see *2 Henry VI*); page to Countess of Richmond; gained favor of Henry VII; Governor of Guisnes under Henry VIII.

Vaux (William) (*2H.VI*). (d.1471); Lancastrian; returned with Queen Margaret in 1471; died in Battle of Tewkesbury.

Vere, Lord Aubrey (*3H.VI,* **III,iii,102**). (d.1462); eldest son of John de Vere, 12th Earl of Oxford; ardent Lancastrian; married daughter of 1st Duke of Buckingham; executed for treason on Tower Hill.

Vernon, Sir Richard (*1H.IV*). (d.1403); Baron Shipbrook; joined rebellion against Henry IV; captured at Shrewsbury and executed shortly afterwards.

Vernon (*1H.VI, II,iv*). Sir Richard Vernon (d.1452); Speaker of House of Commons; knight of the shire for Derby in 1433.

Visor, William (*2H.IV*). Possibly identified as William Vizard of Woncote, a suburb of Dursley, in Gloucestershire.

Walter Lord Ferres (*R.III*, V,v,13). Sir Walter Devereux (d.1485); member of House of Lords in 1461; died at Bosworth Field.

Warham, William. *See* Canterbury, Archbishop of.

Warwick, Earl of (*2H.IV; H.V; 1H.VI*). Richard de Beauchamp (1382–1439); Earl of Warwick; fought against Glendower and the Percies; suppressed Lollards in 1414; campaigned in France with Henry V; supervised education of Henry VI; Lieutenant of France and Normandy. (Shakespeare's reference to him as "cousin Nevil" is an error, presumably through confusion with Richard Nevil, Earl of Warwick and Salisbury. Note that Nevil did not succeed to the title of Warwick until five years after date covered by *1 Henry VI.*)

Warwick, Earl of (*2H.VI; 3H.VI; R.III*). *See* Nevil, Richard.

Waterton, Sir Robert (*R.II*, II,i,284). Master of the Horse to Henry IV; Sheriff of Lincoln. (Thomson)

Westminster, Abbot of (*R.II*). William de Colchester (d.1420); accompanied Richard II to Ireland; delegate to Council of Constance in 1414. (Thomson)

French believes that Richard Harweden, Colchester's successor to the office, was the Abbot in *Richard II.*

Westmoreland, Earl of (*1H.IV; 2H.IV; H.V*). *See* Nevil, Ralph (1364–1425).

Westmoreland, Earl of (*3H.VI*). *See* Nevil, Ralph (d.1484).

White Surrey (*R.III*, V,iii,64). Name Shakespeare attributes to horse Richard III ordered saddled for Battle of Bosworth Field.

Whitmore, Walter (*2H.VI*). Historians fail to identify this character.

Willoughby, Lord (*R.II*). William de Willoughby (d.1409); 5th Baron; M.P. under Richard II and Henry IV.

Wiltshire, Earl of (*R.II*, II,i,215, and *passim*). William Scroop (1351?–1399); served under John of Gaunt; chief favorite of Richard II; Treasurer of England; executed by Henry IV.

Wiltshire, Earl of (*3H.VI*, I,i,14). James Butler (1420–1461); 5th Earl of Ormonde and Earl of Wiltshire; accompanied Richard Plantagenet, Duke of York, to France; became loyal Lancastrian; Lord High Treasurer (1455); wounded by Montague at first Battle of St. Albans; fought at Wakefield, Mortimer's Cross, and Towton; beheaded.

Winchester, Bishop of (*1,2H.VI*). Henry Beaufort (1377?–1447); 2nd son of John of Gaunt and Katherine Swynford; Bishop of Lincoln; Bishop and Cardinal of Winchester; Lord High Chancellor (intermittently 1403–1426); papal legate against Hussites; crowned Henry VI; lifelong rival of Humphrey, Duke of Gloucester; encouraged marriage of Henry VI and Margaret of Anjou; buried in Winchester Cathedral.

Winchester, Bishop of (*H.VIII*). Stephen Gardiner (1483?–1555); prelate; assisted Henry VIII in divorce of Katherine of Aragon; secretary to Henry VIII; confined to Tower during reign of Edward VI; appointed Lord Chancellor on accession of Mary Tudor; procured parliamentary declaration of Elizabeth's illegitimacy; died of gout.

Winchester, Cardinal of. *See* Winchester, Bishop of.

Wolsey, Cardinal (*H.VIII*). Thomas Wolsey (1475?–1530); churchman and statesman; chaplain to Henry VII; Archbishop of York; cardinal (1515); Lord Chancellor (1515–1529); active in national and international politics and intrigue; arrested for high treason in 1530, but died on way to London; famous for magnificence of style of living; established Cardinal College (now Christ Church), Oxford.

Woodstock, Thomas of. *See* Thomas of Woodstock.

Woodvile (*1H.VI*). Richard de Woodvile (d.*c.*1441); Governor of Northampton Castle during reign of Henry IV; loyal servant of Henry V; appointed Constable of the Tower.

Woodville, Elizabeth. *See* Elizabeth Woodville, Queen of Edward IV.

Worcester, Earl of (*R.II; 1,2H.IV*). Thomas Percy (1344?–1403); Earl of Worcester; brother of Henry Percy, 1st Earl of Northumberland; served in Flanders with Geoffrey Chaucer; campaigned in France and Spain; deserted Richard II to support Henry IV; joined Percy Rebellion; captured at Shrewsbury and beheaded.

York, Archbishop of (*1H.IV*). Richard Scroop (1350?–1405); son of Henry, 1st Baron Scroop of Masham; Bishop of Coventry and Lichfield; Archbishop of York (1398–1405); supported Henry IV in 1399 and diverted to Percies in 1404; executed at York. (Was cousin and not brother of William Scroop, Earl of Wiltshire; see *Richard II.*)

York, Archbishop of (*3H.VI*, IV,v and IV,vi,78). George Nevil (1433–1476); Bishop of Exeter and Archbishop of York; brother of Richard Nevil, Earl of Warwick, "the Kingmaker"; Chancellor of England; may have permitted Edward IV's escape from custody in 1470; surrendered Henry VI and himself to Edward IV in 1471; subsequently imprisoned; died in Northumberland.

York, Archbishop of. *See* Rotherham; Wolsey, Cardinal.

York, Duchess of (*R.II*). Joan Holland (d.1434); 2nd wife of Edmund of Langley, Duke of York (married 1395); subsequently married Lord Willoughby (*Richard II*), Lord Scroop (*Henry V*), and Sir Henry Bomflete. Aumerle's mother in history was Isabella, daughter of Pedro the Cruel of Castile; she died in 1393; Aumerle was born *c.*1373.

York, Duchess of (*R.III*). Cicely Nevil (d.1495); daughter of Ralph Nevil, 1st Earl of Westmoreland; granddaughter of John of Gaunt; married Richard Plantagenet, Duke of York in 1438; mother of Edward IV, Richard III, George Duke of Clarence, Edmund of Rutland, and Margaret Duchess of Burgundy; "a princess of spotless character"; known as "the Rose of Raby."

York, Duke of (*R.II; 1H.IV*, I,iii,245; *1H.VI*, II,v,85; *2H.VI*, II,ii,15). Edmund of Langley (1341–1402); 1st Duke of York; son of Edward III and Philippa of Hainaut; married (1) Isabella, Daughter of Pedro the Cruel of Castile and Leon, and (2) Joan Holland; father of Aumerle (Duke of York in *Henry V*) and Richard Earl of Cambridge; campaigned in France, Spain, and Scotland; Regent of England during Richard II's absence from the country.

York, Duke of (*R.II; H.V*). Edward of Norwich (1373?–1415); also Edward Plantagenet, Earl of Rutland, Duke of Aumerle (i.e., Albemarle) (in *Richard II*), and 2nd Duke of York; son of Edmund of Langley, 1st Duke of York; Constable of England; implicated in death of Thomas of Woodstock and in conspiracy against Henry IV; deprived of land and offices but pardoned in 1401; fought valiantly at Agincourt, where he was killed.

York, Duke of (*1,2,3H.VI*). Richard Plantagenet (1411–1460); 3rd Duke of York; grandson of Edmund of Langley; also descended from Lionel of Antwerp; only son of Richard Earl of Cambridge and Anne Mortimer; married Cicely Nevil, daughter of Ralph, 1st Earl of Westmoreland; precipitated Wars of the Roses; acknowledged leader of

Yorkist faction; defeated and killed at Wakefield, after which his head was placed on walls of York; father of Edward IV; Richard III; George, Duke of Clarence; Edmund, Earl of Rutland.

York, Duke of (*3H.VI*). *See* Edward IV.

York, Duke of (*R.III*). Richard (1472–1483); Duke of York and Earl Marshal; 2nd son of Edward IV and Elizabeth Woodville; married Anne, heiress to Duchy of Norfolk, in 1478 (bride and groom being in their sixth year); accompanied his mother into sanctuary in 1483; his mother released him at behest of Cardinal Bourchier; joined his brother, Edward V, in Tower; presumably murdered with Edward V by order of Richard III.

York, Mayor of. *See* Mayor of York.

Yorkshire, Shrieve of. *See* Sheriff of Yorkshire.

Young Clifford. *See* Clifford, Young.

Young Daughter of Clarence. *See* Margaret Plantagenet.

Young Son of Clarence. *See* Edward, Earl of Warwick.

INDEX TO NON-HISTORICAL CHARACTERS IN SHAKESPEARE'S HISTORY PLAYS

In addition to the persons listed in the Biographical Index, there are others whom scholars have failed to identify. Many are presumably fictional, inserted to add dramatic interest or to provide continuity in the action. A list of these follows:

CHRONOLOGY OF SHAKESPEARE'S PLAYS

Differences of opinion exist concerning the dates when Shakespeare wrote his plays. A working order is, nevertheless, helpful, and the following sequence, with a slight overlapping of periods, represents a consensus of leading editors and scholars.

Dates	Comedies	Histories	Tragedies
1589–1595	*Comedy of Errors* *Taming of the Shrew* *Two Gentlemen of Verona* *Love's Labour's Lost*	*1 Henry VI* *2 Henry VI* *3 Henry VI* *Richard III*	*Titus Andronicus*
1594–1602	*Midsummer Night's Dream* *Merchant of Venice* *Much Ado about Nothing* *Merry Wives of Windsor* *As You Like It* *Twelfth Night*	*Richard II* *King John* *1 Henry IV* *2 Henry IV* *Henry V*	*Romeo and Juliet* *Julius Caesar*
1600–1609	*Troilus and Cressida* *All's Well That Ends Well* *Measure for Measure* *Pericles*		*Hamlet* *Othello* *King Lear* *Macbeth* *Timon of Athens* *Antony and Cleopatra* *Coriolanus*
1609–1613	*Cymbeline* *Winter's Tale* *Tempest*	*Henry VIII*	